Foreign Aid and
American Foreign Policy

Foreign Aid and American Foreign Policy

A DOCUMENTARY ANALYSIS

David A. Baldwin

FREDERICK A. PRAEGER, *Publishers*
New York · Washington · London

FREDERICK A. PRAEGER, *Publishers*
111 Fourth Avenue, New York, N.Y. 10003, U.S.A.
77–79 Charlotte Street, London W.1, England

Published in the United States of America in 1966
by Frederick A. Praeger, Inc., Publishers

Preface

The role of foreign aid in American foreign policy is analyzed in this book through the use of annotated documents and a thorough reading of the excerpted material should provide the reader with a critical comprehension of the subject. However, since the analysis will depend to a considerable extent on the efforts of the reader to define for himself the significance of the documents, the first two chapters of the book are aimed at equipping him with the analytic tools and relevant factual background with which to make his own analyses.

Charles S. Hyneman, former President of the American Political Science Association, has questioned whether courses in political science give the student "a sufficient number of analytic jobs of sufficient difficulty."[1] In this book, an attempt has been made to guide the student no further than necessary, and to challenge him to make his own analyses. By avoiding predigested analyses, it was my intention to provide the professor with three alternatives: (1) adoption and elaboration of the analysis indicated in my guidelines, (2) substitution of his own point of view, and (3) encouragement of the advanced student to draw his own conclusions.

Although the major policy issues relating to foreign aid since World War II have been discussed by others, little attention has been given to the foreign-policy context of aid. This book assumes that foreign aid *is* foreign policy; that is, foreign aid is a technique of statecraft. Elsewhere, the economic aspects of aid have been emphasized at the expense of the political aspects. Here, foreign aid will be considered in the context of both domestic and international politics.

Foreign Aid and American Foreign Policy is a by-product of a research project carried out by the editor during his tenure as Research Fellow at the Brookings Institution, in 1964/65. Professor Michael K. O'Leary of Syracuse University was kind enough to sub-

[1] Charles S. Hyneman, "Some Crucial Learning Experiences: A Personal View," in Robert H. Connery (ed.), *Teaching Political Science* (Durham, N.C.: Duke University Press, 1965), p. 223.

v

mit parts of the manuscript to critical review and to make helpful suggestions. The editorial skills of my wife should also be acknowledged. The editing of the documents has involved eliminating some less relevant passages and making minor changes in spelling, capitalization, and punctuation. Errors and omissions, however, are entirely my responsibility. A constant source of inspiration was provided by the interest in, and dedication to, education instilled in me by my parents, to whom this book is dedicated.

Contents

Tables

Charts

Foreign Aid and
American Foreign Policy

I

Foreign-Aid Analysis

The transfer of money from one government to another as a technique of foreign policy is hardly an innovation of the twentieth century. Never before, however, did so few give so much to so many. Foreign aid has been one of the most controversial public issues in the United States since World War II. Although temporary compromises have altered the nature of the debate on foreign aid each year, the basic issues have not changed essentially in two decades. All of the issues discussed in this book are current; most of them also figured in the debates over the Bretton Woods Agreements, the Marshall Plan, Point Four, and the U.S. loan to Great Britain in 1946.

Foreign aid should be studied within the context of foreign policy. The primary assumption of the following pages is that foreign aid is first and foremost a technique of statecraft. It is, in other words, a means by which one nation tries to get other nations to act in desired ways. To the extent that national desires conflict, foreign aid involves international politics. Conflicts over aid appear on the domestic scene as well. Thus, foreign-aid policy is foreign policy, and as such it is a subject of controversy in both the international and the domestic political arenas.

The following chapters contain a documentary analysis of the U.S. foreign-aid program. Obviously, in such a format, fruitful analysis of the documents will depend in part on the interpretive skills of the reader. For this reason, a few pointers on the study of foreign aid are in order.

POINTERS ON FOREIGN-AID ANALYSIS

A nation's foreign policy is governed to some extent by the way in which power is distributed within the national boundaries. We call the system for determining the distribution of power—who gets what, how, and when—a political system. In the United States, no less than in other countries, the political system affects foreign policy. Since foreign-aid policy is foreign policy, one can better understand the readings that follow by bearing in mind certain relevant aspects of the American political system.

The Electorate

Mass public.—The American mass public has little interest in, or knowledge of, the aid program. This is hardly surprising—numerous public-opinion studies in the last fifteen years have shown that only a small part of the public has much interest in any public-policy issue. The relatively sophisticated political and economic concepts involved in foreign aid make it one of the more complex policy issues of our time. Thus, it is probably not clearly understood even among the more attentive public. The commercial pollsters, of course, do find people willing to register an opinion "for" or "against" something called foreign aid. But if the following questions were asked, one could be relatively confident of receiving little more than a blank stare from the vast majority of "the men in the street": What activities are included in the foreign-aid program? What is the Export-Import Bank? What does IBRD stand for? Who are the major recipients of American aid? What proportion of GNP does American aid represent? What is P.L. 480? Is most American aid bilateral or multilateral? Does it take the form of grants or loans? Do you include IMF contributions as part of foreign aid? What is the effect of foreign aid on the balance of payments?

Another characteristic of the American mass public that has been emphasized in several studies is the responsiveness to clearly discernible short-run threats to individual economic well-being. Issues such as taxation or the level of local employment, to mention two, tend to interest the mass public far more than issues that pose no obvious threat to the prosperity of the individual.

These characteristics of the electorate have several implications for American foreign-aid policy, among which are the following: (1) The lack of understanding of aid by the mass public facilitates manipulation of their attitudes by both friends and foes of aid. Thus, public debate tends to be on a low level of sophistication, with one side contending that aid is a "giveaway," and the other side pretending it is a cure-all for the world's miseries. (2) Effective opposition to aid can be mounted by people who do not perceive that their actions are anti-aid efforts; that is, opposition to increased taxes, or a desire for tax reduction, may actually have the effect of causing aid appropriations to be cut since foreign aid is one of the most vulnerable parts of the Federal budget. The mass public may be anti-tax rather than anti-aid, but the net result can be the same. (3) The apathy and relative ignorance of the mass public regarding aid policy tends to increase the influence of organized pressure groups in the policy-making process.

Interest groups.—Briefly put, the interest groups that count in American politics have little enthusiasm for foreign aid, whereas the interest groups that vigorously defend aid tend to be those that do not count. Each year, the League of Women Voters and various church groups ardently support aid in Congressional hearings. No one, however, has ever seriously contended that such groups exercise much influence on issues involving large appropriations of money. Among the financially powerful interest groups, only the AFL-CIO is a consistent friend of aid legislation. Congressmen, however, can easily perceive that aid is not a vital issue to this organization. The U.S. Chamber of Commerce usually gives grudging support for a cut-down version of whatever aid program the Executive Branch submits, while the National Association of Manufacturers maintains an ominous and meaningful silence during most hearings on aid. It is not always necessary to voice an opinion in order to communicate an unsympathetic attitude toward the program. Lack of support from the powerful interest groups increases the difficulty of securing passage of the annual aid bill in Congress.

Political culture.—Certain aspects of the American political culture have a significant bearing on aid policy. By "political culture" is meant the beliefs, values, and attitudes of a people regarding the political system in their country. Beliefs about the economy, government, and the relation between them are especially important to the student of foreign aid. In America, the popular conception is that since the economic system tends to be self-regulating, governmental intervention is required only at rare intervals. Americans tend to believe that government activity in the economic sphere leads to corruption, is likely to be ineptly administered, and constitutes a definite threat to freedom.

American values are closely related to the above beliefs about government and the economy. International capital transfers, it is believed, should normally be private instead of public. The standard argument is that private investment is less likely to lead to corruption, will be more efficiently administered, and will constitute less of a threat to freedom.

This emphasis on the private sphere of the economy is reflected in the emotional attitudes prevalent in the foreign-aid debate. Certain words, such as "sound" and "business-like," tend to lose precise meaning and to become substitutes for "Hurrah!" Other words, such as "giveaway" and "unbusiness-like," tend to become substitutes for "Boo!" The view of America as a business-dominated society is doubtless oversimplified, but it can serve to alert the student of foreign aid to aspects of the aid program that are likely to be controversial.

Congress

Much of the literature on aid has been generated in connection with the Legislative-Executive pulling and hauling that accompanies the annual debate on foreign aid. One must be aware of the bargaining aspects of these Executive-Legislative matches in order to make sense of many of the aid statements issued by Congressional and Executive Branch leaders. Since the system of checks and balances built into the American Constitution prevents any one branch of the government from exercising complete control of foreign aid, many aspects of aid policy represent compromises between the Executive Branch and Congress. For example, the American soft-loan policy was primarily a compromise between the Executive desire for grants and the Legislative preference for hard loans.

Because of the separation of powers in the Federal Government, it is helpful to the student of aid policy to keep in mind the following aspects of Congressional behavior: (1) Congressmen tend to act in ways that they believe will increase the likelihood of their re-election. Voting for foreign aid rarely wins a Congressman votes, and voting against it rarely loses him many. Support for the aid program may even lose votes for a Congressman. (2) Congressmen are elected by constituencies that represent a state or portion thereof, relatively small geographic areas. Since re-election depends on satisfying the needs of this constituency, Congressmen tend to be interested in matters that directly affect their home state or district and to show little interest in matters that affect their constituencies only in a remote sense. Unlike the military program, which often contributes greatly to the economy of a particular state or Congressional district, the aid program is diffuse in its impact on the domestic economy. (3) The term of office for Representatives is two years and that for Senators is six. Due to their interest in re-election, the desire of Congressmen to have the aid program yield quick, easily identifiable results is understandable. The aid program, however, rarely does this, and Congress often equates this lack of fast results with failure. After all, Representatives must account to the people every two years for what use they have made of public funds, and it is unlikely the people will be favorably impressed by a report that $4 billion were spent on an ephemeral thing called "long-term economic development." (4) Although many Congressmen hold law degrees, few have had formal training in either economics or foreign affairs. It should not be surprising to find that they are often confused about foreign aid, one of the most complex policy problems of our time. This problem is compounded by the fact that Congress has less information on the program at its disposal than does the Executive Branch. (5) It has become traditional to place the aid appropriations bill near the end of the legislative agenda. This is a bill in which the Executive Branch, in comparison with Congress, has a high degree of interest. By delaying a vote on the bill, Congressmen can increase their bargaining power vis-à-vis the Executive on issues in which they are more interested. Thus, Congressmen have been known to agree to support the aid bill in return for dams in their home district or for dilution of civil-rights laws that were especially unpopular in their districts. (6) Congress is organized in a way that bodes ill for foreign aid. First, it is difficult to get any piece of legislation through the Congressional obstacle course; the system makes it easy to obstruct legislation and hard to promote it. In short, the organization of Congress favors the opponents of a bill. Second, influence is not evenly distributed on Capitol Hill. The committee system makes a few "key" people very important with respect to any particular piece of legislation. In the case of foreign aid, several committees are involved, including those for foreign affairs, agriculture, banking and currency, and appropriations. The committees involved most often, however, are the ones concerned with foreign affairs and appropriations. It is in the Appropriations Committee of the House of Representatives that one finds the most vigorous and influential opponents of foreign aid. A recent study of the politics of budgeting underlined the significance of this fact:

> Administrative officials are unanimously agreed that they must, as a bare minimum, enjoy the confidence of the appropriations committee members and their staff. "If you have the confidence of your subcommittee your life is much easier and you can do your department good; if you don't have confidence you can't accomplish much and you are always in trouble over this or that."[1]

[1] Aaron Wildavsky, *The Politics of the Budgetary Process* (Boston: Little, Brown, 1964), p. 74.

Few Federal agencies enjoy less confidence from the appropriations committees of Congress than does the aid agency.

The Executive Branch

Knowledge of the following aspects of the Executive Branch may be useful to the foreign-aid analyst: (1) The Constitution gives the Executive Branch primary responsibility for the conduct of foreign relations. Since Executive Branch officials have to face potential aid recipients on a day-to-day basis, they are, compared with Congressmen, more aware of the problems involved and have more interest in foreign aid. It is significant that several Congressmen abandoned opposition to aid and became advocates of it after they had served on a U.N. delegation and had been involved in day-to-day contact with potential aid recipients. (2) Executive Branch officials are more likely to have received formal training in foreign affairs and economics than Congressmen. The aid agency, for example, often employs highly trained analysts. These people have two additional advantages over legislators in understanding aid programs: They can devote a greater perrcentage of their time to learning about aid, and they have access to more information on aid activities. (3) The Executive Branch has a broader constituency than any individual Congressman and can thus afford to give more emphasis to the national—as opposed to the sectional— aspects of any given issue. Foreign aid is an issue that lends itself more to justification in terms of the broad national interest than in terms of advantage to a particular domestic locality. (4) Whereas legislators serve a term of two or six years, the President serves a term of four years, and can usually look forward to eight years in office. He is therefore able to take a longer-range viewpoint than Representatives and even some Senators. Many professional bureaucrats can maintain an even longer-range perspective since they are protected by civil-service regulations. Thus, the Executive Branch need not be so interested in spectacular short-term results from foreign aid. (5) Due partly to the Executive's control over the day-to-day operations of the aid program and partly to the ambiguity that always creeps into legislation on foreign aid, the Executive has little difficulty making aid policy after the funds have been made available. The Executive Branch can usually interpret aid legislation so as to permit an almost endless choice of actions —*given the funds*. The corollary of this proposition is that control of appropriations, i.e., the threat to cut future appropriations, constitutes the single most important Legislative restraint on Executive policy-making in the field of aid. (6) There are several obstacles to effective coordination of the aid program within the Executive Branch. First, the size and complexity of the job of administering the aid program rival that of running the world's biggest corporations. With 15,000 people disbursing $2 billion per year, there are bound to be coordination problems, even with highly efficient personnel. Second, the aid agency does not attract the best civil servants, because continual Congressional harassment of that agency reduces the job security it can offer its employees. It is quite common for people who "know the ropes" to advise those who want to make government service a career to avoid the aid agency. A third obstacle to coordination within the Executive Branch arises from the differing views of aid held by various government departments. For example, the Bureau of the Budget is likely to be most concerned with the impact of aid on the budget, the Export-Import Bank with financing American exports, the Treasury Department with the effect of aid on the balance of payments, the Department of Agriculture with reducing domestic surpluses, the Defense Department with military aspects of aid, and the State Department with the effect of aid on the recipient state's foreign policy. Such a situation is understandable, but these differing estimates of what is important in the aid program do increase the difficulty of effective coordination.

There are several pitfalls the student of foreign aid is likely to encounter when analyzing foreign aid and foreign policy. These pitfalls are discussed under the headings: Failure to Read Between the Lines, "Slippery" Terms, Irrelevant Definitions and Measurements of Aid, Hasty Conclusions About the Goals of Aid, Failure to Consider Alternatives, and Determinism in Aid Analysis.

Failure to Read Between the Lines

One of the most frequent mistakes in aid analysis is failure to read between the lines. Because foreign aid is a controversial public issue, one must be constantly on guard against polemic literature. Many of the concepts and arguments developed for polemic purposes by participants in the policy-making process have been accepted uncritically by scholars, who have thus needlessly confused academic discussion of this issue. One textbook on American foreign policy, for example, draws its supposedly objective definition of soft loans from a report by a Congressional committee in which the legislators were trying to convince people that authorization of such loans was not really an "unbusiness-like" act since the loans were not of "doubtful validity."[2] This Congressional whitewash, however, did not change the fact that in the late 1940's and early 1950's, such loans were generally considered unsound. Even in 1960, testimony in Congressional hearings indicated that "in conventional private or government finance, a soft loan is a self-evident contradiction in terms."[3] Another example of failure to read between the lines is the frequent acceptance at face value of the Executive Branch contention that loans and grants for foreign aid do not compete with private capital. Since private capital is always available on some terms and in the long run, such a contention is nonsensical unless one specifies the time period and the interest rate of the loan. Even then, the contention should be regarded as a hypothesis requiring empirical testing. A polemicist may be forgiven if he disguises the weak points of his argument, but one cannot forgive the scholar who accepts the argument uncritically.

In order to learn to read between the lines, the student of foreign aid should cultivate mental habits: First, he should strive to identify the bargaining aspects of the situation in which a statement is made. He should watch for bargaining within agencies, among Executive departments, among nations, between the Executive Branch and Congress, and among Congressional committees. Second, when reading a statement on foreign aid, he should constantly be aware of who is speaking to whom and in what capacity. Is this the President speaking to Congress? Is it the President speaking to his subordinates, to the public, to representatives of other nations, or to a gathering of party officials? Is the speaker known to be a friend or foe of foreign aid? Are there any reasons to believe that the speaker might mean something other than what he is actually saying? In the 1957 hearings, on the Mutual Security Act, Secretary of State Dulles was asked about the usefulness of surplus agricultural commodities in foreign aid. He replied:

> We have found that our surplus commodities can serve as a very important aid to our foreign policy in ways which are relatively economical, because they dispose of our surpluses which if otherwise

[2] Cecil V. Crabb, Jr., *American Foreign Policy in the Nuclear Age* (Evanston, Ill.: Row, Peterson, 1960), p. 415.

[3] *International Development Association Act*, Hearings before the House Committee on Banking and Currency, 86th Cong., 2d sess. (Washington, D.C.: Government Printing Office, 1960), p. 62.

not disposed of, to some extent, at least, just rot away and cost the taxpayer a large amount of money.

I think we are spending close to a million dollars a day on storage charges. After you store some of these commodities, like wheat, long enough, it just becomes worthless. So you have paid your storage for nothing and dump it out as waste.[4]

On the face of it, Dulles is saying that surplus commodities are useful in foreign policy, but let us read between the lines. First, it was the policy of the administration to use surplus commodities in the aid program. Since he was a part of the administration team, he was not likely to disagree openly with the policy. The first sentence, therefore, can be written off as lip service to an administration position that Dulles may or may not have liked. Second, one should note that the State Department had been complaining about having its dollar appropriations cut as a result of the surplus-disposal program. Also, it was well known that the State Department was concerned lest the "dumping" of American products on the international market have unfavorable repercussions on U.S. foreign policy. Many Congressmen regarded the surplus-disposal program as a good means of making the cost of subsidizing American farmers appear small, even though the cost of the aid program would then appear large. The State Department, on the other hand, was interested in minimizing the apparent costs of aid. With these considerations in mind, one can see that Dulles really meant something like this:

> We don't mind helping the Congress and the Agriculture Department solve a domestic problem, but we do resent the implication that you are doing us a favor by letting us help you out. After all, this stuff would probably rot anyway; so we are really saving the taxpayers' money, while you fellows in Congress make it appear that we are spending money by adding the value of such commodities to the cost of the foreign-aid program.

"Slippery" Terms

Voltaire is reputed to have begun arguments by saying, "If you would speak with me, Sir, you must first define your terms." Whether Voltaire said it or not, it is wise advice for students of foreign aid. Undergraduates often tend to assume that their confusion over the meaning of a word is due to their own ignorance.

[4] *Mutual Security Act of 1957*, Hearings before the House Committee on Foreign Affairs, 85th Cong., 1st sess. (Washington, D.C.: Government Printing Office, 1957), p. 530.

Although this may sometimes be true, the confusion is often due to the carelessness of a scholar who does not define an ambiguous term. In the field of foreign aid, the tendency to leave ambiguous terms undefined is so prevalent that the student would do well to blame the writer instead of himself for any terms he cannot understand. The "slippery" terms discussed below constitute only a few of the ambiguous terms that the student of foreign aid is likely to encounter.

"*Sound*."—This term is liberally sprinkled throughout the literature on foreign aid, and it is almost never defined, although the term "business-like" appears to be a synonym. Everyone, it seems, favors sound loans and sound governmental policy implemented through sound administrative procedures. No one, as far as I know, has ever argued for doing something unsound or against something sound. The problem this term poses for the student of foreign aid is this. Has anything really been said by the man who testifies before a Congressional committee that he favors sound loans to nations with sound fiscal and monetary policies? The term probably has been borrowed from banking circles, where it is not so ambiguous because those who use it share a number of unstated beliefs and values. When the term is used outside private banking circles, however, one cannot be sure that the user intends to imply all that a private banker would in using the term. As a practical matter, the term should be equated with "Hurrah!" Thus, sound policies are those that the speaker likes and unsound policies are those that he dislikes.

"*Ability to repay*."—This term, which is the same as "debt-servicing capacity," refers to the ability of a nation to repay a loan. This is a concept that has long plagued students of international relations. During the interwar period, a controversy raged over whether Germany had the "ability to pay" the reparations levied on her by the Allies. Today, people argue about the ability of poor nations to repay various kinds and amounts of loans. The problem in both cases is the same: Where does *ability* begin and *willingness* end? The reader should be warned that users of the term ability to repay are usually making implicit assumptions about the willingness of a government to repay and about fiscal and monetary policies. The statement that Ruritania lacks the ability to repay additional commercial loans might have any one of several meanings, such as: (1) The Ruritanian Government is unlikely to adopt policies that would enable her to earn enough foreign exchange to repay the loan; (2) the policies that the Ruritanian Government would have to adopt in order to repay the loan would be so harsh that it would be immoral to ask them to do so; or (3) regardless of what policies the Ruritanian Government adopted, the nation could never repay the loan.

"*Economic development.*"—This term, which occurs frequently in the literature on foreign aid, has no consistent definition. For some, it refers to an increase in national per capita income. For others, it denotes the process by which poor agricultural nations are going to be transformed into highly industrialized, urbanized nations such as the United States. One should note that such a definition rules out specialization in agriculture as a road to economic development. In other words, dubious conclusions are sometimes made because of confusions between definitions and empirical observations. If development is defined in terms of increased industrialization, it is truistic to offer the "empirical observation" that most underdeveloped countries are primarily agricultural.

Economic development may be defined by still others as the creation of domestic social institutions that will permit per capita income to increase over the long run at a steady rate. The definition of economic development that is used will often influence the type of aid advocated for a particular development program. For example, one who defines development in terms of per capita income could advocate aid in the form of machine guns to be used to reduce the population and thus increase everyone's income. Such aid, however, might be irrelevant to industrialization, and could hinder the building of social institutions capable of sustaining long-term increases in per capita income. The importation of tractors might impede development of a domestic tractor industry while stimulating agricultural output and increasing per capita income. Would this be economic development? It depends on how one defines the term.

"*Non-self-liquidating projects.*"—References are frequently made to development projects that lack "intrinsic economic merit," but are still deemed worthy of being undertaken. There is probably no quicker way for the student of foreign aid to become thoroughly confused than to start looking for the intrinsic economic merit of a particular project. Economists long ago gave up trying to explain the market price of an object in terms of its intrinsic worth and turned instead to the concept of supply and demand. One is most likely to come across the "non-self-liquidating project" in the grant-loan debate. It is commonly argued that loans are satisfactory for self-liquidating projects but that grants are the appropriate means to finance the non-self-liquidating ones. One former aid official tells the story of how development efforts in a community were stalled until aid was used to build a wall around a local cemetery, after which community spirit picked up and the development effort surged forward.[5] Few would think of a cemetery wall as a self-liquidating project, but it is conceivable that the net impact of this particular wall was to increase per capita income in the community so much that local taxes could be levied in order to pay for the wall. About the best one can do when confronted with the perplexing concept of the non-self-liquidating project is to ask the following questions: (1) What time period does the speaker have in mind? (2) To whom will the project yield an economic return? (3) How much return will it yield? (4) If the return is to the economy as a whole, can taxes be levied in order to collect this return?

"Favorable investment climate."—For over twenty years, spokesmen for the United States have been diagnosing the ills of the poor nations in the following terms: Although you need capital for economic development, it should be private, not public, capital. The reason you do not get more private capital is that you have an "unfavorable investment climate" for private investors. Now as far as I know, there is no instance of a nation that failed to attract private capital and yet was acknowledged to have a favorable investment climate. One may conclude, therefore, that a favorable investment climate is one that attracts private investors, and an unfavorable investment climate is one that does not. It is simply tautological to cite the lack of a favorable investment climate as a "reason" for the dearth of private investors. A favorable investment climate is whatever the private investors think it is; it has no objective existence outside the psyche of the private investor himself. The process of creating a favorable investment climate is thus one of yielding to whatever demands the potential private investors decide to make on the host government. If thought of in these terms, the reluctance of the governments in poor nations to heed the advice of the United States to improve their investment climate will be more readily understood.

"Soft loan."—In the 1940's and early 1950's, "soft loan" was a derogatory term used by opponents of certain types of foreign aid. It was borrowed from the banking world, where it also carried unfavorable connotations. Since it is no longer considered a derisory

[5] Frank M. Coffin, *Witness for Aid* (Boston: Houghton Mifflin, 1964), p. 14.

term, one who reads widely in the aid literature of the last twenty years should be aware of its changing connotation. Scholarly discussions often leave the term undefined, but this is unwise since several definitions—with varying policy implications—are currently in use. One definition labels as soft any loan made initially in foreign exchange and repayable in inconvertible currency. Another includes loans made in foreign exchange and repayable either in inconvertible currency or in foreign exchange at unusually low interest rates or over especially long time periods, say fifty years.[6] A third defines soft loan as the lending of a currency by one nation to the nation in which the currency originated, with the loan being repayable in that same currency. The differences among these definitions are important to the aid analyst. Lending a nation foreign exchange leads to an infusion of additional goods and services, whereas lending it its own currency does not. The nature of a soft loan repayable in inconvertible currency may be more readily visualized when thought of as a transaction in which dollars are lent in return for the play money from a Monopoly game, though the analogy is not exact.

Irrelevant Definitions and Measurements of Aid

When the United States gets together with her allies to discuss economic-aid programs, there is often a squabble over which nations are bearing the largest share of the aid "burden." Nations making large-scale grants insist that grant aid should count for more, while those relying mainly on five- to ten-year hard loans argue that these should count as aid. There is no end in sight to this disagreement, i.e., where charity begins and commercial transactions end. The important point to note is that opinions differ as to whether a dollar loan repayable in dollars over a 5-year period at 5 per cent interest is "aid."

A slightly different problem is posed in the study of foreign aid as a technique of American statecraft. In this case, one is likely to be interested more in the extent to which the U.S. Government has transferred goods and services to other nations in order to influence their behavior than in theoretical distinctions between charity and commerce. The practical problem for the foreign-policy analyst lies in determining which governmental activities to examine in order to learn about foreign aid in American state-

[6] Foreign exchange (convertible currency) can be freely exchanged for other currencies or for gold. Inconvertible currency has legal limits on the extent to which it can be exchanged for gold or other currencies.

craft. Should he, for example, confine his research to hearings and reports on the annual aid bill, or should he also examine the activities of the Export-Import Bank, the P.L. 480 program for disposal of agricultural surpluses, the Peace Corps, the World Bank, the International Development Association (IDA), International Finance Corporation (IFC), U.N. technical assistance programs, and the Inter-American Development Bank (IDB)? One important study of foreign aid rules out consideration of World Bank activities on the grounds that aid channeled through such agencies ceases to be an instrument of American foreign policy.[7]

Although the definition used should suit one's purpose, serious objections can be raised to a definition which ignores the fact that foreign policies are carried on within, as well as without, international organizations. It should be noted here that the term "foreign aid" is often used imprecisely, and one should not assume that all users of the term are thinking of the same governmental activities.

The problem of measuring aid is closely related to that of defining it. Those interested in the impact of aid on recipients might want to measure it in terms of the net goods and services made available to recipients as a result of American efforts, while those interested in domestic aspects might want a measurement of the cost to the taxpayer. These will not necessarily be the same, since costs of administration will make taxpayer cost exceed net aid received. Also, U.S. contributions to such agencies as the IDA have the effect of grants on the taxpayer—they are never repaid to the United States, even though they become loans to the eventual recipients.

Measured in terms of dollars, aid may appear to have increased over a certain period, whereas, if measured as a percentage of gross national product, the same aid during the same period may show a decline. In such a case would the "burden" of foreign aid be decreasing or growing? Such are the headaches of the aid analyst.

Another problem in measuring aid arises in connection with P.L. 480, one of America's biggest aid programs. The goods distributed under this program consist of agricultural commodities bought by the government at artificially high prices. Should such aid be valued at these prices, at prices current on the world market, or at prices that would have prevailed if America had dumped its surplus on the market and thereby driven prices down? What con-

[7] Charles Wolf, Jr., *Foreign Aid: Theory and Practice in Southern Asia* (Princeton, N.J.: Princeton University Press, 1960), p. 80.

cept of taxpayer cost is relevant under the P.L. 480 program? If agricultural price-stabilization programs would be carried out even in the absence of foreign aid, does it make sense to charge the aid program with the costs of these stabilization programs? If one introduces the concept of "opportunity cost"—those goods and services forfeited in order to obtain something else—there is even the possibility that the United States has a negative cost with respect to some P.L. 480 goods. For example, it is possible that the amount saved on storage costs exceeds the value of the goods given as aid. The United States might actually be saving money in some cases by giving stuff away. The important point for the reader to remember is this: Because there are various ways to measure aid, one can expect enemies of the program to use gauges that exaggerate its cost and apologists for the program to use those that minimize its cost.

Hasty Conclusions About the Goals of Aid

The public debate on foreign aid is peppered with calls for "clarification" of the goals of the aid program. The determination of the goals of aid presents the aid analyst with one of his thorniest problems. Should he accept public statements by foreign-policy spokesmen at face value? If not, how can he decide what the "real" goals are? There is no completely satisfactory answer. The analyst will have to depend to some extent on his ability to read between the lines of political statements.

Most techniques of statecraft are used to pursue multiple goals simultaneously; there is no reason to assume that aid is an exception. Then, too, foreign-policy spokesmen might want to give Congress one picture of the objectives of foreign aid while giving foreigners another. Foreign-policy spokesmen thus have reasons for being less than completely candid when publicly discussing the goals of foreign aid.

One must also distinguish between the goals perceived by participants in the policy-making process and the actual impact of aid. An aid grant may be the result of a desire to finance a dam, but the grant may end up being used to finance a hospital. Thus, in the following statement the word "for" is ambiguous: "The United States made $6 million available to Ruritania *for* harbor improvement." This sentence could mean any one of the following: (1) The makers of foreign policy wanted the loan to result in harbor improvement, and it may or may not have resulted in such improvement; (2) the loan was tied in a bookkeeping sense to harbor improvement, but the policy-makers really wanted it to have other effects; or (3) regardless of what the policy-makers wanted and regardless of what the bookkeepers said, the actual impact of the loan was to facilitate harbor improvement. In order to measure the impact of an aid transaction, it is necessary to estimate the way in which resources would have been allocated in the recipient nation if there had been no aid. By comparing this estimate with the actual allocation of resources under the aid program, it is possible to obtain a fair assessment of the real value of aid in the recipient nation. This, of course, is much more difficult than just accepting the bookkeeping figures at face value; but then no one ever said that *relevant* aid analysis was easy.

Failure to Consider Alternatives

One of the most interesting aspects of foreign aid is the process by which the makers of foreign policy choose aid or an alternative technique of statecraft to accomplish a particular goal. Since discussions of the alternatives to foreign aid are scarce, a few examples are in order. If the foreign-policy goal is the increasing of per capita income in underdeveloped nations, one alternative to aid would be to reduce the number of "heads" through population control. Another would be to encourage underdeveloped nations to rely on private investment, or to admonish them to rely on their own efforts and to stop relying on external capital. Other rich nations might be induced to give foreign aid, or trade liberalization might be promoted as a substitute for aid. If a nation could freely sell its goods in the American market, it might earn enough foreign exchange to enable it to get along without American aid. A unilateral lowering of American tariffs, while allowing the raising of tariffs in underdeveloped nations, would be an even more potent substitute for foreign aid. None of these alternative techniques of statecraft is necessarily better than foreign aid. The point is that aid policy can be better understood if one is aware of some of the alternatives.

Determinism in Aid Analysis

Partly because of the polemic nature of much of the literature and partly through intellectual carelessness, deterministic language often creeps into discussions on foreign aid. There are frequent references to the supposedly objective concept of the "needs" of potential aid recipients and to courses of action that "must" be taken to satisfy those "needs." Friends of foreign aid often describe it as "inevitable," "necessary," or as "impelled by external circumstances." They hope thereby to duck the question of whether aid should be a technique of statecraft so that they may concentrate on the question of how it should be used. The student of foreign aid should be on guard against deterministic language, and should remember that policy-makers are capable of choosing, and do in fact choose, from among alternative courses of action. In this respect, of course, discussions on foreign aid are not in any better state than discussions on other aspects of foreign policy. One textbook issues this warning:

> This kind of rhetoric [deterministic statements] *never* means what it appears to mean. The statesman always has alternatives. When he says that a situation compels him to choose a given course, he simply means that he rejects other courses—with his reasons for the choice frequently left unspecified. The first essential of clear thinking about foreign policy and political action in general is to rid oneself once and for all of the notion that statesmen are mere chips in a fast flowing stream of history.[8]

[8] Harold and Margaret Sprout, *Foundations of International Politics* (Princeton, N.J.: Van Nostrand, 1962), p. 123.

II

Foreign Aid in Perspective

A brief description of the background of American aid policy may be no more helpful than a southward wave of the hand would be to a motorist hunting a specific address in Miami; but then, if the motorist is starting from New York, a southward wave at least heads him in the right direction. The following discussion of the broad outlines, goals, and basic components of America's aid strategy is not intended to be exhaustive. If it equips students with a vague sense of direction, it will have served its purpose.

BROAD OUTLINES OF U.S. AID STRATEGY

The End of the War: 1945

During World War II, extensive preparations were made for an orderly transition from wartime to peacetime conditions. The policy-makers foresaw three types of postwar economic problems —relief, reconstruction, and long-term growth and stability. Foreign aid was one of the foreign-policy instruments adopted to attack all three problems.

Relief aid—in the form of food, clothing, and shelter, on a grant basis—was aimed at preventing the famine, disease, and general chaos that are so likely to occur in the wake of war. During 1945 and 1946, the civilian-supply programs of the U.S. armed forces distributed over $2 billion in emergency aid. The American contribution to the U.N. Relief and Rehabilitation Administration (UNRRA) amounted to more than $3 billion.

The policy-makers realized that beyond the immediate need for relief aid was the need for reconstruction of the war-torn economies of Europe. This need was to be met in three ways. (1) Private foreign investment was to be stimulated to provide the bulk of the capital necessary for reconstruction. Toward this end, the International Bank for Reconstruction and Development (IBRD) was founded. Its chief purpose was to guarantee loans of private investors, rather than to grant direct loans from its own capital. As it turned out, of course, the IBRD never operated as a guarantor of private loans. (2) In the event that private lenders provided insufficient funds, it was expected that the IBRD would be able to render the additional assistance necessary to achieve a desirable rate of reconstruction. (3) The economy of Great Britain was to be strengthened by a $3.75-billion non-IBRD loan at a very low interest rate.

In addition to the short-range planning for relief and reconstruction, plans were laid for the promotion of long-term economic growth and stability. These long-range goals were to be pursued in four ways. (1) The International Monetary Fund (IMF) was established to help overcome the difficulties connected with short-term fluctuations in the balance of international payments. (2) Since it was assumed that private investment would furnish the long-term capital needed for growth, private investors were to be encouraged. (3) The IBRD was to supply long-term capital for projects that did not interest private lenders. (4) The International Trade Organization (ITO) was proposed as a means of reviving liberal principles in the area of international trade. The ITO, which had been vigorously championed by American diplomats, foundered in 1950, in the face of a hostile Congress. The policy-makers of 1945 never believed for a moment that private investment, the IMF, and the IBRD would suffice to ensure long-term growth and stability without a regeneration of international trade. Thus, the collapse of the ITO was a serious blow to the aid strategy that had been conceived between 1943 and 1946.

American aid policy, toward the end of World War II, was based on a number of plausible but, as it turned out, incorrect assumptions about the nature of the postwar world. The assumptions were:

1) Postwar economic policies could be carried out in an atmosphere of cooperation and peaceful political relations with the Soviet Union.
2) Security against a revival of German and Japanese militarism would be provided by the permanent elimination of the economic potential for warmaking of these countries.
3) Low levels of industry in Germany and Japan would not be a barrier to economic recovery and prosperity in other parts of the world.
4) China would be able to fill the gap in Far Eastern economic and political affairs that had been caused by the decline of Japan.

5) Recovery and expansion would not be hampered by large military expenditures.
6) Recovery in Great Britain would be the key to economic recovery in other parts of the world.
7) After a short period of transition, a world-wide multilateral system of trade and payments could be restored and maintained through international agreements.
8) Such a system would permit American private enterprise to compete in world markets on equitable terms and would contribute to the general welfare by increasing the volume of international trade and investment.
9) Efforts to return to such a system would not be impeded by a prolonged and intractable "dollar-shortage" problem.
10) The elimination of burdensome war debts not only would remove a source of international friction but would also shorten the transition period and have long-term effects on international trade relations that would be of great advantage to the United States.
11) During the transition period, the emergency needs that had been created by the war could be met by the orderly liquidation of wartime assistance programs, by the British loan and credits extended in connection with other lend-lease settlements, and by loans and credits from the Export-Import Bank and the Bretton Woods institutions.
12) After the transition period, private foreign investment would revive and, together with loans of the IBRD, would again furnish the international investment network needed for an expanding world economy.[1]

It is easy today to ridicule the planning for the postwar world as unrealistic, but the fact remains that never before in history had postwar problems been so well anticipated or such thorough preparations been taken. What is remarkable is not that the planners failed to foresee all the problems but that they foresaw as many as they did.

Foreign-Aid Strategy Reappraised: 1947

As Soviet-American relations deteriorated, the official conception of the international environment changed. Gradually, the pol-

---

[1] These assumptions appear in Commission on Foreign Economic Policy, *Staff Papers* (Washington, D.C.: Government Printing Office, 1954), pp. 24–25.

icy-makers came to see the world in terms of two blocs dominated by the Russian and American superpowers. The idea of a "cold war" involving competition between East and West slowly emerged. This Cold War was to have three successive battle-grounds—Europe, Korea, and the underdeveloped areas. And each change in the battleground occasioned a reappraisal of American aid strategy.

The first reappraisal came in February, 1947, when the British Government announced that it would be unable to continue its aid to the Greek Government in its fight against Communist guerrillas who were being actively supported by Soviet satellites. In response to the British withdrawal, President Truman, in March, 1947, proposed $300 million in aid for Greece and, at the same time, $100 million to help Turkey resist Soviet threats. The Greek-Turkish aid program became known as the Truman Doctrine; it set forth, for the first time, an American aid policy aimed at containing Communism.

In June, 1947, the United States continued revising its aid strategy. Secretary of State Marshall invited the European nations to take the initiative in planning a massive assault on the problem of economic reconstruction. Although he made no commitments, he indicated that the United States would stand ready to provide substantial financial aid. The Communist nations were invited to participate, but refused. If they had accepted, the program would probably have encountered stiffer opposition in Congress; their refusal permitted the Executive to sell the program to Congress as a way to fight Communism. The Marshall Plan, formally known as the European Recovery Program (ERP), disbursed over $13 billion between April, 1948, and June, 1952. More than 90 per cent of this aid was in the form of grants. The basic assumptions underlying the Marshall Plan were:

1) The recovery of Europe as a whole was vital to world recovery, and was a prerequisite for achieving the general aims of U.S. commercial and financial policy.

2) It was necessary, therefore, that Europe be given priority in assistance.

3) In the interests of American security, strong measures had to be taken to check the advance of Communism in Europe.

4) The Communist threat in Europe was primarily one of internal subversion and infiltration—exploitation of situations in which low standards of living and economic stagnation or collapse existed—rather than overt military aggression.

5) The most suitable means of counteracting the Communist threat were of an economic and financial nature.

6) A four-year European recovery program, made possible by U.S. assistance, would serve the double purpose of making Europe independent of extraordinary foreign assistance, and of raising living standards and maintaining high levels of employment; it would, therefore, serve both the economic and security interests of the United States.

7) The success of such a program required: (a) The economic recovery of West Germany; (b) a regional, instead of a country-by-country, approach to Europe's problems; and (c) a continuation of the employment of European resources primarily for recovery, rather than for rearmament.[2]

The Second Reappraisal: 1950

In June, 1950, when war broke out in Korea, the aid strategy of the United States was again re-examined. Military aid, which in 1949 had been negligible, became increasingly important. The initial assumption of the ERP that there should be no substantial diversion of economic resources to defense was abandoned. The decision to begin a large-scale rearmament program in the free world reversed the priorities that had been given to economic recovery and defense; the United States subordinated its foreign-assistance operations to security considerations.[3] From 1951 to 1961, America's major aid activities were grouped together under a label with a distinctly military connotation—mutual security.

The fundamental assumptions underlying the 1950/51 re-evaluation of the aid program were:

1) Rearmament of the free world was necessary for American security.

2) Large-scale military assistance was necessary for the required scale of rearmament, and would have a multiple effect on the rearmament efforts of other countries.

3) Economic assistance in some form should be extended to preserve the achievements of existing aid programs if they were imperiled by the new burdens of rearmament.

4) A greater proportion of U.S. aid should be extended to countries of Southeast Asia.[4]

[2] *Ibid.*, pp. 27–28.
[3] *Ibid.*, p. 34.
[4] *Ibid.*, p. 35.

Third Reappraisal: 1954

With Europe well on the way to recovery, and with the war in Korea ended, the Cold War battleground shifted once again. This time, the battleground was the poor countries in Latin America, Asia, Africa, and the Middle East—countries where annual per capita incomes were often below $150. After the death of Stalin in 1953, the Soviet Union began to take a greater interest in economic techniques of statecraft. For example, in mid-1953, the Soviets ended their boycott of the U.N. technical-assistance programs. Using both aid and trade as foreign-policy instruments, they courted the underdeveloped nations.

During 1954, American policy-makers began to conceive of the Cold War in terms of a long-term competition with the Communist bloc, one which relied primarily on economic instruments and which had the object of keeping uncommitted nations out of the opposing bloc's hands. Since 1954, the basic assumptions underlying the American aid program have remained the same, despite attempts by the Kennedy and Johnson administrations to depict their approach to aid as radically new. These assumptions are:

1) The Cold War is essentially a long-term economic competition, rather than a short-term military one.

2) The primary targets of the Cold War are the uncommitted nations in Latin America, Africa, the Middle East, and Asia.

3) Foreign aid is a useful policy technique for getting the less-developed nations to: (a) Increase per capita income; (b) resist internal Communist subversion; and (c) resist external demands by members of the Communist bloc.

4) Certain countries bordering the Sino-Soviet bloc deserve special attention, e.g., Taiwan, Korea, Vietnam, Turkey, and Thailand.

Aid Expansion: 1958

Although the assumptions underlying the aid program have changed little, the year 1958 marked a rapid expansion of aid activities in the United States. In that year, the lending authority of the Export-Import Bank was increased from $5 billion to $7 billion; the United States initiated steps toward creation of the IDA; a regional development bank through which American funds could flow to Latin America was approved; and the lending capacity of the IBRD was doubled. All of these events reflected an increased emphasis on the less-developed nations as targets of American foreign policy.

TRENDS IN AID STRATEGY

Five trends, relating to the size, composition, and distribution of American aid, emerge from a survey of aid programs since World War II.

1. Although the total volume of aid measured on an absolute scale has been growing slowly, the United States has been allocating a diminishing proportion of its resources to aid. Table 1 shows aid as a percentage of the gross national product between 1946 and

TABLE 1

TOTAL U.S. AID AS A PERCENTAGE OF GNP, FISCAL YEARS 1946–65[a]

Fiscal Year	GNP[b]	Aid[c]	Aid as Percentage of GNP
1946–48	704	15.1	2.1
1949–52	1,219	22.4	1.8
1953–57	1,988	29.2	1.5
1958	445	5.4	1.2
1959	483	5.7	1.2
1960	503	5.2	1.0
1961	518	5.8	1.1
1962	556	6.6	1.2
1963	589	6.9	1.2
1964	629	6.2	1.0
1965	676	6.2	0.9

[a] SOURCE: Agency for International Development, Statistics and Reports Division, *U.S. Overseas Loans and Grants and Assistance from International Organizations*, Special report prepared for the House Committee on Foreign Affairs (Washington, D.C.: Department of State, March 18, 1966).

[b] Billions of current dollars.

[c] Billions of current dollars. Includes military assistance, Export-Import Bank long-term loans, capital subscriptions to international organizations, and other forms of aid. (See Table 3.)

1965. During the late 1940's and early 1950's, nearly 2 per cent of the GNP was being channeled into foreign aid, but since 1957, only about 1 per cent of GNP is being used for this purpose. An even better measure of the declining American aid burden is furnished by comparing total aid with per capita GNP. Table 2 indicates that the aid burden is now one-third lighter than it was in the 1946–52 period.

TABLE 2

AID BURDEN INDEX, FISCAL YEARS 1946–65[a]

Fiscal Year	Aid Burden Index[b]
1946–48	3.1
1949–52	2.8[c]
1953–57	2.4
1958	2.1
1959	2.1
1960	1.9
1961	2.0
1962	2.2
1963	2.2
1964	1.9
1965	1.8

[a] SOURCE: Agency for International Development, Statistics and Reports Division, *U.S. Overseas Loans and Grants and Assistance from International Organizations*, Special report prepared for the House Committee on Foreign Affairs (Washington, D.C.: Department of State, March 18, 1966).

[b] Aid Burden Index $= \dfrac{\text{Total aid in millions of dollars}}{\text{Per capita GNP in current dollars}}$

[c] A decrease in the index number indicates a decrease in the foreign aid burden.

2. The aid program has become increasingly diffuse. In its early years, the program was concentrated in approximately twenty nations; today about three times as many nations receive U.S. aid. This enlargement of the program is illustrated in Chart I, which indicates the per capita expenditure by AID in various regions. Under the ERP, more than $20 per capita per year was distributed, compared with $1 or $2 per capita per year being disbursed today. Those who wonder why today's aid program fails to yield the spectacular results of the ERP would do well to ponder this statistic.

3. A decreasing emphasis on military aid constitutes another trend in foreign assistance. Although there was a sudden spurt in military aid between 1950 and 1954, such aid has diminished since then, as is illustrated in Chart II. Table 3, which is based on more comprehensive data on aid than Chart II, reveals a similar trend. In 1958, total military aid was $2.4 billion, and total economic

CHART I

REGIONAL DISTRIBUTION OF AID FROM AID, FISCAL YEAR 1966[a]

(*In Millions of Dollars*)

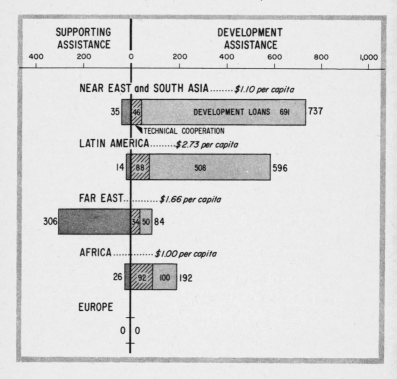

a SOURCE: Agency for International Development, *Proposed Mutual Defense and Development Programs*, FY [*Fiscal Year*] 1966, Summary presentation to Congress (Washington, D.C.: Government Printing Office, March, 1965).

aid was $2.9 billion; by 1965, military aid had fallen to $1.3 billion, while economic aid had climbed to $4.9 billion.

4. Greater emphasis has been placed on loans vis-à-vis grants. Two factors account for this trend. Since military assistance almost always takes the form of grants, the reductions in military aid have resulted in almost equal reductions in total grants, with little or no reduction on the loan side of the ledger. The second

CHART II

TREND OF APPROPRIATIONS FOR U.S. MILITARY ASSISTANCE,
FISCAL YEARS 1948–65[a]

(*In Billions of Dollars*)

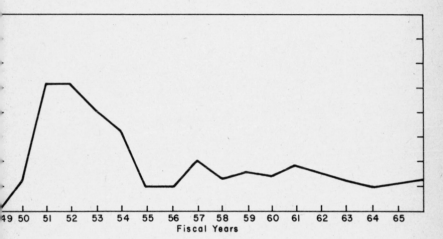

Fiscal Years

[a] SOURCE: Agency for International Development, *Proposed Mutual Defense and Development Programs, FY 1966*, Summary presentation to Congress (Washington, D.C.: Government Printing Office, March, 1965).

factor is the desire of Congress—expressed many times since 1946 —to place economic aid on a loan basis. The increased importance of loans in the activities of AID and its predecessors is illustrated in Chart III. It should also be noted that most of the economic-aid channels outside of AID—IDA, IBRD, Export-Import Bank, etc.—are loan channels. In this respect, Table 3 is likely to be misleading since funds distributed through international lending agencies are shown as grants. Thus, insofar as the United States has placed more emphasis on multilateral lending, Table 3 indicates a growth in grants. This is not to say that Table 3 is wrong—the United States *does give* money to the IDA. The point is that an increased emphasis on loans—both multilateral and unilateral—in American aid strategy may not be adequately reflected in tables that are concerned with the cost to the American taxpayer. The attitudes expressed toward aid by Congress during the last twenty years indicate that the trend toward loans will continue.

SUMMARY OF U.S. AID ACTIVITY BY

(In Millions

| PROGRAM | U.S. OVERSEAS LOANS AND GRANTS: | | | | |
| | Postwar Relief Period 1946–48 | Marshall Plan Period 1949–52 | Mutual Security Act | | |
			1953–57	1958	1959
AID and Predecessor Agencies[b]					
Total	—	14,505	9,142	1,620	1,916
Loans	—	1,577	868	417	626
Grants	—	12,928	8,274	1,203	1,291
Social Progress Trust Fund[c]	—	—	—	—	—
Food for Peace[d]					
Total	—	83	2,668	787	868
Title I[e] *(total sales agreements)*[f]	(—)	(—)	(2,018)	(703)	(796)
Less *(planned for U.S. uses)*	(—)	(—)	(555)	(302)	(216)
Title I: *Planned for loans and grants*[g]	—	—	1,463	400	580
Grants for common defense (104c)	—	—	236	69	35
Grants for economic development (104e)	—	—	210	47	107
Loans to private industry (104e)	—	—	2	68	98
Loans to governments (104g)	—	—	1,015	216	340
Title I: *Assistance from other country sales agreements*[h]	—	—	37	5	—
Title II: *Emergency relief and economic development*[i]	—	—	317	87	48
Title III: *Voluntary relief agencies*[j]	—	83	850	295	240
Title IV: *Dollar credit sales*[k]	—	—	—	—	—
Export-Import Bank Long-Term Loans[l]	2,091	904	1,498	506	704
Other U.S. Economic Programs[m]	12,553	4,049	526	23	19
Total Economic	14,644	19,541	13,833	2,936	3,507
Loans	8,058	3,458	3,443	1,210	1,768
Grants	6,586	16,082	10,391	1,727	1,739
Military Assistance Program					
Charged to appropriations[n]	—	2,517	14,863	2,363	2,110
Credit assistance	15	39	60	—	—
Grants	—	2,517	14,848	2,325	2,050
(Additional grants from excess stocks)	(—)	(513)	(448)	(257)	(197)
Other Military Assistance[o]	481	324	444	41	50
Total Military	481	2,842	15,307	2,404	2,160
TOTAL ECONOMIC AND MILITARY	15,125	22,383	29,141	5,341	5,667
Loans	8,058	3,458	3,457	1,248	1,827
Grants	7,067	18,924	25,683	4,092	3,840

3

FISCAL YEAR AND PROGRAM, 1946–65[a]
of Dollars)

NET OBLIGATIONS AND LOAN AUTHORIZATIONS							REPAYMENTS AND INTEREST 1946–65[q]	TOTAL LESS REPAYMENTS AND INTEREST
Period		Foreign Assistance Act Period				Total 1946–65[p]		
1960	1961	1962	1963	1964	1965			
1,866	2,012	2,508	2,297	2,136	2,026	40,030	1,758	38,272
564	707	1,329	1,343	1,328	1,122	9,881	1,758	8,122
1,302	1,305	1,180	954	808	904	30,150	–	30,150
–	–	226	127	42	101	497	13	484
1,052	1,228	1,550	1,713	1,750	1,527	13,225	446	12,779
(1,055)	(1,035)	(1,292)	(1,198)	(1,248)	(1,059)	(10,404)	(–)	(10,404)
(238)	(285)	(233)	(187)	(231)	(138)	(2,385)	(–)	(2,385)
818	749	1,059	1,011	1,017	921	8,019	429	7,590
19	62	143	113	138	106	921	–	921
309	232	287	252	252	113	1,811	–	1,811
79	60	87	62	60	86	602	61	541
411	396	542	583	567	616	4,685	368	4,317
–	–	–	15	–	7	64	2	62
62	239	169	286	225	184	1,616	–	1,616
172	240	271	325	391	235	3,101	–	3,101
–	–	51	77	118	180	426	16	410
283	876	396	455	531	772	9,015	5,844	3,172
97	88	234	363	254	470	18,675	4,091	14,585
3,298	4,204	4,915	4,956	4,714	4,895	81,443	12,152	69,291
1,340	2,039	2,647	2,726	2,670	2,893	32,252	12,152	20,100
1,958	2,166	2,267	2,229	2,043	2,002	49,191	–	49,191
1,718	1,374	1,448	1,809	1,498	1,310	32,909	302	32,607
21	30	21	44	83	71	556	302	254
1,697	1,344	1,427	1,765	1,415	1,239	32,354	–	32,354
(289)	(328)	(248)	(188)	(125)	(201)	(2,847)	(–)	(2,847)
127	91	79	71	26	2	1,738	–	1,738
1,845	1,466	1,527	1,881	1,523	1,313	34,647	302	34,345
5,143	5,670	6,441	6,836	6,237	6,208	116,090	12,454	103,636
1,361	2,069	2,668	2,770	2,753	2,964	32,807	12,454	20,353
3,782	3,601	3,773	4,066	3,484	3,244	83,283	–	83,283

[Notes to Table 3 begin on page 33.]

CHART III

AID COUNTRY AND REGIONAL PROGRAMS FINANCED BY LOANS,
1953–66[a]

(*In Per Cents*)

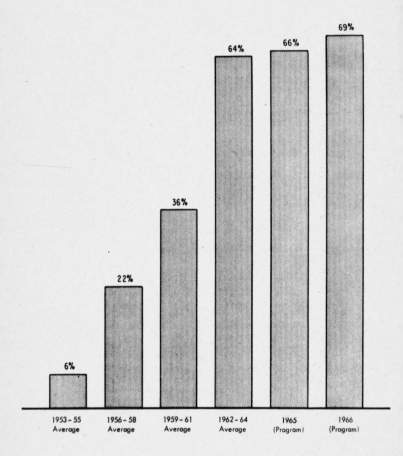

[a] SOURCE: Agency for International Development, *Loan Terms, Debt Burden, and Development*, Summary report (Washington, D.C.: Department of State, April, 1965).

5. Another trend is related to the geographic distribution of funds. Europe, as one can see in Table 4, was by far the most important recipient of aid in the first decade after the war. Since

TABLE 4

REGIONAL DISTRIBUTION OF U.S. AID, FISCAL YEARS 1946-65[a]

(*In Per Cents*)

Fiscal Year	Europe	Latin America	Near East and South Asia	Far East	Africa
1946–48	69	2	6	15	b
1949–52	69	3	9	16	b
1953–57	45	7	16	27	1
1958	26	8	30	30	2
1959	22	11	29	29	3
1960	22	8	38	25	4
1961	15	18	31	23	8
1962	11	20	34	20	8
1963	12	16	32	23	8
1964	11	21	31	21	7
1965	11	22	33	23	6

a SOURCE: Agency for International Development, Statistics and Reports Division, *U.S. Overseas Loans and Grants and Assistance from International Organizations*, Special report prepared for the House Committee on Foreign Affairs (Washington, D.C.: Department of State, March 18, 1966). The data include all United States overseas loans and grants which were allocated on a regional basis—including AID and predecessor agencies, Food for Peace, Export-Import Bank, and military assistance. The percentages do not add to 100 because of the omission of nonregional funds, such as gifts to international organizations, and of funds for Oceania.

b Less than 1 per cent.

then, it has received relatively little aid; in fact, Europe has now become an important aid giver. Latin America became a large-scale recipient of aid only after 1960, with the establishment of the

NOTES TO TABLE 3

a SOURCE: Agency for International Development, Statistics and Reports Division, *U.S. Overseas Loans and Grants and Assistance from International Organizations*, special report prepared for the House Committee on Foreign Affairs (Washington, D.C.: Department of State, March 18, 1966). Figures in columns may not add to totals due to rounding.

b *Agency for International Development.*—The data cover commitments for economic and technical assistance made by AID and its predecessor agencies. Commitments may be defined as development loans authorized and obligations of other AID funds. All annual commitment data as well as the cumulative totals are on a "net" basis, that is, new obligations from funds appropriated for that fiscal year, plus or minus reobligations or deobligations of prior year funds. Data for FY 1949 cover 15 months, from the start of the Marshall Plan, April 3, 1948, to June 30, 1949. Commitments made by AID and its predecessor agencies are shown separately for loans and grants. The loan total covers development loans, Alliance for Progress loans, supporting assistance loans, and

IDB and the Alliance for Progress. The Near East, South Asia, and the Far East have been receiving relatively large amounts of aid since the mid-1950's. Africa, however, remains the stepchild of the American aid program. The small proportion of aid channeled to that area probably reflects both its low priority vis-à-vis other areas in the eyes of policy-makers and a belief that former colonial powers, such as France and Britain, should be responsible for the bulk of aid to Africa. The over-all trend has been to concentrate less on Europe and more on the underdeveloped areas; this trend may be expected to persist.

GOALS OF AID STRATEGY

Since 1945, the United States has expended more than $100 billion on various forms of foreign aid. About one-third has gone into military programs, and almost another third has gone into programs for postwar relief and reconstruction. (See Chart IV.) Thus,

---

any other loans from AID or predecessor agency funds. The loans made from the Social Progress Trust Fund by the Inter-American Development Bank (IDB) are shown separately.

c *Social Progress Trust Fund.*—The data represent loans authorized by the IDB from the $525-million Social Progress Trust Fund which the Bank administers; they also include minor amounts of technical assistance grants from the Trust Fund. This Fund was established in FY 1961 as part of the Alliance for Progress program and is available for Latin American countries only.

d *Food for Peace.*—P.L. 480 (Agricultural Trade Development and Assistance Act of 1954) and amendments thereto.

e *Title I: Sales for foreign currency.*—Title I of the Act provides for the sale of surplus agricultural commodities for foreign currency, and in Section 104, specifies the ways in which these currencies may be used.

f The figures for sales agreements shown as a parenthetical item, not added into total assistance, represent the export market value of sales agreements signed during each year with minor adjustments for subsequent shortfalls in deliveries. An additional parenthetical item, "Planned for U.S. Uses," is also shown. These figures represent the portion of the sales proceeds planned for U.S. uses such as payment of U.S. obligations or for special foreign currency programs to develop agricultural markets, provide military family housing, promote trade fairs and the like. They include any amounts used under Section 104d to purchase aid goods for other countries (see footnote g). The "Total Sales Agreements" amount less the "Planned for U.S. Uses" represents the country aid portion of the sales agreements and is equal to the entries shown on line "Title I: Planned for Loans and Grants."

g The figures for "Planned for Loans and Grants" represent those portions of the foreign currency proceeds of the sales which are planned as loans or grants to the recipient country under Sections 104c, e, and g, or as Cooley Amendment loans to private industry in the foreign country under Section 104e. The portion of each sales agreement which is "Planned for Loans and Grants" is

CHART IV

Composition of Total U.S. Overseas Loans and Grants, Fiscal Years 1946–65[a]

(In Billions of Dollars)

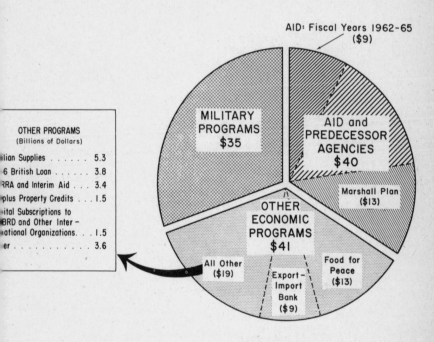

AID: Fiscal Years 1962-65 ($9)

MILITARY PROGRAMS $35

AID and PREDECESSOR AGENCIES $40

Marshall Plan ($13)

OTHER ECONOMIC PROGRAMS $41

All Other ($19)

Export-Import Bank ($9)

Food for Peace ($13)

OTHER PROGRAMS
(Billions of Dollars)

...lian Supplies	5.3
...6 British Loan	3.8
...RRA and Interim Aid	3.4
...plus Property Credits	1.5
...ital Subscriptions to BRD and Other Inter-national Organizations	1.5
...er	3.6

$116 Billion

a SOURCE: Agency for International Development, Statistics and Reports Division, *U.S. Overseas Loans and Grants and Assistance from International Organizations*, Special report prepared for the House Committee on Foreign Affairs (Washington, D.C.: Department of State, March 18, 1966).

since the Marshall Plan, only about one-third of the $100 billion has been in the form of economic aid. The question often asked is: What did America get for its money? The many goals of foreign aid make it difficult to answer this question. Several views re-

included in the assistance totals in the year the sales agreement was signed. A few agreements are more than a year's requirement. These have been pro-rated. In addition, adjustments have been made for actual shortfall of deliveries from annual agreements.

h Under "Title I: Assistance from Other Country Sales Agreements" are shown the Section 104d Triangular Trade transactions whereby a third country receives, on a loan or grant basis, foreign currency generated by a surplus commodity sales agreement between the United States and another foreign country.

i *Title II: Famine relief and other emergency assistance.*—Title II authorizes funds for the transfer of commodities held in stock by the Commodity Credit Corporation (CCC) to help friendly foreign people to meet famine or other urgent or extraordinary relief requirements or to promote economic development. The data represent commodities authorized at CCC cost, plus ocean freight distributed by country.

j *Title III: Donations for voluntary relief agencies.*—The data included under Title III cover only the donations of surplus commodities to voluntary relief agencies such as CARE, National Catholic Welfare Conference, Lutheran World Relief, etc., for distribution to needy people abroad. Barter transactions are not included. The figures represent authorizations for voluntary relief agency donations, valued at CCC cost. For years prior to FY 1955, the data represent transfers authorized under Section 416 of the Agricultural Act of 1949 (P.L. 81-439). The data for FY 1952 represents transfers during FY's 1950–52.

k *Title IV: Dollar credit sales.*—Title IV, added to the Act in September, 1959, provides for dollar credit sales of surplus agricultural commodities, repayable within 20 years. The data shown represent the export market value of the credit sales agreements signed. Some agreements have covered more than a 1-year program and these have been prorated.

l *Export-Import Bank long-term loans.*—These data were compiled from the reports of the Export-Import Bank. They represent authorizations for loans by the Export-Import Bank with maturities of five years or more. They exclude credits with maturities of less than five years, and those loans bought by private banks and other institutions. The data also exclude all export guarantees and insurance authorized by the Bank. Cancellations and terminations are deducted from loans authorized. Repayments have not been taken into account. The fiscal year data have been constructed so that if a loan made in one year is increased in a later year, the increase is included at the time it occurred; but if the loan is decreased or canceled in a later year, the loan has been decreased in the year originally authorized.

m *Other non-AID economic programs.*—In general, the programs included here predated the Mutual Security Program (MSP). The major items (not shown) included are "UNRRA," "Civilian Supplies (including Government and Relief in Occupied Areas)," "Surplus Property Credits," "Civilian Relief in Korea," "Greek-Turkish Aid," and "Philippine Rehabilitation." A few items are also included which ran concurrently with MSP, such as "Inter-American and Related Highways" and "Elimination of Foot and Mouth Disease in garding the purposes of the aid program may be found even among those who participate in building a consensus in support of aid policy. Another problem is that it is sometimes impossible to determine if the goals of the aid program are being realized due to the

---

Mexico." "Occupied Areas Commodity Credits" are not included since these were short-term credits generally not over 15 months. To the extent possible, these early programs have been presented on an obligations basis. Programs obligated prior to June 30, 1945, such as Lend Lease, have been excluded even though expenditures continued in 1946 and later. For UNRRA, Civilian Supplies, and certain minor programs, obligations by fiscal year were not available. For these programs, therefore, it was necessary to present data on an expenditures basis, and to include an unknown portion obligated prior to July 1, 1945, but delivered in FY 1946 and subsequently. In recent years, the principal programs in this category have been capital subscriptions to the IDB and the IDA; the Peace Corps; Philippine War Damage Claims; and the United Nations bond issue.

n *Foreign Assistance Act military program.*—The data represent primarily grants of military equipment, supplies, and services purchased with appropriated funds. They also include the cost of repair and rehabilitation of excess stocks furnished without cost to the Military Assistance Program, and the cost of packing, crating, handling, and transportation of equipment and supplies. The loan portion represents sales to recipient countries of military equipment and supplies initially credit-financed with MAP funds. The annual data represent deliveries. The cumulative total represents the total amount programmed for each country for the period 1950–65 and, therefore, the difference between the sum of the fiscal years and the cumulative total is the value of goods programmed but not yet delivered. The line "From Excess Stocks" represents the *acquisition* value of equipment and supplies excess to the requirements of the U.S. military departments granted to countries *without charge* to MAP-appropriated funds. These amounts are shown for information only, and are not included in the total.

o *Other military assistance.*—Included here are the military portion of the items (not shown) "Greek-Turkish Aid," "China Naval Aid," "P.L. 454 Philippine Aid," and "Vessel Loans." Since the latter are essentially transfers on an indeterminate basis, generally requiring only the return of the vessel, if available, they are treated here as grants. For these vessel loans, the data represent the estimated value of the vessels; the activation cost is included in MAP data.

p The commitment data for all economic and military programs are shown by U.S. fiscal years arranged in four broad groupings: Postwar Relief Period (1946–48); Marshall Plan Period (1948–52); Mutual Security Act Period (1953–61); and Foreign Assistance Act Period (1962–65). AID has been in existence only during the latter period.

q The "Repayments and Interest" column shows the cumulative principal repaid and interest collected for the period 1946–65 against loans made during that period. It excludes any repayments or interest collections against loans made prior to July 1, 1945. These data include repayments and interest collections in dollars and in foreign currencies; the latter are expressed in dollar equivalents. For loans fully or largely repaid on which interest has been collected for a number of years, the total repayment and interest figure will frequently be in excess of the original loan.

program itself or to extraneous circumstances. With these difficulties in mind, we shall examine four hypotheses about the effectiveness of aid in realizing different goals.

1. *Aid limits Communist influence.*—If the borders of the Communist bloc had expanded rapidly during the last twenty years, the hypothesis that aid impedes the spread of Communism would probably have been rejected. Since 1950, however, there has been relatively little change in the size of the Sino-Soviet bloc. Although China fell to the Communists in 1949, Greece and Turkey were able to fend off Communist threats to their security. The uncommitted nations have usually been able to play off the two superblocs against each other without joining either. In Europe, where aid was disbursed at an annual rate of $20 per person under the Marshall Plan, the influence of domestic Communists has dwindled rapidly since the early postwar years. The efficacy of aid in limiting the expansion of Communist influence is probably due to three factors: (1) The existence of alternative sources of aid weakens the bargaining value of the Soviet Union's aid program; (2) aid helps the recipient countries strengthen military defenses against external threats; and (3) aid enables recipient governments to take steps toward reducing the economic causes of social and political unrest.

2. *Aid stimulates recovery from war.*—The most spectacular success of aid as a technique of statecraft developed during the first five years after the most destructive war in history. By 1950, Marshall Plan participants—Germany excepted—were producing more industrial and agricultural products than they had before the war. And the volume both of intra-European trade and European trade with the rest of the world had passed the prewar mark. By 1955, Europe was enjoying a better standard of living than it had ever known. One measure of the success of the Marshall Plan was the absence of charges that it was a failure, even from the harshest critics of foreign aid. Ironically, it is more common to hear that aid did too good a job in helping Europe recover, thus putting American industry at a competitive disadvantage.

In some ways, helping to promote European recovery was easier than is the task of trying to foster economic growth in less-developed areas. In Europe, most people knew how to read and write; they were familiar with machinery; they had the social values of an industrial society; and they had a fierce desire to recover. In underdeveloped countries, aid administrators cannot assume that any of these factors prevail.

3. *Aid spurs economic development.*—Since 1949, when President Truman delivered his inaugural address containing the famous Point Four proposal, promoting economic growth in poor countries has been one goal of American aid strategy. Although aid administrators can point to some impressive accomplishments, there have been, and are likely to be, no results so spectacular as those of the Marshall Plan. It is true that deaths from such diseases as cholera and malaria have declined sharply, but it is also true that the falling death rate has meant more mouths to feed. It is true that total production in Asia, Africa, and Latin America has risen at an average of over 4 per cent a year since 1950, but it is also true that population has increased by about 3 per cent a year. Although the results to date may be unimpressive, one should remember that the United States is spending only one-tenth as much per person in these areas as it did in Europe between 1948 and 1952.

4. *Aid wins friends.*—It is sometimes alleged that if a government of a nation that has ever received any American aid criticizes the United States, the aid to such a nation has "failed." This is not to say that policy-makers think in these terms, but many people—usually foes of the aid program—claim that gratitude should be the goal of foreign aid. Whatever the policy-makers think, it should be noted that aid has been less effective in winning friends than it has been in obtaining other objectives. In other words, of the four hypotheses, this one is least likely to be valid. All, however, should be regarded as tentative and subject to further testing as the aid program evolves.

Major Components of the Aid Program

AID and Its Predecessors

In the minds of most Americans, foreign aid is associated with the activities of the "aid agency"; that is, AID and its predecessors. Largely because of continuing Congressional dissatisfaction with the aid program, this agency has been reorganized many times. In 1948, the Economic Cooperation Administration (ECA) was set up to administer the Marshall Plan. In 1951, ECA was replaced by the Mutual Security Agency (MSA), reflecting the shift in emphasis toward military aspects of aid. Two years later, it was replaced by the Foreign Operations Administration (FOA). In 1955, in an effort to reorient the aid program toward long-term economic goals, the International Cooperation Administration

(ICA) was established. This agency continued until it was replaced by AID, in 1961.

AID and its forerunners have provided aid in the form of grants and soft loans. Approximately $30 billion out of a total of $40 billion have been in the form of grants. Grants, however, are on the way out. Whereas more than 90 per cent of ERP aid was in the form of grants, only 30 per cent of today's AID funds are so allocated. Two types of soft loans have been used by the aid agency. Between 1954 and 1961, the emphasis was on dollar loans that could be repaid over a period of thirty or forty years at low-interest rates and in inconvertible currency. But since 1961, all AID dollar loans have been repayable only in dollars, although on lenient terms. Interest rates on AID loans have been raised by Congress from three-quarters of 1 per cent in 1961 to 2.5 per cent in 1964. Recent AID loans have also been repayable over thirty or forty years. Future aid from AID will probably take the form of dollar-repayable soft loans, but the agency will have to fight hard to keep Congress from hardening the terms of its loans.

Food for Peace

In 1954, the domestic farm price support program had filled government storage bins with huge quantities of "surplus"[5] agricultural commodities. Primarily to get rid of these surpluses, and secondarily to augment foreign aid, Congress passed the Agricultural Trade Development and Assistance Act of 1954, better known as P.L. 480. This law authorized the transfer abroad of surplus agricultural products in a variety of ways, e.g., by sale, by barter, and as gifts. Without question, the most important section of P.L. 480 is Title I, which authorizes the sale of surpluses for inconvertible foreign currency. Under Title I, nearly $10 billion worth of sales agreements (valued at world market prices) have been negotiated. About three-fourths of the foreign currency received in Title I transactions is given or loaned back to the country from which it came. P.L. 480 is easily the most popular aid program in Congress, and it is therefore likely to enjoy a long and vigorous life.

Export-Import Bank

One of America's oldest aid agencies is the Washington-based

[5] Note that surplus merely means that they could not be sold on the American market at the minimum support price. It does not mean that they could not have been sold at lower prices.

Export-Import Bank. Originally established in 1934, it has always been especially interested in promoting the exports of the United States. In 1945, the Bank was revamped and given a lending authority of $3.5 billion. This authority has been increased since then —in 1953, 1954, 1958, and 1963—to the present level of $9 billion. The Export-Import Bank enjoys the enviable position of not having to face the House Appropriations Committee to get its money. It relies instead on what is commonly called "backdoor financing"; that is, the lending authority lets the Bank borrow directly from the Treasury. When loan repayments come in, the Bank can re-lend them without seeking new authority. The only requirement is that total loans outstanding at any one time cannot exceed $9 billion.

The Bank is known as a hard lender. All of its dollar loans are repayable in dollars at about 5 per cent interest; most of these loans extend over a period of from five to twenty-five years. Between 1946 and 1965, the Bank made long-term loans of $9 billion. As Table 5 shows, Europe was the main borrower in the

TABLE 5

REGIONAL DISTRIBUTION OF EXPORT-IMPORT BANK LOANS,
FISCAL YEARS 1946–65[a]

(*In Per Cents*)

Fiscal Year	Europe	Latin America	Near East and South Asia	Far East	Africa
1946–48	87	8	3	2	[b]
1949–52	8	55	18	13	5
1953–57	4	74	5	6	10
1958	12	42	35	12	[b]
1959	23	58	6	12	1
1960	29	36	10	22	2
1961	11	54	17	13	5
1962	16	40	16	16	13
1963	41	18	13	26	2
1964	42	30	16	10	2
1965	41	33	10	11	5

[a] SOURCE: Agency for International Development, Statistics and Reports Division, *U.S. Overseas Loans and Grants and Assistance from International Organizations*, Special report prepared for the House Committee on Foreign Affairs (Washington, D.C.: Department of State, March 18, 1966). Percentages do not add to 100 because of rounding.

[b] Less than 1 per cent.

1946–48 period. After Europe, Latin America received the bulk of the Bank's attention until about 1960. The figures for 1963, 1964, and 1965 indicate that Europe is again drawing heavily on the Bank. No area other than Europe or Latin America has ever received as much as 40 per cent of the Bank's funds. The survival of the Export-Import Bank for the last thirty years suggests that it will probably still be around thirty years hence.

IBRD–IFC–IDA

The International Bank and its two affiliates, the International Finance Corporation (IFC) and the International Development Association, are the main multilateral channels through which nations disburse foreign aid. The IBRD, also known as the World Bank, has lent nearly $9 billion since it came into existence in 1945. At first, the IBRD concentrated on European reconstruction, but after 1948 its attention shifted to the less-developed areas. (See Table 6.) Although the IBRD total capitalization ex-

TABLE 6

REGIONAL DISTRIBUTION OF IBRD LOANS, FISCAL YEARS 1946–65[a]

(*In Per Cents*)

Fiscal Year	Europe	Latin America	Near East and South Asia	Far East	Africa
1946–48	97	3	—	—	—
1949–52	15	34	17	3	19
1953	20	17	24	—	8
1954	12	30	9	12	21
1955	37	31	13	—	6
1956	10	19	31	11	29
1957	31	13	28	7	5
1958	14	15	31	23	16
1959	15	20	30	19	16
1960	11	21	30	13	25
1961	9	25	40	22	5
1962	4	47	19	9	10
1963	21	29	26	17	8
1964	18	32	10	24	11
1965	29	21	17	22	12

[a] SOURCE: Agency for International Development, Statistics and Reports Division, *U.S. Overseas Loans and Grants and Assistance from International Organizations*, Special report prepared for the House Committee on Foreign Affairs (Washington, D.C.: Department of State, March 18, 1966). Percentages do not add to 100 because of rounding.

ceeds $20 billion, most of its activities are financed by floating bonds in private-capital markets. Nine-tenths of the $20 billion is merely a guarantee of the IBRD's credit by member governments. The IBRD has long been a favorite of American policy-makers because it uses a system of voting weighted according to financial contributions. The United States, as the biggest contributor, thereby wields about one-third of the votes. Similar voting systems prevail in the IDA and IFC.

Like the Export-Import Bank, the World Bank is a hard lender. Its loans are repayable in foreign exchange at interest rates of 5 or 6 per cent, and they usually extend over ten to twenty-five years.

The IFC was established in 1956 in order to provide equity financing for development projects. The organization was small when it started and it has remained that way. Its originally authorized capital was $100 million, which was increased by $10 million in 1963. Few people have been impressed by this agency's activities, and it is unlikely that its funds will be expanded much in the future.

The IDA, which came into being in 1960, dwarfs the IFC. The IDA acquired about $750 million in usable foreign exchange from its initial subscriptions, and recent subscriptions have doubled this amount. The United States' share in each case was $312 million. IDA loans are repayable in dollars over fifty years, with no repayment for the first ten years, then 1 per cent per annum for the next ten years, then 3 per cent per annum for thirty years. No interest is charged, but there is a service charge of three-quarters of 1 per cent to meet administrative costs of the IDA. During its first four years of operations, IDA distributed almost $800 million; because of the popularity of this type of aid among recipients, we can expect to see IDA activities expand rapidly in coming years.

Inter-American Development Bank

Since 1958, the United States has taken an increased interest in Latin American problems. In that year, the United States Government acquiesced to Latin America's desire for a regional lending institution; in 1959 it was established, and in 1961 it made its first loan. For its regular operations, the IDB originally commanded $850 million, of which $450 million was callable but not paid in. The callable portion serves as a guarantee of the IDB's credit, thus helping it to raise money in the private capital market. In 1964, the total was raised to $2 billion, with three-fourths of this callable but not paid in. By 1965, the IDB had made hard loans amounting to more than $500 million. These loans were repayable in dollars at interest rates of about 6 per cent.

The IDB also has a soft-loan window, the Fund for Special Operations. The Fund began with $150 million and has since acquired another $70 million. Loans from the Fund are usually repayable in inconvertible local currency at very low interest rates. In view of these lenient terms, it is not surprising that over $170 million was committed by January, 1965. In 1964, the popularity of this fund led the IDB Board of Governors to approve an increase in its resources of $900 million, of which the United States was to furnish $750 million.

In addition to its own operations, the IDB administered the Social Progress Trust Fund on behalf of the United States from 1961 to 1965. This fund, amounting to $525 million, made loans on terms similar to those of the Fund for Special Operations. Although the future of the Social Progress Trust Fund is unclear, it will probably soon be merged with the Fund for Special Operations.

III

The Roots of American
Foreign-Aid Policy

It is widely believed that economic development first became a goal of American foreign policy when the Truman Administration moved to implement the President's Point Four proposal in 1949. Actually, American policy-makers had evinced an interest in this goal several years earlier. During the 1943–48 period, the techniques of statecraft that were envisaged as appropriate means for encouraging economic development included trade liberalization, stimulation of private investment, and establishment of the International Bank. The readings in this chapter are intended to give the reader a perspective on the early postwar aid policies of the United States.

The *Statement of the Foreign Loan Policy of the United States Government* (see Document 2), issued in 1946, is especially important, for two reasons. First, it provides a good picture of the basic assumptions of American aid policy in the early postwar period; second, it provides a basis for estimating the degree of change represented by later policies.

Four basic ideas in this statement should be noted: (1) Economic stability and the maintenance of peace are interconnected. This idea has had a telling influence on American policy from that day to this. It is, perhaps, the single most important assumption in the planning and operation of the aid program. (2) The United States Government cannot do much; primary responsibility rests with the potential aid recipient. Time and again, since 1946, American spokesmen have advised poor nations to rely on their own domestic efforts and to secure necessary external capital from private sources and the World Bank. (3) American trade barriers should be lowered. This has also been a fundamental principle of American statecraft during the past twenty years. Executive Branch spokesmen have consistently argued that the lowering of American tariffs would reduce the need for aid and would permit foreigners to service their private foreign loans. (4) The United States must stimulate its exports in order to stave off depression and maintain

45

full employment. Here we see an important change in American policy. Although this idea figured prominently in early postwar planning, it no longer plays much part in the thinking of foreign-policy planners. The belief still exists, of course, that higher levels of international trade will benefit the participants, but one rarely hears such goals related to countercyclical economic policy. More efficient economic tools have been developed to control the business cycle. With the exception of this fourth point, the policy assumptions of 1946 and those of today are strikingly similar. Considering the revolutionary changes that have been taking place in the world, one is led by this similarity to question the significance of the "agonizing reappraisals" of foreign policy that are alleged to have occurred in the last twenty years.

1. *The United Nations Monetary and Financial Conference*[1]

[EDITOR'S NOTE: *In July, 1944, forty-four nations met at Bretton Woods, New Hampshire, to draw up articles of agreement for the establishment of the IMF and IBRD. This statement to the closing session of the conference, delivered by Secretary of the Treasury Henry Morgenthau, Jr., who was Chairman of the American delegation, indicates what policy-makers hoped these institutions would do with regard to both postwar reconstruction and long-term economic development.*]

I am gratified to announce that the Conference at Bretton Woods has successfully completed the task before it.

It was, as we knew when we began, a difficult task, involving complicated technical problems. We came here to work out methods which would do away with the economic evils—the competitive currency devaluation and destructive impediments to trade, which preceded the present war. We have succeeded in that effort.

The actual details of an international monetary and financial agreement may seem mysterious to the general public. Yet at the heart of it lie the most elementary bread-and-butter realities of daily life. What we have done here in Bretton Woods is to devise machinery by which men and women everywhere can freely ex-

[1] SOURCE: "The United Nations Monetary and Financial Conference: Address by the Secretary of the Treasury," *Department of State Bulletin*, XI, No. 266 (July 30, 1944), 111–13.

change, on a fair and stable basis, the goods which they produce through their labor. And we have taken the initial steps through which the nations of the world will be able to help one another in economic development to their mutual advantage and for the enrichment of all.

The representatives of the 44 nations faced differences of opinion frankly and reached an agreement which is rooted in genuine understanding. None of the nations represented here has altogether had its own way. We have had to yield to one another not in respect to principles or essentials but in respect to methods and procedural details. The fact that we have done so, and that we have done it in a continuing spirit of good will and mutual trust, is, I believe, one of the hopeful and heartening portents of our times. Here is a sign blazoned upon the horizon, written large upon the threshold of the future—a sign for men in battle, for men at work in mines and mills, and in the fields, and a sign for women whose hearts have been burdened and anxious lest the cancer of war assail yet another generation—a sign that the peoples of the earth are learning how to join hands and work in unity.

There is a curious notion that the protection of national interests and the development of international cooperation are conflicting philosophies—that somehow or other men of different nations cannot work together without sacrificing the interests of their particular nations. There has been talk of this sort—and from people who ought to know better—concerning the international cooperative nature of the undertaking just completed at Bretton Woods. I am perfectly certain that no delegation to this Conference has lost sight for a moment of the particular national interests it was sent here to represent. The American delegation, which I have had the honor of leading, has at all times been conscious of its primary obligation—the protection of American interests. And the other representatives here have been no less loyal or devoted to the welfare of their own people.

Yet none of us found any incompatibility between devotion to our own countries and joint action.[2] Indeed, we have found on the contrary that the only genuine safeguard for our national interests lies in international cooperation. We have come to recognize that the wisest and most effective way to protect our national interests is through international cooperation—that is to say, through united effort for the attainment of common goals. This has been

[2] Morgenthau is a bit optimistic here. The Soviet Union sent a delegation to Bretton Woods, but never joined the IMF or the IBRD.—ED.

the great lesson taught by the war and is, I think, the great lesson of contemporary life—that the peoples of the earth are inseparably linked to one another by a deep, underlying community of purpose. This community of purpose is no less real and vital in peace than in war, and cooperation is no less essential to its fulfillment.

To seek the achievement of our aims separately through the planless, senseless rivalry that divided us in the past, or through the outright economic aggression which turned neighbors into enemies, would be to invite ruin again upon us all. Worse, it would be once more to start our steps irretraceably down the steep, disastrous road to war. That sort of extreme nationalism belongs to an era that is dead. Today the only enlightened form of national self-interest lies in international accord. At Bretton Woods we have taken practical steps toward putting this lesson into practice in the monetary and economic field.

I take it as an axiom that after this war is ended no people—and therefore no government of the people—will again tolerate prolonged and widespread unemployment. A revival of international trade is indispensable if full employment is to be achieved in a peaceful world and with standards of living which will permit the realization of men's reasonable hopes.

What are the fundamental conditions under which commerce among the nations can once more flourish?

First, there must be a reasonably stable standard of international exchange to which all countries can adhere without sacrificing the freedom of action necessary to meet their internal economic problems.

This is the alternative to the desperate tactics of the past—competitive currency depreciation, excessive tariff barriers, uneconomic barter deals, multiple currency practices, and unnecessary exchange restrictions—by which governments vainly sought to maintain employment and uphold living standards. In the final analysis, these tactics only succeeded in contributing to world-wide depression and even war. The International Fund agreed upon at Bretton Woods will help remedy this situation.

Second, long-term financial aid must be made available at reasonable rates to those countries whose industry and agriculture have been destroyed by the ruthless torch of an invader or by the heroic scorched-earth policy of their defenders.

Long-term funds must be made available also to promote sound industry and increase industrial and agricultural production in nations whose economic potentialities have not yet been developed.

It is essential to us all that these nations play their full part in the exchange of goods throughout the world.

They must be enabled to produce and to sell if they are to be able to purchase and consume. The Bank for International Reconstruction and Development is designed to meet this need.

Objections to this Bank have been raised by some bankers and a few economists. The institutions proposed by the Bretton Woods Conference would indeed limit the control which certain private bankers have in the past exercised over international finance. It would by no means restrict the investment sphere in which bankers could engage. On the contrary, it would greatly expand this sphere by enlarging the volume of international investment and would act as an enormously effective stabilizer and guarantor of loans which they might make. The chief purpose of the Bank for International Reconstruction and Development is to guarantee private loans made through the usual investment channels.[3] It would make loans only when these could not be floated through the normal channels at reasonable rates. The effect would be to provide capital for those who need it at lower interest rates than in the past and to drive only the usurious moneylenders from the temple of international finance. For my own part I cannot look upon this outcome with any sense of dismay.

Capital, like any other commodity, should be free from monopoly control and available upon reasonable terms to those who will put it to use for the general welfare.

The delegates and technical staffs at Bretton Woods have completed their portion of the job. They sat down together, talked as friends, and perfected plans to cope with the international monetary and financial problems which all their countries face. These proposals now must be submitted to the legislatures and the peoples of the participating nations. They will pass upon what has been accomplished here.

The result will be of vital importance to everyone in every country. In the last analysis, it will help determine whether or not people have jobs and the amount of money they are to find in their weekly pay envelopes. More important still, it concerns the kind of world in which our children are to grow to maturity. It concerns the opportunities which will await millions of young men when at last they can take off their uniforms and come home and roll up their sleeves and go to work.

[3] Although it was expected that this would be the chief function of the IBRD, the supposition proved to be mistaken.—ED.

This monetary agreement is but one step, of course, in the broad program of international action necessary for the shaping of a free future. But it is an indispensable step and a vital test of our intentions.

2. *The National Advisory Council on the Foreign Loan Policy of the United States*[4]

1. The foreign loan program of the United States, by assisting in the restoration of the productive capacities of war-devastated countries and by facilitating the sound economic development of other areas, is directed toward the creation of an international economic environment permitting a large volume of trade among all nations. This program is predicated on the view that a productive and peaceful world must be free from warring economic blocs and from barriers which obstruct the free flow of international trade and productive capital. Only by the reestablishment of high levels of production and trade the world over can the United States be assured in future years of a sustained level of exports appropriate to the maintenance of high levels of domestic production and employment.

By far the greatest part of the program of reconstruction is being carried out with the resources of the war-devastated countries. UNRRA takes care only of those immediate relief needs which cannot be met out of the resources of the countries involved. Another part of this program is being carried out through sales of surplus property, such sales being made on credit terms or for local foreign currencies where sales for cash payment in U.S. dollars cannot be made. The rest of the job must be handled on a loan basis.

2. The International Bank will be the principal agency to make foreign loans for reconstruction and development which private capital cannot furnish on reasonable terms. It provides a means by which the risks as well as the benefits from international lending will be shared by all of its members. It is expected that the In-

[4] SOURCE: National Advisory Council on International Monetary and Financial Problems, *Statement of the Foreign Loan Policy of United States Government* (National Advisory Council Document No. 70-A [Washington, D.C., February 21, 1946]); here reprinted from *Report of Activities of the National Advisory Council on International Monetary and Financial Problems* (80th Cong., 1st sess., H.R. Doc. 365 [Washington, D.C.: Government Printing Office, 1947]), pp. 16–21.

ternational Bank will begin lending operations in the latter half of 1946 and that during the calendar year 1947 the International Bank will assume the primary responsibility for meeting the world's international capital requirements that cannot be met by private investors on their own account and risk. With its present membership, the International Bank will be authorized to lend approximately $7.5 billion. The bulk of the funds for the loans made through the International Bank will be raised in the private capital markets of member countries, particularly in the United States. However, since this new institution will take time to develop a lending program, it will probably not be in a position to enter into more than a small volume of commitments this year.

3. The proposed loan to Britain, requiring congressional authorization, is a special case, but one which is an integral part of the foreign economic program of this Government. No other country has the same crucial position in world trade as England. Because of the wide use of the pound sterling in world trade, the large proportion of the world's trade which is carried on by the countries of the British Empire, and the extreme dependence of England upon imports, the financial and commercial practices of Britain are of utmost significance in determining what kind of world economy we shall have. The early realization of the full objectives of the Bretton Woods program, including the elimination of exchange restrictions and other barriers to world trade and investment, requires an immediate solution to Britain's financial problem. The International Monetary Fund agreement permits the continued imposition of certain of these restrictions for as much as 5 years; in the financial agreement of December 6, 1945, the British agree to their removal within 1 year from the effective date of that agreement. It is the view of the Council that the British case is unique and will not be a precedent for a loan to any other country.

4. In July, 1945, the Congress, for the purpose of making loans to war-devastated areas during the period prior to the inauguration of the International Bank and for the promotion of American exports and other special purposes, increased the lending power of the Export-Import Bank by $2.8 billion, making its total lending power $3.5 billion. At the end of 1945 the Export-Import Bank had outstanding commitments, including money authorized for cotton loans, of $1,560 million of which $1,040 million was committed in the last half of 1945. The $1,040 million of commitments made during the last half of 1945 consisted of (a) 655 million dol-

lars for the purchase of goods which originally had been included in the lend-lease program to Belgium, Netherlands, and France; (b) 165 million dollars for the purchase of other goods and services necessary for the reconstruction of Belgium, Denmark, Netherlands, and Norway; (c) 100 million dollars available to various European countries, including Finland, Belgium, Czechoslovakia, France, Italy, Netherlands, and Poland, for the purchase of raw cotton; and (d) 120 million dollars for specific export and development programs, mostly to Latin-American countries.

On January 1, 1946, the Export-Import Bank had unused lending power of $1.9 billion for making additional commitments. In addition to the $1.9 billion, there will be available during the fiscal year 1947 about $50 million from repayment of principal and an additional sum (possibly $100 million) from the cancellation of earlier commitments.

5. Pending the effective operation of the International Bank, it has been the policy of this Government to limit loans through the Export-Import Bank for reconstruction and development to the immediate minimum needs of the borrower. Among the factors taken into consideration in making loans of this character are (1) the urgency of the need of the borrower; (2) the borrower's own resources; (3) the possibility of obtaining the loan from other sources: private capital markets and other governments; (4) the ability of the borrower to make effective use of the funds; (5) the capacity of the borrower to repay; and (6) the impact of the loan on our domestic economy.

6. It is the view of the Council that, pending the establishment and operation of the International Bank, this Government can meet only a small proportion of the undoubtedly large needs of foreign countries for credits for reconstruction and development.

After careful consideration of all factors, the Council has concluded that the most urgent foreign needs will involve negotiations for loan commitments by the Export-Import Bank of approximately $3.25 billion in the period from January, 1946, through June, 1947. This is exclusive of the proposed credit to Britain.

Since the available funds of the Export-Import Bank are about $2 billion, it will be necessary in order to carry out this program to ask Congress to increase the lending authority of the Bank by $1.25 billion. Although this is a substantial increase, the Council believes that it is a minimum figure.

It is only through careful screening that it will be possible to carry out the program within the limits of the additional funds which the Congress will be asked to make available to the bank. It is the established policy of the United States Government carefully to scrutinize each loan application to determine that the need is urgent and that the funds can be obtained from no other source than the Export-Import Bank.

7. On balance the loan program will be beneficial to our domestic economy. In the transition from war to peace, expanded foreign trade will not only assist the reconstruction of foreign countries, but also ease the reconversion problem of a number of domestic industries.

During the war many of our important industries, particularly in the field of capital goods, were built up to capacities far in excess of any foreseeable peacetime domestic demands. With the elimination of war demands, much of this American productive capacity may be unused. Such a situation has already arisen, for instance, with reference to railroad equipment, machine tools, power and transmission equipment, and certain types of general industrial machinery. This is also true for some of the metals, heavy chemicals, synthetic rubber, and other industrial materials. Similarly, we have quantities of cotton, tobacco, and other agricultural products which are surplus to domestic needs. It is fortunate that this excess productive capacity is for many items which are most urgently needed by the war-devastated countries.

However, a part of the foreign demand will fall on products which are at present scarce in American markets. The Department of Commerce estimates that perhaps one-fourth of the proceeds of foreign loans will be spent on such products. In these cases the export demand, although small in relation to current domestic demand, contributes to inflationary pressures in the U.S. economy, and allocation and export controls must be maintained in order both to prevent any undue drain on domestic supplies and to assure that the minimum essential needs of other countries are met.

In this connection, account must be taken not only of the fact that there is an inevitable delay in the spending of the loans but also that the Export-Import Bank discourages the employment of loan proceeds for the purchase of commodities in scarce supply. It is also the policy of the Government to prevent the proceeds of loans from being used to purchase goods in the U.S. market when similar supplies are for sale as surplus property.

The figure of $3.25 billion in requirements through the fiscal year 1947 represents anticipated commitments and not amounts which will be actually loaned or spent. For example, on January 1, 1946, the net outstanding loans of the Export-Import Bank amounted to only $252 million although the total amount committed was $1.6 billion. In order to permit foreign governments to plan their import programs and to permit U.S. producers to schedule their production, loan commitments by the Export-Import Bank must be made well in advance of actual use of loan funds.

In view of these considerations, it is believed that a foreign lending program adequate to meet the minimum needs of foreign countries will provide additional production and employment in many American industries, and that any temporary sacrifice involved in other areas of the economy will be small compared to the long-range advantages to the United States of a peaceful, active, and growing world economy.

8. A basic question to be considered is whether at a later period foreign countries will be able to service large American loans and investments. There is little doubt regarding the ability of debtor countries after their economies have been fully reconstructed to increase their national income sufficiently to handle the service charges on American loans and investments, providing an undue part of national income of borrowing countries is not diverted to military expenditures.[5] This increase can be brought about through the modernization of economically backward areas, increased employment, and the utilization of new productive techniques, and well-directed foreign loans will make an important contribution to this development.

The ability of borrowing countries to develop an export surplus sufficient to meet service charges on foreign loans will depend in large measure upon the level of world trade. A high level of world trade will in turn depend upon the maintenance of a high level of world income and a reduction of the barriers to international trade which have grown up in the past. A high level of world income, and of national income in the United States, will be greatly influenced by the domestic economic policies of the United States and of other major countries. It is expected that the proposed International Trade Organization will play an important role in securing the international economic environment necessary for the maintenance of high levels of world trade. The operation of the International Monetary Fund should assure the orderly functioning of a system of multilateral payments, and this will make it possible

[5] Note this important qualification.—ED.

for debtor countries to convert their export surplus with any country into the currency in which their obligations must be discharged.

9. Fundamentally, however, the ability of foreign countries to transfer interest and amortization on foreign loans to the United States depends upon the extent to which we make dollars available to the world through imports of goods and services, including personal remittances and tourist expenditures, and through new investments abroad. As a last resort, the world outside of the United States has a current gold production of possibly $1 billion per year to add to their present foreign exchange reserves, which can be dipped into to insure payment.

As long as new American investment exceeds interest and amortization on outstanding foreign investment, the question of net repayment on our total foreign investment will not arise, although as individual investments are paid off the composition of our foreign investment may shift. It is impossible to prophesy when receipts on foreign investment will exceed new investment, as American investment abroad will depend on many future developments. In a world of peace, prosperity, and a liberal trade policy, there may well be a revival and continuation of American private investment on a large scale, including a reinvestment of the profits of industry, that will put the period of net repayment far in the future. Such an increase of investment is a natural and wholesome development for a wealthy community.

When net repayment begins, whether this be a few years or many decades from now, it will involve an excess of imports of goods and services (including foreign travel by Americans) over our total exports of goods and services. The growth in our population and the depletion of our natural resources and the increase in our standard of living will increase the need for imported products, and these developments together with the maintenance of a high and stable level of employment will facilitate this adjustment. The annual interest and amortization payments on the entire present and contemplated Export-Import Bank program, the British loan, and the International Bank loans floated in U.S. markets will be less than $1 billion. The receipt of payments on our foreign loans in the form of goods and services is entirely consistent with increased exports from this country and rising production at home, and will contribute to a rising living standard in the United States in the same way that a private individual's earnings on his investments make possible an increase in his own living standard.

10. The loan policies stated here are in full accord with the basic political and economic interests of the United States. The National Advisory Council, which was established by the Congress in the Bretton Woods Agreement Act and consists of the Secretary of the Treasury, as chairman, the Secretary of State, the Secretary of Commerce, the Chairman of the Board of Governors of the Federal Reserve System, and the Chairman of the Board of Directors of the Export-Import Bank, has the responsibility of coordinating the lending and credit programs of this Government, and of achieving maximum consistency between American Government lending and the lending operations of the International Bank.

This country is supporting the United Nations Organization wholeheartedly, and the success of the United Nations Organization depends not only on political agreement but also on economic improvement. These loans are for economic reconstruction and development. They will enable the borrowing countries to increase their own production, relieve their foreign trade from excessive regulation, and expand their trade with us. Economic stability will foster peace. This program of foreign lending is essential to the realization of the main objective of the foreign economic policy of the United States, which is to lay the economic foundations of the peace.

FRED M. VINSON
Secretary of the Treasury
Chairman of the National Advisory Council
on International Monetary and Financial Problems

JAMES F. BYRNES
Secretary of State

H. A. WALLACE
Secretary of Commerce

M. S. ECCLES
Chairman of the Board of Governors
of the Federal Reserve System

WM. McC. MARTIN, JR.
Chairman of the Board of Directors
of the Export-Import Bank of Washington

3. *Marshall's Harvard Commencement Speech*[6]

[EDITOR'S NOTE: *This famous speech, delivered by Secretary of State George C. Marshall on June 5, 1947, at Harvard University, initiated the establishment of the Marshall Plan.*]

I need not tell you gentlemen that the world situation is very serious. That must be apparent to all intelligent people. I think one difficulty is that the problem is one of such enormous complexity that the very mass of facts presented to the public by press and radio make it exceedingly difficult for the man in the street to reach a clear appraisement of the situation. Furthermore, the people of this country are distant from the troubled areas of the earth and it is hard for them to comprehend the plight and consequent reactions of the long-suffering peoples, and the effect of those reactions on their governments in connection with our efforts to promote peace in the world.

In considering the requirements for the rehabilitation of Europe, the physical loss of life, the visible destruction of cities, factories, mines, and railroads was correctly estimated, but it has become obvious during recent months that this visible destruction was probably less serious than the dislocation of the entire fabric of European economy. For the past 10 years conditions have been highly abnormal. The feverish preparation for war and the more feverish maintenance of the war effort engulfed all aspects of national economies. Machinery has fallen into disrepair or is entirely obsolete. Under the arbitrary and destructive Nazi rule, virtually every possible enterprise was geared into the German war machine. Long-standing commercial ties, private institutions, banks, insurance companies, and shipping companies disappeared, through loss of capital, absorption through nationalization, or by simple destruction. In many countries, confidence in the local currency has been severely shaken. The breakdown of the business structure of Europe during the war was complete. Recovery has been seriously retarded by the fact that two years after the close of hostilities a peace settlement with Germany and Austria has not been

---

[6] SOURCE: George C. Marshall, "European Initiative Essential to Economic Recovery," *Department of State Bulletin*, XVI, No. 415 (June 15, 1947), 1159–60.

agreed upon. But even given a more prompt solution of these difficult problems, the rehabilitation of the economic structure of Europe quite evidently will require a much longer time and greater effort than had been foreseen.

There is a phase of this matter which is both interesting and serious. The farmer has always produced the foodstuffs to exchange with the city dweller for the other necessities of life. This division of labor is the basis of modern civilization. At the present time it is threatened with breakdown. The town and city industries are not producing adequate goods to exchange with the food-producing farmer. Raw materials and fuel are in short supply. Machinery is lacking or worn out. The farmer or the peasant cannot find the goods for sale which he desires to purchase. So the sale of his farm produce for money which he cannot use seems to him an unprofitable transaction. He, therefore, has withdrawn many fields from crop cultivation and is using them for grazing. He feeds more grain to stock and finds for himself and his family an ample supply of food, however short he may be on clothing and the other ordinary gadgets of civilization. Meanwhile people in the cities are short of food and fuel. So the governments are forced to use their foreign money and credits to procure these necessities abroad. This process exhausts funds which are urgently needed for reconstruction. Thus a very serious situation is rapidly developing which bodes no good for the world. The modern system of the division of labor upon which the exchange of products is based is in danger of breaking down.

The truth of the matter is that Europe's requirements for the next 3 or 4 years of foreign food and other essential products—principally from America—are so much greater than her present ability to pay that she must have substantial additional help or face economic, social, and political deterioration of a very grave character.

The remedy lies in breaking the vicious circle and restoring the confidence of the European people in the economic future of their own countries and of Europe as a whole. The manufacturer and the farmer throughout wide areas must be able and willing to exchange their products for currencies the continuing value of which is not open to question.

Aside from the demoralizing effect on the world at large and the possibilities of disturbances arising as a result of the desperation of the people concerned, the consequences to the economy of the United States should be apparent to all. It is logical that the United States should do whatever it is able to do to assist in the return of normal economic health in the world, without which there can be no political stability and no assured peace. Our policy is directed not against any country or doctrine but against hunger, poverty, desperation, and chaos. Its purpose should be the revival of a working economy in the world so as to permit the emergence of political and social conditions in which free institutions can exist. Such assistance, I am convinced, must not be on a piecemeal basis as various crises develop. Any assistance that this Government may render in the future should provide a cure rather than a mere palliative. Any government that is willing to assist in the task of recovery will find full cooperation, I am sure, on the part of the United States Government. Any government which maneuvers to block the recovery of other countries cannot expect help from us. Furthermore, governments, political parties, or groups which seek to perpetuate human misery in order to profit therefrom politically or otherwise will encounter the opposition of the United States.

It is already evident that, before the United States Government can proceed much further in its efforts to alleviate the situation and help start the European world on its way to recovery, there must be some agreement among the countries of Europe as to the requirements of the situation and the part those countries themselves will take in order to give proper effect to whatever action might be undertaken by this Government. It would be neither fitting nor efficacious for this Government to undertake to draw up unilaterally a program designed to place Europe on its feet economically. This is the business of the Europeans. The initiative, I think, must come from Europe. The role of this country should consist of friendly aid in the drafting of a European program and of later support of such a program so far as it may be practical for us to do so. The program should be a joint one, agreed to by a number, if not all, European nations.

An essential part of any successful action on the part of the United States is an understanding on the part of the people of America of the character of the problem and the remedies to be applied. Political passion and prejudice should have no part. With foresight, and a willingness on the part of our people to face up to the vast responsibility which history has clearly placed upon our country, the difficulties I have outlined can and will be overcome.

4. *Inaugural Address of Harry S. Truman,* *January 20, 1949*[7]

[EDITOR'S NOTE: *In this abridgment of President Truman's ad-dress, the famous Point Four is presented in conjunction with the seldom-mentioned other three points.*]

In the coming years, our program for peace and freedom will em-phasize four major courses of action.

First. We will continue to give unfaltering support to the United Nations and related agencies, and we will continue to search for ways to strengthen their authority and increase their effectiveness. We believe that the United Nations will be strength-ened by the new nations which are being formed in lands now ad-vancing toward self-government under democratic principles.

Second. We will continue our programs for world economic re-covery. This means, first of all, that we must keep our full weight behind the European recovery program. We are confident of the success of this major venture in world recovery. We believe that our partners in this effort will achieve the status of self-supporting nations once again.

In addition, we must carry out our plans for reducing the bar-riers to world trade and increasing its volume. Economic recovery and peace itself depend on increased world trade.

Third. We will strengthen freedom-loving nations against the dangers of aggression.

We are now working out with a number of countries a joint agreement designed to strengthen the security of the North Atlan-tic area. Such an agreement would take the form of a collective defense arrangement within the terms of the United Nations Charter.

We have already established such a defense pact for the West-ern Hemisphere by the treaty of Rio de Janeiro.

The primary purpose of these agreements is to provide unmis-takable proof of the joint determination of the free countries to resist armed attack from any quarter. Each country participating in these arrangements must contribute all it can to the common defense.

[7] SOURCE: *Public Papers of the Presidents of the United States: Harry S. Truman* (Washington, D.C.: Government Printing Office, 1964), pp. 112–16.

If we can make it sufficiently clear, in advance, that any armed attack affecting our national security would be met with overwhelming force, the armed attack might never occur.

I hope soon to send to the Senate a treaty respecting the North Atlantic security plan.

In addition, we will provide military advice and equipment to free nations which will cooperate with us in the maintenance of peace and security.

Fourth. We must embark on a bold new program for making the benefits of our scientific advances and industrial progress available for the improvement and growth of underdeveloped areas.

More than half the people of the world are living in conditions approaching misery. Their food is inadequate. They are victims of disease. Their economic life is primitive and stagnant. Their poverty is a handicap and a threat both to them and to more prosperous areas.

For the first time in history humanity possesses the knowledge and the skill to relieve the suffering of these people.

The United States is pre-eminent among nations in the development of industrial and scientific techniques. The material resources which we can afford to use for the assistance of other peoples are limited. But our imponderable resources in technical knowledge are constantly growing and are inexhaustible.

I believe that we should make available to peace-loving peoples the benefits of our store of technical knowledge in order to help them realize their aspirations for a better life. And, in cooperation with other nations, we should foster capital investment in areas needing development.

Our aim should be to help the free peoples of the world, through their own efforts, to produce more food, more clothing, more materials for housing, and more mechanical power to lighten their burdens.

We invite other countries to pool their technological resources in this undertaking. Their contributions will be warmly welcomed. This should be a cooperative enterprise in which all nations work together through the United Nations and its specialized agencies wherever practicable. It must be a worldwide effort for the achievement of peace, plenty, and freedom.

With the cooperation of business, private capital, agriculture, and labor in this country, this program can greatly increase the industrial activity in other nations and can raise substantially their standards of living.

Such new economic developments must be devised and controlled to benefit the peoples of the areas in which they are established. Guaranties to the investor must be balanced by guaranties in the interest of the people whose resources and whose labor go into these developments.

The old imperialism—exploitation for foreign profit—has no place in our plans. What we envisage is a program of development based on the concepts of democratic fair dealing.

All countries, including our own, will greatly benefit from a constructive program for the better use of the world's human and natural resources. Experience shows that our commerce with other countries expands as they progress industrially and economically.

Greater production is the key to prosperity and peace. And the key to greater production is a wider and more vigorous application of modern scientific and technical knowledge.

Only by helping the least fortunate of its members to help themselves can the human family achieve the decent, satisfying life that is the right of all people.

Democracy alone can supply the vitalizing force to stir the peoples of the world into triumphant action, not only against their human oppressors, but also against their ancient enemies—hunger, misery, and despair.

On the basis of these four major courses of action we hope to help create the conditions that will lead eventually to personal freedom and happiness for all mankind.

5. *Aid to Underdeveloped Areas as Measure of National Security*[8]

[EDITOR'S NOTE: *This excerpt from Secretary of State Dean Acheson's testimony before the Senate Committee on Foreign Relations, on March 10, 1950, relates to legislation to implement President Truman's Point Four proposal. Note that two months before the outbreak of the Korean War, the aid program was already acquiring a national-security orientation.*]

Four Courses of Action

This proposed measure is the underlying legislative authority for carrying out a program to assist the people of the underdevel-

[8] SOURCE: Dean Acheson, "Aid to Underdeveloped Areas as Measure of National Security," *Department of State Bulletin*, XXII, No. 562 (April 10, 1950), 552–55.

oped areas of the world in their efforts to develop their economic
resources. It is an integral part of a general program outlined by
the President as a basis for assuring peace and personal freedom
in the world. This program contained four interrelated courses of
action. The first course is the continuing of our unfaltering support of the United Nations and its related agencies. The second
course is the continuing of our programs for world economic recovery. The third is the strengthening of freedom-loving nations
against the dangers of aggression by providing military advice and
equipment to those nations which will cooperate with us in the
maintenance of peace and security. The fourth course of action is
the program which you are now considering. It involves making
available to peace-loving peoples the benefits of our technical
knowledge and skills. It also involves cooperation with other free
nations in fostering capital investment in areas needing development. Its aim is to help the free peoples of the world through their
own efforts to produce the things they need for a decent life.

The legislation before you is the product of more than a year of
careful study in which 43 agencies of the Federal Government
have participated. It is the product also of consultation with interested members of the Congress and with leading members of
business and labor and scientific groups. I would say that it represents the best combined judgment of all who were concerned in
shaping it.

As you know, this legislation does two things: It establishes the
objectives and the broad policy to guide the whole program of
American aid to underdeveloped areas, and it authorizes the President to carry out that part of the program dealing with technical
cooperation.

As this Committee well knows, the activities proposed are not
new. For many years Americans have been sharing technical skills
with other peoples and investing their capital abroad. This is part
of the American experience. It is in the American tradition.

Why, then, did the President propose to raise these activities to
the level of a national policy and a great national enterprise? Why
did he single out this policy and this enterprise as one of the four
cardinal aims of American foreign policy?

Only by answering these questions can we, in my opinion, appreciate the overriding importance of the legislation that is before
you.

Today, democracy is on trial for its life. The free way of life is
under attack in every part of the world, including those areas of
the world which we call "underdeveloped."

These areas include parts of Latin America, Africa, the Middle East, and the Far East where two-thirds of the world's people live, many of them in the shadow of hunger, poverty, and disease.

Increasing numbers of these people no longer accept poverty as an inevitable fact of life. They are becoming aware of the gap between their living standards and those in the more highly developed countries. They are looking for a way out of their misery. They are not concerned with abstract ideas of democracy or communism. They are interested in practical solutions to their problems in terms of food, shelter, and a decent livelihood. When the Communists offer quick and easy remedies for all their ills, they make a strong appeal to these people.

These are the facts we must face. What do they mean to our national security? To the peace and well-being and freedom of the American people, in short, to the fundamental aims of our foreign policy?

We are spending billions for military defense—as we must. We are spending other billions for economic reconstruction in Europe and vital points in the Far East—as we must. We are organizing joint defense through the North Atlantic Treaty and the Military Assistance Program. We are organizing joint action to remove trade barriers through tariff and reciprocal trade agreements and through the International Trade Organization. We are attempting to remove the causes of international friction and misunderstanding by playing an active role in the United Nations.

All the things we do are, in the last analysis, measures of national security—the broadest kind of security for our free and democratic way of life.

This legislation that is before you, this "Act for International Development" has the same broad purpose. In a very real sense, it is a security measure. And as a security measure, it is an essential arm of our foreign policy. For our military and economic security is vitally dependent on the economic security of other peoples.

But our foreign policy is not based on security alone. We have never been satisfied merely to resist a threat—of communism or any other "ism." Our policy is broader than this. It is essentially constructive. It is based on the assumption that, in the world today, our own welfare is closely related to that of other peoples. We can participate in this kind of a program because it serves both the interest of other peoples and our own interest as well.

Economic development will bring us certain practical material benefits. It will open up new sources of materials and goods we need, and new markets for the products of our farms and factories. Our friends in Europe, who depend far more than we do on foreign goods and markets, will benefit in similar ways. The volume of world trade will inevitably expand.

And finally, the peoples of the underdeveloped areas will begin to see new opportunities for a better life, and they will associate those opportunities in their minds with the helping hand of the American people. Even more important, they will associate economic progress with an approach to the problems of daily life that preserves and enlarges the initiative, dignity, and freedom of the individual.

The bill now before you establishes economic development of underdeveloped areas for the first time as a national policy.[9] Its purpose is to encourage the exchange of technical skills and promote the flow of private investment capital where these skills and capital can help to raise standards of living, create new wealth, increase productivity, and expand purchasing power.

There are other conditions. American aid will be furnished only where it contributes to the development of a balanced economy. It may go only where it is actually needed, and where the country receiving it cannot provide skills and capital for itself.

Most of the capital needed for economic development must come from the underdeveloped areas themselves. However, foreign capital will be needed from three main sources: from private investors, from the International Bank for Reconstruction and Development, and from the Export-Import Bank. The latter two should supplement, not compete with private capital. They should finance projects, such as transportation and irrigation, which are foundations for economic development and which are not ordinarily attractive to private investment. We put primary emphasis, however, on the need for stimulating an expansion of private investment not only to provide capital but also to provide the technical and managerial skills that come with capital. . . .

I want to make one last observation. We talk about this program as a long-term business, which it must be. But the fact is, we are not going to have to wait long to get results. Some results can be seen in a year. . . . Others may take 5 or 10 years or even longer to produce tangible benefits.

Well, 10 years is a minute in the life of a nation and less than a second in the life of a civilization. The fight for freedom and

---

[9] This was not true. See, for example, Morgenthau's Bretton Woods speech (Document 1, Chapter III).—Ed.

democracy has been going on for more than 2,000 years. It will not be won in a decade. The question that concerns us is whether it will be going our way 10 years from now. And part of the answer, I am convinced, lies in the energy, the skill, and the faith we put into this Point Four Program.

Here, indeed, is a chance to prove that our civilization which has grown to vigor and maturity with the help of science, can bend science to its will—not to destroy but to serve humanity.

IV

Grants vs. Loans: Part I

No issue has been more prominent in the debate on foreign aid than the loan-grant controversy. During the late 1940's and early 1950's, the Executive Branch favored grants in all situations in which hard loans were deemed inappropriate. Soft loans were taboo. Congress, however, has always been hostile to grants and has tended to prefer any kind of loan to a grant. Although saving the taxpayers' money has probably been the primary concern of Congress, other arguments for loans have also been put forth. It has been argued that exercise of the discipline to repay a loan strengthens the moral fiber of the borrower. Another argument is that loan recipients will use their resources more economically than grant recipients because of the repayment obligation. And still another argument is that loans are not humiliating to the recipient, whereas grants are; thus, the giving of loans eliminates a possible source of political friction.

The loan-grant controversy has not been confined to the U.S. Congress and Executive Branch; it has involved international agencies as well. The United Nations has been the main source of agitation for more grants and soft loans; between 1948 and 1955, the World Bank opposed such proposals. In 1949, a U.N. Economic Development Administration with authority to make soft loans was proposed. This was followed, in 1951, by a proposed International Development Authority that would give money away. And, in 1953, still a third agency was suggested by a U.N. study committee—the Special United Nations Fund for Economic Development (SUNFED). This institution was designed to make both grants and soft loans. All three of these proposed organizations would have decreased the importance of the IBRD in international public finance. In 1955, the SUNFED proposal was finally modified to guarantee close cooperation with the IBRD. Although the IBRD then relaxed its opposition, SUNFED, as originally conceived, was never established.

The documents in this chapter highlight the domestic and international political aspects of the debate of loans vs. grants in foreign aid. It should be noted that this debate relates mainly to economic aid, since it is generally agreed that military assistance should take the form of grants.

6. Grants for Development[1]

[EDITOR'S NOTE: *In 1950, President Truman appointed Gordon Gray, a former Secretary of the Army, to study the foreign economic policies of the United States. The Gray Report, issued in November, 1950, contained the following discussion of the circumstances under which the United States should use grants.*]

While the major instruments for the external financing of development on a continuing basis should be private and public investment, for the next few years there is also a need for public grants for development. In contrast to the large-scale grants required to assist in the recovery and rearmament of Europe, the size of grant aid needed to support development is limited. In emergency situations related to military action, as in Korea, the United States may have to bear a major share of the United Nations' burden of providing for minimum consumption and rehabilitation needs. As a general matter, however, grants to underdeveloped areas should be confined to the moderate amounts needed to finance necessary increases in productivity which the particular underdeveloped country cannot finance through loans without dangerously retarding its development.

While a country's ability to repay depends upon its foreign exchange position, this in turn depends upon the extent to which it makes resources available for export or for producing goods which it formerly imported. Resources so used to repay loans are, of course, not available for building up domestic capital equipment. In some cases, they may constitute a significant portion of its net capital investment. Thus, a basic question for the United States in deciding whether to extend grants instead of loans is whether the need to repay external capital assistance would slow up a country's development below a rate which the common interests of the free nations require. In general, this decision must be made in the light of a comprehensive assessment of the country's resources and urgent needs. Such an assessment was the basis for deciding whether to provide loans or grants in the case of aid to the Western Euro-

[1] SOURCE: Gordon Gray, *Report to the President on Foreign Economic Policies* (Washington, D.C.: Government Printing Office, 1950), pp. 66–67.

pean countries under the ERP; the basic principle is the same in the case of the underdeveloped countries, though its application may be made difficult.

The extension of aid in the form of grants instead of loans may increase productivity in a recipient country by considerably more than would result merely from the amount of capital involved in repayment. If active steps are to be taken to attack the basic problems of the underdeveloped countries, then limited grants, extended on condition that they are effectively used, may be a spur to the governments and peoples concerned to take these steps. Grant aid of this character is an instrument of great usefulness to our foreign economic and political policy toward underdeveloped areas, especially in connection with basic agricultural problems in Southern and Eastern Asia.

7. *Determination of Loan and Grant Assistance to Southeast Asia and Other Underdeveloped Areas*[2]

[EDITOR'S NOTE: *From 1945 to 1954, the Executive Branch stoutly resisted Congressional pressure to place aid on a loan basis in situations where repayment prospects were doubtful. Since 1954, the Executive has gradually acquiesced to the Legislative desire to place a greater proportion of foreign assistance on a loan basis in all types of aid situations. This statement summarizes the Executive's position in 1951.*]

It is the policy of the Administration with respect to the countries of Southeast Asia, as well as with respect to all underdeveloped areas, to place assistance on a loan basis insofar as there is reasonable prospect of repayment and the programs are of such a character as may reasonably be financed on a loan basis. It is also the policy of the Administration that the lending operations for development of the underdeveloped areas should be undertaken by the established lending institutions, namely, the Export-Import Bank and the International Bank. It would be fundamentally unwise to place a greater portion of foreign assistance on a loan basis than could be justified reasonably through an analysis of capacity to repay. To saddle countries with an external debt structure which they cannot handle over the longer term will place barriers against

2 SOURCE: *Mutual Security Act of 1951*, Hearings before the Senate Committee on Foreign Relations and Committee on Armed Services, 82d Cong., 1st sess. (Washington, D.C.: Government Printing Office, 1951), p. 605.

the flow of private investment to such areas, which we are most interested in encouraging, and lead to trade and exchange restrictions which are inimical to the private enterprise system of world trade. In addition, the making of loans which we and the rest of the world know at the outset have little chance of repayment will discredit the entire lending process and is likely to lead to widespread repudiation of debt.

With specific reference to the Southeast Asia area, these countries have in general very low standards of living and will need substantial foreign capital over an extended period of time if their peoples are to have any real prospect of escaping their present poverty. A substantial portion of this assistance can be placed on a loan basis through the International Bank and the Export-Import Bank. If, however, we are to meet the threat of communism in this area we will need to push development more rapidly than could reasonably be expected to be financed by loans. It is for that reason, plus the fact that these areas need substantial technical assistance which is not suitable to be placed on a loan basis, that there is a significant grant component in programs for these areas. But it should be noted that such grant elements will be but a small part of the total investment programs being planned by these countries.

Another factor to be considered is that the uncertain political and military situation in SEA [Southeast Asia], together with the internal defense effort in these areas, tends to limit loan opportunities. This is particularly true in areas marked by civil strife and warfare as are Burma and Indochina. Too heavy an extension of loans in unstable areas would tend to depreciate the traditionally high loan standards maintained by the Export-Import Bank and the IBRD. In the case of the latter, this would have particularly unfortunate reactions on the willingness of the private financial community to direct its funds through the bank into overseas development.

8. Congress and Loans[3]

[EDITOR'S NOTE: *The following interchange between Senator Bourke Hickenlooper (R., Iowa) and Mutual Security Director Harold E. Stassen typifies the loan-grant dialogue between the*

[3] SOURCE: *Mutual Security Act of 1954*, Hearings before the Senate Committee on Foreign Relations, 83d Cong., 2d sess. (Washington, D.C.: Government Printing Office, 1954), pp. 68–69.

*Executive and Congress in the late 1940's and early 1950's. Note
the Senator's preference for loans, even in situations where repayment is uncertain.*]

SENATOR HICKENLOOPER: That comes to my next question which
applies to all of these countries in similar circumstances. If their
economic potential is such that it justifies an investment at this
time, why can't they pay for it over the long run? Why do we have
to donate it? It would seem to me the investment in development
operations should be paid for out of the increased economic developments that will occur. Why do we not loan them the money
on the easiest possible terms—let us say, substantially deferred periods of payment on principal—at probably a very low interest
rate?

MR. STASSEN: We are moving toward more loans and less
grants, including the matter of loaning for repayment in local currencies because as you are aware, there are two problems in a repayment. One is whether you have the internal finances to do it,
and the second is whether you have the international exchange or
the balance of payment to be able to make payment on the loan.
It is our view that if it cannot in fact be repaid, that it is not wise
foreign policy to set it up as a loan when really a grant is needed,
because under those circumstances a loan loses both itself and
the friend.

SENATOR HICKENLOOPER: I will suggest that gifts do the same
thing; the givers lose the gifts and also the friend who receives. I
think that has been very well established in recent years.

MR. STASSEN: Under some circumstances, but not under others;
but the allied war debt approach after World War I—I think most
of those who analyze it in retrospect agree—was a dislocating and
unfavorable economic and foreign policy factor, and was one of
the things that set in these chain reactions that ultimately led to
the worst depression in our history and to the background for
World War II. So the matter of when to make a loan and when
to make a grant must be very carefully analyzed in each situation;
but I would agree with your basic premise that we should move
more to loans and less to grants.

SENATOR HICKENLOOPER: I think that philosophy is sound, and
ever since 1948 and 1949 we have moved more to loans and less to
grants, but yet we keep right on giving this money in the shape of
grants.

MR. STASSEN: Well, Senator, may I point out that we have

granted to Europe this past year less money than you had authorized us to do. We have loaned to Europe $100 million for the coal and steel community, which we believe will be a good loan; this will be repaid with interest at 3.8 percent. That is some affirmative evidence that we have administratively been moving in the direction in which you advocate. We feel that we are moving that way as rapidly as it is sound for the United States' own foreign policy to move.

SENATOR HICKENLOOPER: I am not advocating what you would call a bankable loan which has an immediate presumed due date or one which is assured of being repaid. But if the economy of a country is worthy of development, I see no reason why that country should not assume the technical development costs as an obligation. At a later date, when their economy begins to develop, they should certainly pay back the costs of the technical advice and the assistance we put in there. I cannot justify too much approaching the American taxpayer and asking him to put up the money for these things which will increase substantially the material wealth of these countries. I am not talking about the direct military assistance and certain items that may have to go along with it.

MR. STASSEN: I recognize the merit of your viewpoint, Senator. There are two answers to your comment; first, the situation is somewhat as if you had an individual who had been, we will say, a heavy machinery operator, and he lost a leg, and he was in a hospital. You might deduce that from his skill and his ability you could train him as a tool and die worker, and he could be more productive than he ever was before, and that when once so trained that he could be self-supporting and a good member of the community. You then might decide that you would provide for him a vocational education to train him as a tool and die worker, and you might even provide an artificial limb for him. It can be argued that when that man becomes a tool and die worker and a very high earner, that he could afford to pay back the cost of the artificial limb and costs of the vocational education, but, on the other hand, it may well be that it would be better public policy to say when he becomes a tool and die maker, if he is then no longer a charge upon the community and can use his then earnings for his future participation in the economy, that that would be wiser community policy. Likewise, from the standpoint of the U.S. foreign policy in relationship to these nations which, for one reason or another, are not today self-supporting and are not able to move in this postwar situation in the way we want to see them move as stable members of a world community. It does appear that it is a wise expenditure of a moderate amount of U.S. funds for this purpose.

Now, I grant that the $131 million for the world technical cooperation program is substantial money but, at the same time, it is also important to realize that it amounts to just about 10 cents a month for each adult in the United States, and that investment per month in the development of the education, the skills, the self-supporting ability of these countries around the world appears to me to be a wise investment on a grant basis of United States funds for technical cooperation.

SENATOR HICKENLOOPER: Well, I have been in some countries in the world where a program is going on, and most of these have very substantial resources. Some of them, fortunately, have as much natural resource potential as we had in the United States when we started out here. I am aware that our industry and our agriculture in this country was built in substantial degree by foreign capital, but we paid back every dollar of it, and we retained our pride in our development.

It has been my impression that we have not gained any friendship in quite a number of countries by donations. There is no sense of obligation on their part; it is just a handout from a bountiful country that is far away. They do not assume an obligation under which they can say, well, we have done this over a period of years, we have paid for it.

9. *The United Nations Position on Financing Economic Development*[4]

[EDITOR'S NOTE: *U.N. General Assembly Resolution 400(V), passed on November 20, 1950, set forth the majority position of Assembly members on the financing of economic development. Expressed in the following excerpt from the resolution are the basic ideas on such financing that have prevailed in U.N. debate from that day to this.*]

The General Assembly . . .

Recognizing that a more rapid economic development of under-developed countries, in particular an increase of their production,

[4] SOURCE: *Official Records*, U.N. General Assembly, Fifth Session (U.N. Doc. No. A/1775 [New York, 1950]), Supplement No. 20, pp. 26–27.

is essential for raising the level of productive employment and the living standards of their populations, for the growth of the world economy as a whole and for the maintenance of international peace and security,

Recognizing further that, although the economic development of underdeveloped countries depends primarily upon the efforts of the people of those countries, the necessary acceleration of that development, on the basis of their own plans and programs, requires not only technical but also financial assistance from abroad, and particularly from the more developed countries,

Considering that the domestic financial resources of the underdeveloped countries, together with the international flow of capital for investment, have not been sufficient to assure the desired rate of economic development, and that the accelerated economic development of underdeveloped countries requires a more effective and sustained mobilization of domestic savings and an expanded and more stable flow of foreign capital investment,

Being convinced that the volume of private capital which is currently flowing into underdeveloped countries cannot meet the financial needs of the economic development of the underdeveloped countries and that those needs cannot be met without an increased flow of international public funds,

Taking account of the fact that some basic development projects are not capable of being adequately serviced through existing sources of foreign finance although they contribute directly or indirectly to the increase of national productivity and national income,

1. Recommends that the Economic and Social Council in giving further study to the problem of the financing of economic development consider practical methods, conditions, and policies for achieving the adequate expansion and steadier flow of foreign capital, both private and public, and pay special attention to the financing of non-self-liquidating projects which are basic to economic development . . .

10. *Grants, Loans, and SUNFED*[5]

[EDITOR'S NOTE: *On January 12, 1952, the underdeveloped countries in the United Nations were able to push through U.N. Gen-*

[5] SOURCE: *Official Records,* U.N. General Assembly, Tenth Session (U.N. Doc. No. A/2906 [New York, 1955]), Supplement No. 17: "Special United Nations Fund for Economic Development," pp. 8–9.

eral Assembly Resolution 520A(VI), which called for establish-
ment of a special U.N. fund to make grants and soft loans. Not
one industrialized nation supported the resolution. In 1953, a
committee of experts, known as the Committee of Nine, made
suggestions for setting up such a fund (SUNFED). Since then,
the less-developed nations have tried to get the richer nations to
support the establishment of SUNFED. Although they did get a
small Special Fund (UNSF) approved in 1958, they did not get the
large capital fund they had called for. Each time their efforts to es-
tablish SUNFED were rebuffed, they were able to secure agreement
on a recommendation that the proposal be studied further. The
study that was undertaken in 1955 contained the following discus-
sion of grants and loans.]

The Committee devoted considerable time to the methods of disbursement of the Special Fund's resources. A satisfactory solution
of this question appeared to us essential for two reasons. First, a
solution of the problems of structure and of coordination with existing international organizations is closely linked with the particular ways in which the Special Fund uses its resources. Second,
the methods of disbursement will largely determine the distribution of resources of the Special Fund between different countries,
and perhaps more important, between different types of projects.

Our point of departure was the report of the Committee of
Nine. Their recommendations, roughly speaking, provided that the
resources of the Special Fund should be disbursed both through
grants-in-aid and through "low-interest loans." The interest on
these loans would be lower than that on loans from the International Bank and the terms of repayment would generally be easier.
Considerable scope for readjustment of the terms of these low-
interest loans and for renegotiability was also provided for by the
Committee of Nine.

Grants-in-aid.—Like our predecessors and all serious students of
the problems to be solved by the creation of the Special Fund, we
have no doubt that the Special Fund should be authorized to give
grants-in-aid and that these would be the most important, and also
the preponderant, method through which the Special Fund would
disburse its resources.

The reasons which led us towards unanimity on this point
largely arise from the very *raison d'être* of a Special Fund: the
true repayment of the Fund's assistance lies in the effective use of
its resources by the recipients for their own self-sustaining and
universally beneficial economic development.

In addition, grants-in-aid have distinct advantages as compared with loans. No negotiations concerning terms of repayment are required; no subsequent consultations or friction in case of difficulty of repayment will arise; no estimate of capacity to repay need be made. All of this will obviously tend to simplify administration and reduce administrative work.

Any confusion in the public mind—or in the minds of governments—between the Special Fund and lending institutions such as the International Bank is avoided. With the Special Fund making grants-in-aid, these institutions would be in an even better position to resist the temptation—if any—to apply other than strictly business standards to their borrowers in the case of "marginal projects." The debt-carrying capacity of assisted countries is not reduced, and thus their position as borrowers from other sources of finance is not weakened. It is even likely to be strengthened as a grant-in-aid from the Special Fund would lead to a more resilient and more diversified economy, or possibly to the development of new lines of exports, or of import substitutes. This effect of grants-in-aid appears to us to be consistent with the desired aim that the Special Fund should complement other sources of finance.

These are the main and sufficiently conclusive arguments which led us to endorse grants-in-aid by the Special Fund. . . .

Combination of grants and loans.—There is a further argument in favour of the making of grants-in-aid by the Special Fund; a grant from the Fund could be combined with a loan from the International Bank or some other lending agency. Such a combination has several specific advantages which are additional to those of grants-in-aid considered by themselves. A grant-in-aid from the Special Fund could be combined with a loan from another institution in any proportion. Thus a combination of grant and loan could produce the desired rate of interest for the loan-grant transaction considered as a whole, as well as a maturity equivalent to any desired repayment schedule. The combination of loan and grant would thus achieve the maximum degree of flexibility—as long as the loan-grant transaction could be carried through conjointly—and this without the disadvantages and uncertainties attached to other methods. The incentive to make effective use of a grant from the Special Fund might be increased by such a combination, since a "good" grant proposition would increase the capacity to repay and thereby enhance a country's prospects of obtaining loans linked with the grant. Claims on the resources of the Special Fund might be smaller, since part of the submitted programs could be covered by the loan sector of the combination. The last point might also be presented in a more positive form: each dollar spent by the Special Fund would have a multiplier effect in so far as it made possible the granting of further loans to the assisted countries.

This combination of loans and grants would obviously require concerted action by the Special Fund and the loan-making institutions. The real economic advantages of combined grants and loans would in fact only apply if the grants-loans were made during the same period to the same country in support of the same projects or different sectors of the same development programs. Such combinations would, of course, be greatly facilitated by a close integration of the structure of the Special Fund with that of the International Bank. . . .

Loans repayable in local currency.—Having agreed on the desirability of grants-in-aid, in particular, in combination with loans, we next considered whether the advantages of this method of financing were sufficient to suggest that the Special Fund should confine itself to this method of disbursement.

The transactions of the Special Fund, other than grants-in-aid which have received our unanimous agreement, can be presented in various ways, although their final economic effect may be similar. One form is the provision of loans which would be repayable at a full rate of interest (i.e., loans of the International Bank type) but which, unlike International Bank loans, could be repaid in the currency of the borrowing country. As is well known, a loan made by the International Bank has to be repaid in the currency in which it is made.

This novel proposal impressed the group and stood up well to further examination and discussion. We would therefore recommend it to the close consideration of governments. It should be emphasized that it is essential that such loans should be made at a normal rate of interest, and not at the concessional rates of interest envisaged by the Committee of Nine. The terms of these loans would be definite and would not include any clause permitting their revision. There would thus be no competition between the International Bank and the Special Fund in respect of interest rates or the obligatory nature of repayment. The maturity of the loan might, however, be rather longer than that of a normal International Bank loan, i.e., thirty years or more.

This proposal maintains so many of the advantages of loans, while permitting the Fund to achieve its purpose, that we consider that this method of financing should also be provided by the Fund. Among the advantages of the loan procedure are the fact that the lender-borrower relation is generally more satisfactory than the donor-beneficiary relation; that, because it must be repaid, a loan is more likely to be effectively used than a grant-in-aid; that the discipline of servicing a loan has a beneficial effect on the policy of the borrowing country; that a loan repayable in local currency could be as readily combined with a grant as a loan from the International Bank or any other loan-making institution; that contributions to the Special Fund might be more easily obtained if the money was to be lent and ultimately repaid, thus making it unnecessary to call for the continual replenishment of all the Fund's resources.

The last point is of particular importance as the establishment of the Special Fund must be conditional upon the conviction and willingness of some larger contributing countries and contributions might be more readily given if the Fund made loans of this type.[6] If this is the case, an arrangement might have to be considered under which contributing countries would be given an option (which, of course, they need not exercise) whether they wished their contributions to be used to give grants or to make loans. The establishment of a separate grant-in-aid fund and a separate loan fund (the latter for the local currency loans here described) would not appear to introduce any insuperable administrative or structural complications.

[6] The experts probably had been listening to American Congressmen extol the merits of soft loans as opposed to grants.—Ed.

V

Grants vs. Loans: Part II

After 1954, the Executive Branch modified its desire for grants in order to accommodate the Congressional preference for loans. By emphasizing a form of aid that is neither a grant nor a normal loan —the soft loan repayable in local currency[1]—the Executive was able to achieve economic effects comparable to those which could be achieved with grants and at the same time to protect itself from Congressional attacks on foreign "giveaways." The trouble was that in order to secure Legislative approval of soft loans, the Executive had to exaggerate the usefulness of the local currency in which the loans were to be repaid. Later, when Congress began to advocate the use of local currencies instead of dollars in aid programs, the Executive had to emphasize the limited usefulness of such currency.

Between 1954 and 1961, the United States placed increasing emphasis on soft loans repayable in local currency. The Mutual Security Act of 1954 contained two soft-lending provisions. Section 505 authorized loans repayable in inconvertible local currency, and Section 402 authorized the selling of surplus agricultural products for such currencies. Since these currencies were often loaned back to the country of origin, the United States frequently ended up holding local-currency IOU's as a result of the transactions permitted by Sections 402 and 505. Insofar as the United States traded real resources for IOU's, the net effect of these surplus commodity "sales" was comparable to the effect of granting soft loans.

The year 1954 also marked the passage of P.L. 480, under which even more surplus commodities were exchanged for local currency that was in turn exchanged for IOU's repayable in local currency. In 1957, the Development Loan Fund (DLF) was established under the Mutual Security Act. Between 1957 and 1961, this organization disbursed about three-quarters of its funds in the form of soft loans repayable in local currency. In 1961, the Kennedy Administration, faced with the prospect of rapid increases in huge

---

[1] As used here, the term "local currency" refers to inconvertible foreign currency.

amounts of American-owned inconvertible currency, announced that all soft loans would henceforth be repayable in dollars. Since 1961, however, the United States has continued to acquire inconvertible currency through P.L. 480 operations.

Soft loans, especially of the local-currency type, have caused much confusion and misunderstanding in Washington. The debate revolves primarily around these questions: (1) What is local currency? (2) How can one measure it? (3) In what sense is it a "problem" for American foreign policy? (4) What can we do with it?

11. *The Monroney Resolution*[2]

[EDITOR'S NOTE: *In 1958, Senator A. S. Mike Monroney (D., Oklahoma) suggested that the American-owned local currencies, which were rapidly piling up, be contributed to a new international development fund to be known as the International Development Association. His proposal involved two controversial ideas—the phasing out of DLF activities and increased use of inconvertible currencies. Although neither of these was realized, an institution bearing the name he had suggested was eventually set up. The speech in which he presented his proposal to the Senate, in February, 1958, provides an interesting illustration of Congressional misunderstanding of the "local-currency problem."*]

MR. MONRONEY: Mr. President, I submit for appropriate reference a resolution, and I ask unanimous consent that it may be printed at this point in the Record.

(There being no objection, the resolution was referred to the Committee on Banking and Currency and ordered to be printed in the Record, as follows.)

Resolved, That, recognizing the desirability of promoting a greater degree of international development by means of multilateral loans based on sound economic principles rather than a system of unilateral grants or loans, it is the sense of the Senate that consideration should be given to the establishment of an International Development Association, in cooperation with the International Bank for Reconstruction and Development.

[2] SOURCE: *International Development Association*, Hearings before the Senate Committee on Banking and Currency, 85th Cong., 2d sess. (Washington, D.C.: Government Printing Office, 1958), pp. 7–11.

In order to achieve greater international trade, development, and economic well-being, such an agency should promote the following objectives:

1. Provide long-term loans available at a low rate of interest and repayable in local currencies[3] to supplement World Bank loans and thereby permit the prompt completion of worthwhile development projects which could not otherwise go forward.

2. Permit maximum use of foreign currencies available to the United States through the sale of agricultural surpluses and through other programs by devoting a portion of these currencies to such loans.

3. Insure that funds necessary for international economic development can be made available by a process which eliminates any possible implications of interference with national sovereignty.

It is further the sense of the Senate that as a part of the U.S. economic aid program funds be subscribed to the capital stock of the International Development Association in cooperation with investments made by other participating countries.

MR. MONRONEY: Mr. President, the resolution I have submitted would put the Senate on record as favoring a greater degree of international development by means of multilateral loans based on sound economic principles, rather than on a system of unilateral grants or loans. In this regard, it recommends that consideration be given to the establishment of an International Development Association, in cooperation with the International Bank for Reconstruction and Development.

In my judgment the United States must avoid the folly of rigid fixation on policies once valid but no longer effective. The world is not a static, unchanging picture. It is more like a growing family, with maturing and improving standards of knowledge and economic status, and with members desirous of achieving a rising standard of living through economic independence.

New challenges, such as those of Russia in the international development arena, should be met with better ideas, ideals, and plans.

If we insist on retreading badly worn Democratic tires, good in their day, but now worn down to the fabric, our foreign-aid program will be broken down while the world passes us by. A continuation of propaganda-inspired growing antagonisms, summed up in such disrespectful tags as Uncle Sugar, Uncle Shylock, and even Uncle Sap, must cease. But they will not be stopped by re-

[3] Note that, to date, the IDA has never made a loan repayable in inconvertible currency.—ED.

calcitrant attitudes of a barren, holier-than-thou, false morality.

The Russians have started an intense economic offensive by offering loans for development purposes that are a better deal than ours. We can best meet this challenge by taking a lead in creating an international program of multilateral loans for economic development, mixing dollars and foreign local currencies.

The United States took the lead in helping to establish the International Bank for Reconstruction and Development, which has financed the construction of many worthwhile development projects. However, the World Bank cannot, over the 20-year term required by it, make project loans which might be good, but would be impossible of repayment in dollars or other hard currencies. Therein lies our opportunity.

Nor can we rely on unilateral grants and gifts to promote the risky but valuable projects. Times have changed. The free and uncommitted nations of the world now want progress on a basis of self-respect and equality. There is no longer any place for anything that even implies a handout.

We need to help set up a system of multilateral loans which can be made on a completely self-respecting basis. We must eliminate as quickly as possible the type of aid which, despite our honest intention, has been the subject of Communist propaganda which labels it not only as a charity program, but also as Uncle Sam's efforts to subvert the recipient nations. These untrue allegations that our aid implies a superior-inferior relationship with the receiving countries, have, in many cases, helped to destroy the leaders of governments friendly to us.

My resolution urges consideration of the establishment of an International Development Association to work in cooperation with the International Bank for Reconstruction and Development. Such an institution should probably have its capital stock subscribed from hard currencies of the United States and other participating countries, so as to give it a dollar and hard currency base. It should also have the use of local currencies, including a large portion of those which this Nation has accumulated from its large-scale disposal of agricultural surpluses.

Thus, much of the usable capital of the IDA would come [from] local currencies which are now frozen and of little or no use to any country. There may be some residual funds from the Marshall Plan aid program which would also be available. The foreign aid dollar, already appropriated and spent, might well be recycled, for use again in world economic development. The IDA would give a greater flexibility to the use of foreign currencies and would promote international trade.

For example, one of the world's troubled spots is in the relationship between India and Pakistan. At the root of this dispute is far more than Kashmir. The struggle is for the use of the waters of the six-river watershed that originate in India and Tibet and flow through Pakistan.

Should India alone develop the waters of this great river system, Pakistan will perish through loss of water indispensable to its economy.

For a year or more, engineers of both Pakistan and India have worked together in trying to arrive at a joint plan for a huge TVA type of development for this section of Asia. The program probably would cost $400 million. Under the World Bank rules—requiring repayment in 20 years' time, at 4 percent interest, in hard currencies—this is not a bankable loan.

Under the plan of the International Development Association, however, the plan could be financed with safety and with tremendous good for the development of two friendly nations whose disagreements now threaten trouble or perhaps even war in the Far East.

As a second-mortgage operation, the International Development Association could take perhaps 50 percent of the $400-million loan, subordinating its loan to the first claim of the World Bank. The loan could be made for 40 years, at 2 percent interest, to be repaid, not in dollars or hard currencies, but in local currencies of India and Pakistan.

In designating the dam, for example, the IDA could loan engineering funds in German deutschmarks. For earth-moving equipment, it could provide funds in French francs, with certain dollar or hard-currency additions. Cement could come from some 10 countries, and could be purchased in large part with local currencies, with only 10 or 20 percent in dollars. Thus, with a worldwide shopping list and a vault filled with many local currencies, for the first time wise banking administration could make full use of local currencies, including those accumulating from the sale of our agricultural surpluses.

Undoubtedly other members of the World Bank also could contribute local currencies which they have on hand, thus making flexible and judicious use of many frozen assets.

MR. GORE: Mr. President, will the Senator from Oklahoma yield to me?

MR. MONRONEY: I am happy to yield to my distinguished colleague, the Senator from Tennessee.

MR. GORE: To what beneficial use—unless it be in some international development program—is the United States to put the enormous quantities of foreign currencies now within its call?

MR. MONRONEY: I am very glad the Senator from Tennessee has asked that question, because we have seen such currencies pile up until now they have reached a total of nearly $2.5 billion. We are lending some of these local currencies back to the countries which buy our surplus agricultural commodities. However, as the Senator from Tennessee found last year when he was in Burma, they are loath and unwilling to accept a unilateral loan from the United States, for fear that their governments would be charged with being satellites of Uncle Sam. Consequently, the money which the United States might be willing to loan unilaterally is not designed [desired?] by many such countries. I am told that $78 million from the sale of our agricultural surpluses to Indonesia lies idle in the Bank.

If we are not careful, in the next 5 years we may accumulate additional billions of local currencies, from the sale of our agricultural surpluses. If we do not find a means of using these section [Public Law] 480 funds, we shall find that we have sacrificed bales of cotton in warehouses for bales of currency.

We cannot justify a continuation of this very fine program of section 480 sales, which I have supported thoroughly, unless we find a way now to put the funds to work.

By mixing hard currencies with soft currencies in connection with a second-mortgage type of program, the necessary funds could be made available to countries which today cannot deal in dollars. Such second-mortgage loans could be made by an international development association. In that way the necessary funds could be made available.

MR. GORE: Mr. President, will the Senator from Oklahoma yield further to me?

MR. MONRONEY: I am very glad to yield.

MR. GORE: Although the amount of foreign currencies now belonging to the United States is enormous, it would still appear to be within manageable proportions. However, if no constructive measure is advanced and if no realistic program is adopted, so as to put this enormous amount of currency to some good use, in the years ahead, shall we not run the risk of accumulating foreign currencies in such enormous quantities as to create a real danger to international exchange?

Mr. Monroney: If we attempted to use them unilaterally, in large-scale amounts, the stability of the foreign currencies might be destroyed.

Mr. Gore: Mr. President, will the Senator from Oklahoma yield once more?

Mr. Monroney: Mr. President, I am happy to yield, because of the great contribution the Senator from Tennessee is making to the development of the idea of recycling the aid given by the United States to other countries, so that those countries might in turn extend aid to others.

Mr. Gore: I thank the able Senator. If I understand the situation correctly, this foreign currency has no purchasing power in the United States. Is that correct?

Mr. Monroney: Absolutely none. We intended to use more for strategic materials, but our stockpile is apparently now considered adequate. We use a small part of it for our military expenditures and for our diplomatic establishments within the issuing countries; but it is only a fraction of the billions of dollars being generated by the sale of our agricultural commodities.

Mr. Gore: But all three instances of expenditure to which the Senator has alluded occur in other countries, not in ours. Is that correct?

Mr. Monroney: That is correct.

Mr. Gore: This quantity of foreign currency, however, does have a value in international exchange, does it not?

Mr. Monroney: Indeed, it does, and the use of it in a world bank that could carefully release amounts of foreign currencies in a judicious way, so it would not create inflation, would result in foreign currency beginning to move in world trade, instead of having all world trade tied to the American dollar. It is bad to have a dollar-scarce world. The more freely other countries can use their own currencies, the better off we all are.

Mr. Gore: Would it not be possible, since we possess more than $2 billion of foreign currency, representing good international exchange, to substitute the use of the international currency for the appropriation of American dollars, at least to some extent?[4]

Mr. Monroney: The Senator is reading my mind, because that is part of the proposed program. There cannot be a complete substitution of foreign currency. There must be a dollar or hard-currency base. But given such a base, there will be more oppor-

[4] It is highly misleading to describe inconvertible currency as "good international exchange."—Ed.

tunity to make use of currencies which today have little value in the world market.

MR. GORE: I wish to thank the Senator for making the constructive suggestion by which foreign currencies might be put to beneficial use—a use for which the world is in great need, a use which will contribute to the development of foreign countries, and a use which will prevent a dangerous accumulation of unmanageable quantities of foreign currency.

MR. MONRONEY: I am sure my distinguished friend and colleague also recognizes the dangers of tying up trade on a unilateral basis which makes the countries of the world indebted to us and gives us an unusable stockpile of currencies of many nations of the world. At some future time a movement will be started for total forgiveness of the increasing foreign aid debt. Uncle Sam will probably be asked to forgive world loans. The Senator from Oklahoma proposes to put such loans through an international banking association, so such transactions will be handled on an international basis. The International Development Association would be similar to the World Bank, except it would furnish a second-mortgage market for the 20 percent or 30 percent of projects which otherwise would not be bankable. The head of the World Bank confidentially told me he could have made 50 or 60 more bank loans, which would have made unnecessary some grants-in-aid, had he had available such a second-mortgage operation.

MR. SYMINGTON: Mr. President, will the Senator yield?

MR. MONRONEY: I yield to the distinguished Senator from Missouri.

MR. SYMINGTON: I am much impressed with the idea of the distinguished Senator from Oklahoma. In the cost to the people of the United States of the farm program, there was a difference of opinion as it was presented by the Department of Agriculture, and some members of the committee, as to the true cost. The difference ran into several billions of dollars. One of the charges placed in the cost balance sheet of the Department of Agriculture was that resulting from depreciation in foreign currencies received as a result of the operation of Public Law 480. As I listened to what the distinguished Senator had to say on the subject, it occurred to me that inasmuch as there probably would be an increasing flow of foreign currency, we probably would prevent further devaluation of such foreign currency; and therefore there would be less cost chargeable against the farmers for the price-support program.

Mr. Monroney: The Senator is hitting an important note, as he always does. Certainly, the farmers of America should not be charged with the depreciation in the value of foreign currency. But if the world is tied to the dollar standard instead of the gold standard, then the other currencies that are used will decline in value. Only through usefulness in world trade do currencies have value. The bank I propose would for the first time provide for the use, in international trade, of local currencies of many small and new nations which have recently emerged from colonial status.

Mr. Symington: I should like to associate myself also with the statement of the distinguished Senator from Tennessee and congratulate the Senator from Oklahoma, who, as usual has been constructive in the presentation of an idea to the Senate. As I have listened, it is my understanding that such a bank would further reduce the cost of the agricultural programs; and also would probably increase our good-will relations with other countries.

Mr. Monroney: I thank my distinguished colleague. I may say that with such multilateral loans we could look forward to more sales of our agricultural surpluses, because the receiving nations would prefer to have their currency working rather than hanging over their heads like the sword of Damocles. I think by judicious diplomacy we can negotiate to remove the strings by which countries are now tied. All the world will recognize the benefits from the establishment of an international development bank, and trying to bring other countries to an adequate economic development.

Mr. Gore: Mr. President, will the Senator yield?

Mr. Monroney: I yield to the Senator from Tennessee.

Mr. Gore: Does not this discussion illustrate once again that it is not money, currencies, but goods and services which cross international boundary lines, and oceans to balance trade?

Mr. Monroney: The Senator is entirely correct. We hope to remove some of the problems brought about by having dollars and the pound sterling as the only currencies in which the world can deal. The shortage of those currencies could result in multiple disasters.

Mr. Gore: If our country continues to accumulate bales of lira, bales of yen, and bales of francs, will that not inevitably worsen the imbalance which presently exists?

Mr. Monroney: Sooner or later these currencies must be forgiven or written off or they must be used. If they are used injudiciously, then there will be an impact on the country of issue which could cause inflation, and could destroy instead of help the country to whom we have sold agricultural surpluses.

Thus other nations, which have been helped in their economic recovery, can in turn help others. However, a hard-currency base of dollars and other well-rated moneys will be necessary to make the IDA work.

Final details of the IDA would have to be worked out after careful hearings before the Senate Committee on Banking and Currency. Then the experts of the State Department, the World Bank, and those of other leading nations could refine the program to give it a sound charter and capital structure.

As a starter, it seems to me the International Development Association would need an original capital of $1 billion in dollars or hard currency. The United States would probably put up 30 percent of this amount or $300 million, based on our contribution to the establishment of the World Bank.

It might be possible, after full hearings, to commit the $300 million appropriated by the Congress last year for the establishment of the U.S. development loan program. It is my understanding that few, if any, of these millions have yet been used.

If the Congress chose this method and if the U.S. development loan program's funds were authorized for use in the IDA, no new appropriated funds would be required for the U.S. capital stock in the association.

Secretary Dulles is now asking in the current foreign program for an additional $625 million for his own U.S. development loan program.

This is a unilateral lending program which is operated in conjunction with the State Department. We appropriated $300 million last year, and we are being asked to appropriate $625 million this year, yet there has not been a single loan to date. I see no need for this additional money for more unilateral lending.

The U.S. share of the capital stock of the proposed International Development Association would be less than half of the total which Secretary Dulles is asking as additional capital for his own unilateral development fund.

It is likely that more hard currency capital might be needed for 2 or 3 years. If this should prove true, the Congress could commit the $75 million in annual dollar earnings from interest on foreign loans made under previous aid programs and thus meet additional requirements without new appropriations.

The idea of subordinated loans is not a new one. It was used successfully in many programs under the Reconstruction Finance Corporation. The guaranty of home mortgages released a flood of home building because of the guarantees behind private mortgages. Our reclamation loans are another example. They are gilt-edged when the projects are used for the construction of a new dam which generates hydroelectric power. Power revenues pay off quickly and handsomely, while the long-term loans for irrigation pay off slowly but surely through development of undeveloped areas of the United States and from the sale over 50 years of irrigation water.

The IDA would have the triple advantage of (a) ultimately lessening the need for direct economic aid by making more effective use of local currencies, (b) promoting the sale of agricultural surpluses, and (c) promoting international trade and economic well-being.

This is not a sudden inspiration. I have discussed the idea with many leaders both in America and abroad over a period of 18 months. The response has been overwhelmingly favorable, both to the establishment of such an international association and to the judicious use of multilateral currencies. About the only argument I have heard against the proposal is that the local currencies under our control are already committed. This, of course, can be changed either by the unilateral action of the United States or by agreement among the countries affected.

I have sought bipartisan support for this matter, and have discussed it with leaders in the present administration at several levels, who are giving it continuing study. As of now there has been no final determination of the administration's position on the proposal.

12. *The State Department on United States-owned Local Currencies*[5]

During a hearing before the Subcommittee on International Finance of the Senate Banking and Currency Committee on March 19 [1958], at which the proposed International Development Association was under discussion, Senator Fulbright asked Deputy

[5] SOURCE: Department of State, "United States-owned Local Currencies: Their Uses and Limitations in Economic Development," in *International Development Association*, Hearings before the Senate Committee on Banking and Currency, 85th Cong., 2d sess. (Washington, D.C.: Government Printing Office, 1958), pp. 123–24.

Under Secretary of State Dillon to submit a statement explaining, as simply and briefly as possible, why U.S.-owned local currency holdings are of limited use multilaterally for economic development purposes. This paper is submitted in response to that request.

The currencies of the less developed countries now comprise, and in the future are likely to constitute, the great bulk of the holdings of the United States of the local currencies of foreign countries. Of the $1.8 billion of foreign currencies owned by the United States and unexpended under existing Public Law 480 agreements at the end of last year, some $1.6 billion represented the currency of less developed countries.

The usefulness of a less developed country's local currency is determined by the economic position of that country. For the currency of any country is simply a claim against that country's existing economic resources. It is to a nation's economy what a checkbook is to a checking account. Expenditure of its own currency by a less developed country does not make more resources available to it, any more than writing checks increases a bank balance.

The less developed countries face a deficit rather than a surplus of useful resources. They need all the resources that they have in order to meet their own essential needs; and, in addition, they need more resources, which they do not now have, in order to carry forward economic development. The fact that these countries have a shortage of resources for development is the reason why they are considered as "less developed" countries.

It is clear, therefore, that unless they receive at least equivalent resources in return the less developed countries cannot provide resources to other countries without a setback to their own economic growth. If the United States were to use a less developed country's local currency to remove resources from it for use by other countries we would cause such a setback.

It has been suggested, however, that U.S.-owned local currencies could be used to exchange resources between less developed countries which have complementary needs: We would give country X resources from country Y and vice versa, by lending each country the other's local currency.

To the extent that it is feasible, this sort of exchange is already going on through normal commercial channels. The less developed countries trade with each other to their mutual advantage. They trade jute for oil, rice for textiles, spices for lumber, and so forth.

In a few cases they may even trade steel, but they get needed physical resources in return. If, however, Brazil borrowed rupees from the United States or from a multilateral fund and used those rupees to procure steel from India, by that act Brazil would be taking out of India a physical resource which India needs for its own development; and India would get no compensatory physical resource in return. As a developing country, India is in no position to make resources available to other countries on any significant scale without receiving essential goods in return.

It should be noted, moreover, that the local currencies of less developed countries—cruzeiros, rupees, pesos, hwan, bolivianos—cannot be used to procure the agricultural machinery, the power equipment, the harbor dredges, the railroad cars, etc., that are especially needed for development, for the reason that these things are not produced within the less developed countries and must be imported from the industrialized countries.

There is no present obstacle to trade between the less developed countries which would be removed by United States governmental action in lending these countries each other's local currencies. Such lending would not, therefore, increase the exchange of goods that is now going on between these countries.

Although local currencies are not a useful way of adding to the total resources of the less developed countries, they can help to mobilize resources already within such countries. They may enable a less developed country's government to direct existing economic resources to particular internal uses more effectively. This will be especially true where obstacles exist to the government's securing local currency for this purpose by borrowing from the central bank or other internal means.

The United States is now using local currencies to help governments of less developed countries mobilize their resources in this way. We do this by lending them the local currencies for specified development purposes. By the end of 1957, $463 million of local currencies had been allocated to approved development projects and actual disbursements of funds totaled $259 million.

It is clear from what has been said above that local currency loans for internal purposes cannot have the effect of reducing the need of a less developed country for U.S. external assistance.[6] The basic element of that assistance is foreign exchange, which can be used to acquire goods and services that the less developed coun-

[6] This, of course, was the basic source of disagreement between the Executive and Congress.—ED.

tries do not now possess. These countries will continue to need such goods and services, even if they use their own local currencies to make the most effective possible use of their internal resources.

So long as local currencies cannot be used to provide a net addition to a country's resources, by transferring resources to it from some other country, they cannot be used to reduce the requirement for U.S. dollar assistance.

Eventually, we believe that it will be possible to use some of these local currencies to remove resources from some presently underdeveloped countries for United States or other uses. As these countries' development and production increases, it should be increasingly possible to do this without economic damage to the country concerned. This is not expected to be the case for a considerable period, however. Premature use of these local currencies to remove resources from less developed countries would only set back their development and increase their needs for other types of assistance from the United States.

To sum up, the limitations on the usefulness of our local currency holdings result from the economic condition of the countries in question and not from the fact of U.S. ownership. The utility of these local currencies of less developed countries as an instrument of multilateral economic development will remain very limited until their economic growth reaches the point where they begin to pass out of the category of less developed countries and develop a capacity to contribute to the development of the countries that have not yet made the transition.

13. *The Local-Currency Problem*[7]

[EDITOR'S NOTE: *In 1960, a study group that included the distinguished student of foreign aid Professor Edward S. Mason of Harvard reported to the Under Secretary of State on the "local-currency problem." This excerpt from the report provides an especially interesting discussion of the political aspects of the problem.*]

At the request of the Under Secretary of State, we have undertaken an examination of the growing accumulation of those local

[7] SOURCE: Consultants on International Finance and Economic Problems, *The Problem of Excess Accumulation of U.S.-Owned Local Currencies: Findings and Recommendations Submitted to the Under Secretary of State* (multilithed; Washington, D.C.: Department of State, April 4, 1960), pp. 1–10.

currencies which are owned or controlled by the United States. In so doing, we have studied the size, trend and composition of the U.S. holdings; we have sought to identify those policies and concepts which are causes of the accumulation or which impede its reduction; we have weighed the urgency of required action; and we have considered alternative approaches to a solution in terms of policy and of operations.

As a result of this examination, we have arrived at certain general conclusions which may be summarized as follows:

1. The magnitude of U.S. local currency holdings, in terms of both size and trend, is much larger than is generally assumed. This fact is further accentuated by the uneven pattern of distribution of our local currency holdings.

2. There are certain basic but widespread misunderstandings about the nature of local currency which are responsible for accelerated accumulation and which have served also as impediments to the solution of the problem of excessive accumulation.

3. The excess accumulation of certain currencies is producing increasingly serious problems for the foreign relations of the United States, problems which seem likely to become acute unless corrective action is taken.

4. Contrary to general assumptions, the excess accumulation of local currencies by the United States is a political as well as an economic problem. The real difficulty lies not in finding an economic solution to this problem, but in discovering a solution which is both economically acceptable and politically possible.

5. Finally, we are convinced that the principal cause of the problem is to be found not in the operational field but in the policy and concepts which have dominated thinking and action with regard to local currency. Consequently, we believe that the focus of any remedial effort must center on a revision of policy, based upon a careful analysis of the situations as they are. . . .

I. Magnitude of the Local Currency Problem

In discussing the size of U.S. local currency accumulations, it has been customary to speak in terms of the unexpended or unobligated cash balances on the U.S. books as of a given date. It is our belief that any attempt to analyze the local currency situation as a political problem in terms of the foreign and domestic policies of the United States—and not just as an economic issue—requires a basically different statistical approach. For such purposes, we believe that the magnitude of the problem should be measured in terms of a country's total local currency indebtedness to the United States (cash balances held by the United States plus outstanding loans repayable in local currency), rather than just in terms of unexpended cash balances.

1. The use of cash balances alone may frequently be misleading. For example, the cash balance statistics for June 30, 1958, may show that the United States owns $300 million of Country X's currency. If, before June 30, 1959, Country X draws down a loan of $250 million of its own currency, the next cash balance will show the United States owning only $50 million of Country X currency. The casual observer will assume that we have actually reduced our currency problem by $250 million, which has frequently led to the expression: "We no longer have a problem in Country X." Actually, the $250 million will return to the U.S. account as loan repayments, bringing with it additional amounts of local currency as interest charges and possibly as maintenance of value payments. The loan may have spread the economic burden over a longer period of years; it has not changed the political implications based on the size of the indebtedness.

2. In terms of impact on U.S. foreign policy, it is a country's total indebtedness to the United States—and not just cash balances on the U.S. account—which may well, in the days ahead, subject us to charges that the United States "owns" some of these less developed nations.

3. Total indebtedness, and not cash balance, is important in measuring ability to service loans. There are limits to a country's capacity to service loans, even in local currency, without resort to undesirable monetary practices; this is accentuated in cases where U.S. loans provide for maintenance of value.

4. From the standpoint of the foreign country, the cash balance approach is also inadequate. In deciding whether it can afford to increase its local currency obligations to the United States, a foreign country must consider two aspects: the fiscal problem (in the context of total indebtedness already incurred) and the political problem (the concentration of its indebtedness in the hands of a single foreign creditor). Both have potential foreign policy implications. . . .

II. The Nature of Local Currency

In our opinion, the greatest single impediment to the proper handling of the local currency situation is the widespread confusion and misunderstanding over the nature of the currency itself, its possible uses, and its inherent limitations. The very words "currency" and "money" customarily denote something which is desirable to own, definitely worth saving, and only too easy to use. It is difficult, therefore, to convince people that these local currencies which we are accumulating have little in common with dollars or with other freely convertible money, and that these funds have limitations which frequently make it difficult for the United States to use them for purposes which are either in our interest or in the interest of the countries we are assisting.

There is also a tendency to generalize from the specific and to assume that because local currencies have proved useful in Country X they will prove equally useful in Countries Y and Z. Finally, there is a tendency to assume that if a small amount of local currency proved useful or usable in Country X, a large amount of local currency would prove equally useful. The fact is that, in many cases, there are de facto limits to the quantity of U.S.-held local currency which the United States or the foreign country can constructively employ, and that accumulations above this amount are of no practical value. This is the situation with which we are confronted today in an increasing number of countries. And this is the situation which produces strain on, and potential damage to, U.S. foreign relations without producing any compensating gain to the U.S. Treasury. . . .

2. The governments of most underdeveloped countries are under tremendous pressure to hasten economic development; therefore, their budget expenditures for this purpose are usually greater than borrowing from real savings plus tax revenues will finance. This means that these countries are typically in a semi-inflationary or inflationary condition.

3. One must be careful to differentiate between the dollars and commodities which generate local currency on the one hand, and the local currencies themselves on the other. The former are real resources which make a contribution to the total wealth of the recipient country; the local currencies are not. How much local currency will in fact be generated will depend upon the fiscal policy of the government receiving the commodities.

Money itself is not a resource; it is a claim on a country's resources.[8] When the United States supplies a foreign country with the latter's own local currency, we are not increasing the real re-

[8] Unfortunately, the report fails to point out that local currencies in United States accounts do *not* constitute an effective claim on foreign resources, because of legal, political, and economic restrictions on their use.—ED.

sources available to it—we are giving it an additional claim on its own resources. In fact, because such loans or grants are primarily to governments, we may be adding to the already heavy concentration of claims on the country's resources in the hands of government, at the expense of the private sector.

Another important characteristic of these local currencies, and an inherent limitation, is that they are inconvertible. Therefore, the United States cannot use them freely to buy from third countries the goods which we or one of our aid-receiving countries may require. Nor can we freely exchange this currency for some other money which we might be able to use.

A third characteristic of the local currencies which the United States is accumulating is the number of restrictions put on their "use" by the agreements which generate the accumulations. This type of limitation is caused by the fact that these negotiations have domestic and foreign policy objectives and are not commercial deals designed merely to obtain an economic quid pro quo. For this reason, they require concessions and restrictions on both sides. . . .

III. Political Implications for U.S. Foreign Policy

A second fairly widespread misunderstanding concerns the negative implications which this local currency accumulation holds for U.S. foreign policy. In many quarters, there is a vague uneasiness about what is called the local currency "problem," based largely on the fact that somehow the size of our holdings keeps growing each year, even when measured in terms of cash balances. However, the serious potential which this situation holds for U.S. foreign relations seems little understood. A word or two about the objectives and methods of U.S. foreign assistance is, in our opinion, a necessary prerequisite to a discussion of the specific political problems produced by an excess accumulation of local currency.

Since 1954, and increasingly in more recent years, there has been a shift in emphasis in U.S. foreign assistance programs away from grants and gifts to loans and sales. With regard to the programs which generate local currency, this shift in emphasis has resulted in an insistence on selling U.S. agricultural surpluses for local currency rather than in giving them away, and on making loans repayable in local currency rather than the continuation of a large program of grants-in-aid.

These changes in emphasis and in the form of U.S. foreign assistance are the result of a strong political reaction in this country against so-called "giveaway" progams; they represent an attempt to put our foreign assistance on a sound and businesslike basis. Some people have supported these changes because they think of foreign assistance in fiscal rather than in foreign policy terms. Others have supported these changes because they are convinced that foreign assistance appropriations can be obtained more easily by accenting the commercial and business form of loans and sales rather than grants and gifts, which sound like "giveaway" procedures.

In order to clear the record, let us examine the meaning of "giveaway" as it relates to the objectives and form of U.S. foreign assistance. In cases where the U.S. is piling up sizeable excess accumulations, such excess currencies which we receive as payment for U.S. assistance, have little present or foreseeable economic value to the United States. Thus, in a purely economic sense, the United States is still not being compensated and its programs continue to be a "giveaway" despite their new businesslike form and the economic terms used in describing them.

In our opinion, however, it is irrelevant that the United States is not receiving an economic quid pro quo for its foreign assistance. Foreign assistance was not instituted primarily to achieve economic gain for the United States but as an instrument for the achievement of U.S. foreign policy objectives. Those programs which generate local currency were not originated with the objective of collecting local currency but with the political and security interests of the United States as their goal. Therefore, the test of value received—the test of whether such programs are really a "giveaway"—is not whether an equivalent amount of money accrues to the United States in repayment for its assistance but whether our basic foreign policy objectives are, in fact, achieved. That this cannot be measured until considerable time has elapsed, and therefore may be difficult for the public to understand, does not alter the fact that this is the only valid yardstick.

The danger which currently faces the United States is that in the pursuit of an unobtainable economic quid pro quo, we are adopting measures and pursuing methods which seem destined inevitably to undermine the real political and security objectives of foreign assistance. A few examples may be in order:

1. Among the damaging consequences is the already evident political reaction in certain underdeveloped countries against the excessively large claims on local resources which are represented by the size of the country's indebtedness to the United States. Pakis-

tan's local currency obligations to this country are already over $235 million. In relation to the Pakistan national income, this would be the approximate equivalent of $20 billion in the United States. It is unlikely that American citizens or the American Government could regard such holdings by a single foreign power with equanimity, even though they were not convertible into other currencies.

Such a situation is even less acceptable to newly independent states who are jealous of their recently gained independence and sovereignty. The inevitable reaction is already in evidence in certain Asian countries—not always from the governments themselves but from the Communists and from the opposition parties, both of whom embarrass governments friendly to the United States by questioning the size of the indebtedness and speaking in terms of U.S. imperialism.

2. As discussed in a subsequent section of this report, U.S. officials find themselves under pressures to get local currency accumulations "off the books" by loans to underdeveloped countries. We have noted in the previous section that such loans may not be an unmixed blessing to the recipient, and, accordingly, U.S. pressure is sometimes resisted by the foreign country. This puts the United States in the awkward position of persuading and even coercing foreign governments to borrow their own currency from us. For its part, the foreign government, having obliged the United States by signing a loan agreement, may prove quite slow and reluctant to draw down local currency balances under the agreement. It is the size of the accumulation which creates U.S. domestic pressures to remove visible cash balances from the books; it is the effort of the foreign country to avoid such pressures which leads to conflicts with U.S. foreign policy interests.

VI

Multilateral Aid

The controversy over channeling American aid through international organizations is as lively today as it was ten or fifteen years ago. Historically, this debate has been tied closely to the grant-loan issue. Because the International Bank could make hard loans, any argument for new multinational machinery had to explain why the Bank could not do the job adequately. The arguments for more multilateral aid were often couched, therefore, in terms of an attack on hard loans.

The explanations of the alleged inadequacies of hard lending, however, tended to conceal the equally important but more delicate issue of control over aid distribution. The proposals generated in the United Nations, e.g., SUNFED, usually gave potential aid recipients an equal say with potential donors in deciding who would get what and when, an arrangement for which the U.S. Government, as the biggest potential contributor, showed little enthusiasm. It tended to prefer a system of weighted voting, such as that used by the IBRD, which apportioned votes according to the amount of money each nation contributed. The United States has also been reluctant to contribute to multilateral agencies to which the Soviet Union might belong. Since 1945, the United States has contributed some money to the U.N. technical assistance programs, including the U.N. Special Fund; but most of its multilateral aid has been channeled through organizations with weighted voting, such as the IDA, IFC, IBRD, and IDB, none of which includes the Soviet Union as a member.

14. *Dulles on Multilateral Aid*[1]

[EDITOR's NOTE: *During the hearings on the Mutual Security Act of 1956, Secretary of State John Foster Dulles was questioned on the advisability of channeling more American aid through the*

[1] SOURCE: *Mutual Security Act of 1956*, Hearings before the Senate Committee on Foreign Relations, 84th Cong., 2d sess. (Washington, D.C.: Government Printing Office, 1956), pp. 41–44.

United Nations. On this point, he found himself in an awkward disagreement with the American Ambassador to the United Nations, Henry Cabot Lodge.]

SENATOR MORSE [D., Oregon]: Mr. Secretary, I read the statement of Ambassador Lodge that has been referred to by Senator Knowland [R., California], and I interpret this statement to mean that he advocated greater use of the United Nations in the handling of economic foreign aid.

Am I correct in my interpretation of your remarks that you have at least a modified opinion about that proposal and hold to the point of view which you commented on in regard to answering one of Senator Knowland's questions, that you thought only a minimum amount of economic aid should be handled through the United Nations?

SECRETARY DULLES: I think that when I said it was minimum, I was referring to the program as a whole. He pointed out, I think, that the greater part of the program is related to our defense arrangements.

As I said in my statement, approximately 83 percent of the program is either direct military assistance or what we call defense support—

SENATOR MORSE: What about the 17 percent in your statement?

SECRETARY DULLES: That would probably not lend itself to any United Nations supervision. That leaves the balance of the program, some part of which could be and indeed some part of which does go through the United Nations.

Whether the United Nations can usefully be used to a greater degree or not with advantage is a very close question which we are considering and which I think is one of the questions which should be considered if we have a new study made of certain aspects of this program. I mentioned that in my statement as one of the things which might be studied.

There are advantages and also disadvantages in a proposal to combine with the Soviet Union in this effort. We know, Senator, because it appears so dramatically from the facts of the case that the Soviet Union is doing this only for its own political purposes.

Now, whether you can effectively sterilize it by putting it through the United Nations I am not quite clear, and there is some question as to whether we want to admit that Soviet activities and ours can be equated in that way.

So there are both advantages and disadvantages in this proposal. That whole subject is being very closely studied by various members of the administration at the present time. We have not come to any clear conclusion on it, and it would be a subject on which I would be glad to get the views of the kind of people that we might be able to make a study of some phases of this program.

SENATOR MORSE: Taking the 17 percent which you mentioned in your statement, which is the economic aid that we could say generally speaking is not directly connected with the military program, do you think that a substantial portion of that 17 percent might possibly be administered along the lines of the suggestion made by Ambassador Lodge this morning?

SECRETARY DULLES: The entire amount?

SENATOR MORSE: A substantial portion of that 17 percent that is not connected directly with our so-called military aid might be administered along the lines of Ambassador Lodge's suggestion this morning.

SECRETARY DULLES: I would doubt that anything like $700 million ought to be administered in that way. I believe that approximately $45 million now does go through the United Nations in one form or another, but I doubt very much whether it would be wise to increase that to any such figure as $500 or $600 million.

SENATOR MORSE: I think some $15.5 million goes to the United Nations now for the technical assistance program.

SECRETARY DULLES: That is right.

SENATOR MORSE: I hope this is a proper question.

Did you have any idea that Ambassador Lodge was going to make the suggestion that he made in the press today? Have there been any conferences between you and Ambassador Lodge on this matter of administering economic aid through the United Nations?

SECRETARY DULLES: Yes; we have had a very full exchange of views on this subject over recent weeks.

SENATOR MORSE: Are we to understand, therefore, that there is this apparent difference of opinion between his proposal of today, if I interpret it correctly, and your testimony of today?

SECRETARY DULLES: Well, I would not say there was a difference of opinion. I would say that as far as the executive branch of the Government is concerned, we have not yet come to any decision.

SENATOR MORSE: Now a question or two about the relationship of the United Nations . . . as far as its originally intended purpose is concerned, and the problem of building up the economic productive power of the areas of the world that we are trying to win over to the side of freedom.

Is it your opinion that we should seek to try to get the nations that we are helping to recognize that our intentions are not intended unduly to influence their internal policies, which the line of Russian propaganda tries to represent to the world, but that our intention is to try to help them build up their economic productive power so that they can stand firmly on their own political legs of self-government?

Would you say that that is clearly our objective?

SECRETARY DULLES: That is clearly our objective. I think the President put it very well when he said we have no desire or intention to make over the world in our own image.

Our desire is that these different peoples of the world should have the opportunity to work out their own future in accordance with their own culture, their own aspirations, their own best judgment as to how best their form of government can serve their own community.

That may be in a way quite different from what we judge as the best way for us. I think we are trying to make that quite clear, Senator.

SENATOR MORSE: Does it not follow though that if we are going to meet that Russian propaganda, that wherever we can do it without in any way weakening our own security, we ought to make a maximum use of the procedures of the United Nations and our freedom-loving allies within the United Nations in carrying on this program of economic aid to even the neutral countries and the weaker free countries so that it cannot be said that we are using economic weapons as a means of holding in line countries that may at the present time be neutral?

SECRETARY DULLES: The United Nations is a wonderful organization, and as I think you know, I have had a great deal to do with it since its beginning and perhaps had something to do with the creation in this country of the public sentiment which led to its creation with strong American support.

However, it is important to remember that the United Nations, like every other organization, is not an abstraction. It operates through human beings like every organization does, and you have to measure it by the people, by the governments who play the role.

The idea of the United Nations trusteeship is a fine conception, but when you boil it down, you have to find out who administers this trusteeship, is it country X or is it country Y?

When you begin to think of it in those terms, it does not seem quite so glamorous as when you just talk about the United Nations.

In the same way here I think it must be admitted that some of the economic organizations of the United Nations have not measured up to the high standards in terms of personnel and so forth which we would like to see.

And while it is quite true that we have no desire to make the world over into our image, we equally have the desire that it should not be made over into somebody else's image.

15. *Mutual Aid Through the United Nations*[2]

[EDITOR'S NOTE: *In this statement by Henry Cabot Lodge, speaking with the authority of his position as Ambassador to the United Nations, the standard arguments for multilateral aid are succinctly summarized. The speech was made on March 7, 1960, before a conference of the American Association for the United Nations, in Washington, D.C.*]

The advantages of the multilateral way are clear, and I should like to list them:

1. In these programs our dollars are more than matched by the dollars put in by those countries which also contribute.

2. Then the countries which receive make further matching efforts of their own. Thus we get more for our money from both contributors and from recipients—sometimes as much as $7 for every dollar which the United States puts in.

3. The necessary experts are recruited not only from the United States but from scores of other countries. Well-qualified experts can often be obtained outside the United States at salaries half that which it costs to get an American expert.

4. These programs are so obviously insulated against political manipulation that they are welcomed in places where bilateral programs—however unjustifiably in our case—would be suspect. Thus there is less risk of having our purposes misunderstood and resented. Instead we get credit for helping an altruistic United Nations program.

[2] SOURCE: Henry Cabot Lodge, "Mutual Aid Through the United Nations," *Department of State Bulletin*, XLII, No. 1084 (April 4, 1960), 525–27.

5. It is also true that you get more for your money when the recipient nation feels that it is participating in the planning and carrying out of the program. This was proved time and again in the operation of the Marshall Plan when the Organization for European Economic Cooperation formulated the plans which were then carried out by the members.

6. Nor should we lose sight of the fact that the United Nations can push a recipient government in a way that no sovereign government can ever push another. No consideration of prestige is involved, nor can the cry of "imperialism" or of "intervention" be raised when it is the gentle friendly pressure of the ever-helpful United Nations—particularly when the recipient nation itself is a member of the United Nations.

7. Decisions must be taken in operating any economic program which disappoint or displease. How much better it is for us not to be the ones who cause disappointment or displeasure and for this to be done by an international organization which is not a "foreign country."

8. There is another selfish reason, from the U.S. point of view, why reliance should be placed on an international method of operation. As Paul Hoffman recently said, "The countries of Western Europe, now fully recovered, are able to invest more in underdeveloped areas than they are now doing. Their gold and foreign exchange holdings, as well as their capacity to earn more, are increasing. The United States, on the other hand, is facing a continued deficit in its balance of payments, and its gold stocks are declining. It is clearly to our interest to spread the responsibility for investment in the underdeveloped areas and to induce other countries to make their maximum contribution." The way to do this is through the multilateral economic programs bearing the United Nations label.

9. Finally, because of the major part we play in these programs, we are fully protected against unsound use of the money. Some very intelligent and well-disposed people have not understood this fact.

Let me illustrate:

I have actually heard some persons say that our funds, when put into a multilateral United Nations program, would be subject to the Soviet veto—or that they would be subject to an adverse vote in the General Assembly. Nothing could be more wildly inaccurate and more totally impossible. In the World Bank and in the IDA, for example, voting is on a weighted basis, according to the capital subscribed. In the United Nations Special Fund the governing body is so constituted as to make impossible any action opposed by the nations of the free world. The same is true of United Nations technical assistance.

Now there are enough real complications in the world without manufacturing extra ones which do not exist. The influence of the United States and of the free world in all these multilateral programs is such that, while they cannot—and should not—be used to promote our special interests, it is absolutely impossible for them to be turned against us. They do, obviously, serve our long-range interest in a peaceful, more prosperous world.

For all these reasons it is in the U.S. interests to use the multilateral aid of the United Nations to the maximum, and I believe this will be done increasingly in the future.

It is significant that to date the Soviet Union has made only a token contribution to these United Nations aid programs. This is not good for humanity in general and for the underdeveloped countries in particular, because multilateral aid frees a weak underdeveloped country from the natural fear that it will become a battleground for politics between the superpowers. As long as the Soviet Union refuses to support these programs wholeheartedly it will be suspected of using its economic aid for selfish motives—for attaching "strings" to its aid.

Prime Minister Khrushchev said to the General Assembly last September that the United Nations has a duty to "contribute to the utmost to the economic advancement of the new states which are rising from the ruins of the colonial system, to help them speedily to develop their national economies." And he said that this must be done "without any political or other strings attached." But the Soviet Government has not yet carried out this policy.

If the Soviets should ever choose to compete, not for political advantage but for the honor of having done the most to help peoples who seek a better life, the United Nations offers them an unmatched way to do so. They could, if they chose, contribute many times more to United Nations technical assistance programs—and in convertible currency. They could even join the World Bank and the Monetary Fund and the International Development Association.

I do not expect them to do these things soon, but, until they do, the nations will inescapably judge for themselves whether Soviet aid is disinterested or not.

In the midst of all these events the United Nations has continued to grow. In fact, that growth—from 60 to 82 members—is the greatest single change in the United Nations in recent years.[3] Still others will join this year, mostly from Africa. In another 10 years the Organization may well have 100 members. It seems as though everyone wants to get in and no one wants to get out.

Now there is no need to pretend that this growth in membership has not caused more work for the United States. There are more people whom one must try to persuade, and that means more work. More people are trying to persuade us. It is certainly harder now for any nation to muster a two-thirds majority in the General Assembly on a controversial question than it used to be. But this may not be a bad thing, because an organization as influential and as weighty as the United Nations should not express itself too glibly.

As we look ahead it seems certain that the United Nations will remain what diplomats call a "power fact," with which countries will have to cope whether they like it or not. There is certainly no reason for the United States to fear its growth. For us it is a priceless asset and an unceasing opportunity. Neither we nor any nation is so powerful that we do not need friends or that we can with impunity disregard world opinion. Indeed, as a wise Englishman wrote 50 years ago, the sheer power of a great nation will only "inspire universal jealousy and fear" unless its policy is designed "to harmonize with the general desires and ideals common to all mankind." Our United States policies have been successful because they do so harmonize.

The United Nations has always been important as a great center for that harmonizing. Now it is more so than ever. To an increasing number of new nations membership in it is the greatest tangible proof to the world that they are now sovereign. That is the main reason why they attach such great importance to it. There is no better way for the United States to keep their confidence, and to prove that we ungrudgingly and wholeheartedly welcome their sovereignty, than for us to work with them through the United Nations.

Our foreign policy must have more than physical strength, vital though that is. It must also have great and magnanimous purposes, and it must find ways to express those purposes so that the peoples of the world will understand and welcome them. Economic cooperation through the United Nations is, preeminently, such a way. Indeed it can be one of the indispensable ingredients of peace on earth.

[3] Most of the new members were low-income countries.—ED.

16. *Multilateral Aid on the New Frontier*[4]

[EDITOR's NOTE: *The role of multilateral aid in American foreign-aid strategy was described in 1961 by Richard N. Gardner, a spokesman for the Kennedy Administration in his capacity as Deputy Assistant Secretary of State for International Organization Affairs.*]

The executing agencies are identified by a range of initials which might bewilder even as well-informed a group as this committee. Their programs cover a wide range of activities from medical research to security forces—from surveys of natural resources to the care of refugees. At first glance, one might get the impression that this is a miscellaneous hodgepodge of unrelated programs with no clear relation to the national interest.

I should like to begin by assuring the committee that this is not the case. Each of these appropriation requests is in direct support of one or both of two basic aims of U.S. foreign policy: First, the promotion of peace and security; and second, the promotion of economic and social growth.

Each program listed has, in our view, a high priority in support of our national foreign policy objectives. Each has been pioneered or cosponsored by the United States, and stands as a symbol of U.S. leadership in both the security and development fields.

Many of these activities are analogous in character to programs carried out directly by the United States under bilateral programs of cooperation and assistance. I therefore should explain briefly why the programs represented in this part of the presentation are carried out through multilateral agencies and how they complement the rest of the program before you.

But first I should like to say that we do not see any conflict between bilateral and multilateral assistance. Both types are needed —and probably will be needed for the indefinite future—for solid, practical reasons.

The choice between national and international institutions for maintaining peace and security or for channeling economic and technical assistance is not a theoretical but a pragmatic choice. In any given case, one route may be more feasible or desirable than the other or both may prove necessary.

[4] SOURCE: *International Development and Security*, Hearings before the Senate Committee on Foreign Relations, 87th Cong., 1st sess. (Washington, D.C.: Government Printing Office, 1961), pp. 402–3.

Let me list quickly some inherent advantages of the multilateral approach when that is the practical thing to do.

First, the use of international agencies for the maintenance of peace and order can avoid competitive intervention by rival nations with all the explosive implications of such action. The United Nations can intervene without being accused of intervention because it is done in the name of the world community; because it is clearly in the interests of peace; and because its motivation is beyond suspicion of national ambition. This is the case of the United Nations Emergency Force in the Middle East and, more recently, the United Nations operation in the Congo.

Second, some of the newly emerging nations are understandably sensitive about accepting even technical conditions for assistance from one of the great powers. This is eliminated or greatly reduced when the aid is furnished through an international organization of which they are members and from which they are willing to accept conditions for aid. This is often the case in technical assistance, especially when it concerns such delicate areas as the improvement of public administration.

Third, international agencies offer a device for raising the contributions of other nations which can afford to help. It is pleasant to be able to report to this committee a gratifying increase in both the number and size of contributions from other countries to the international agencies. There are several cases where international agencies have expanded their total effort while reducing the proportionate U.S. contribution to them. And in the case of the development agencies, the nations receiving assistance contribute substantially from their own resources—at times more than half of the total cost of the cooperative projects.

Fourth, the international agencies can draw on a worldwide pool of technical personnel which may not be available in the United States and which frequently can be employed at a lower cost. In many cases, non-American technicians have experience which is more relevant to conditions obtaining in the less developed world and, as I have suggested, internationally sponsored technical assistance is likely to be more economical than bilateral assistance.

For these reasons we have supported the growth of the United Nations and regional technical assistance programs and hope they will be able to absorb an ever greater share of this work in the years ahead.

Fifth, international agencies are better equipped to help on regional projects overlapping national boundaries. The Indus Basin project before you is a case in point.

Sixth, the healthy growth of international agencies is in itself a highly desirable objective. Multilateral organizations endowed with the capacity to act in the interest of security and development, can promote that open world society of independent and prosperous nations which is the goal of our foreign policy, and which stands at the opposite extreme from Soviet dreams of a world Communist state.

At least several of the projects being carried out by these agencies are imaginative in concept, dramatic in scope, and require an unprecedented degree of international cooperation in the service of human aspirations.

Our national interest is well served by a leading role in such enterprises.

These are the major reasons, Mr. Chairman, why our contributions to international agencies are part and parcel of our total program for what the President has called the decade of development. . . .

17. *Multilateral Aid in the Great Society*[5]

[EDITOR'S NOTE: *For the past several years, the Chairman of the Senate Foreign Relations Committee, J. W. Fulbright, has led a campaign to increase the proportion of American aid flowing through multinational channels. In the following excerpt from the 1965 hearings on foreign aid, Senator Fulbright's fellow committee member Senator Joseph S. Clark (D., Pennsylvania) questions David E. Bell, Administrator of AID, with regard to international aid.*]

SENATOR CLARK: Now it occurs to me as a new member of the committee that one of the problems over which seems to be some controversy is the relative effectiveness of the multilateral as opposed to bilateral aid. I would like to get your opinion on several of these questions. The first one would be: in your opinion are international agencies any more successful than the AID program in accomplishing results? If you don't want to answer it, just say so.

MR. BELL: No; I am perfectly prepared to answer that, Senator.

[5] SOURCE: *Foreign Assistance, 1965*, Hearings before the Senate Committee on Foreign Relations, 89th Cong., 1st sess. (Washington, D.C.: Government Printing Office, 1965), pp. 117–20.

I would say that the aid that is going to—leave aside if we may the supporting assistance type of case in which the international agencies are not normally involved—the aid that is going to development under our bilateral program is today being administered as effectively as the aid going for development being administered by the international agencies.

Now they will vary. Some of the international agencies are clearly stronger, more strongly administered, have longer traditions than some others. But in general I think the development aid that we are providing today is very effective, and as effective in general as the aid going under the international agencies.

This is of course in part true because, as I pointed out in my statement and as the Secretary did yesterday, so much of our aid is going, even if it is bilateral aid, to the developing countries under a system of multilateral coordination, such as CIAP [Inter-American Committee for the Alliance for Progress] for Latin America, such as the consortiums organized by the World Bank. We are therefore in constant and continuous contact and collaboration particularly with the World Bank, the IMF, the Inter-American Development Bank, and we are all trying to use similar standards for decisions as to the kinds of projects we undertake and the ways in which we carry them out, and so on.

SENATOR CLARK: Now in terms of enlisting self-help from the countries to which we give assistance, what is your opinion as to whether the international agencies such as the World Bank are generally more successful than you have been able to be in getting the maximum amount of self-help from these countries?

MR. BELL: Well, now here again, Senator, of course, you are asking me questions on which I am sure different people would have different judgments.

SENATOR CLARK: I understand. That is why I want to get your opinion.

MR. BELL: My own feeling is that again the international agencies have varied. The best of them, the World Bank, has done an extremely good job of requiring careful standards to be met for the projects which they have been willing to finance. Indeed I would say that Eugene Black and the World Bank led the world some years ago in establishing high standards. I think we have been catching up to those standards since.

There is another area of self-help standards, however, which goes beyond the individual project, and relates to the over-all economic policies of a country. When, for example, we worked out with the Brazilians plans for bringing this very severe inflation to a halt, and overcoming the other very difficult economic circumstances that the new government had inherited from the Goulart Administration, there was a long period of discussion as to what the proper and appropriate Brazilian program was. We were eventually quite well satisfied that the Brazilians understood their problem well and were tackling it well.

We had made it quite plain that until we were satisfied along those lines, we were not prepared to provide major assistance to them. Now that is the kind of discussion leading to very strong self-help commitments on the part of the country receiving assistance, and very strong support from us, which we and the IMF have been doing very well, and in which the banks by and large have not usually participated on quite the same basis.

In this sense I think it has been fair to say that the American bilateral program and the IMF have in some respects been developing stronger ideas about how to look at the over-all economic position of a country and how to relate an aid program to the over-all economic policies of the country than other international agencies have.

These are distinctions which I do not in any sense want to exaggerate. I repeat the main point, the main response to your comment is that the World Bank, the Inter-American Development Bank, the IMF, the United States, the other donor nations are increasingly working together and increasingly under multilateral arrangements, increasingly trying to apply the same kinds of standards. This is a direction in which we are making progress and we all expect to continue to make progress.

I certainly would be wrong, however, to denigrate or not to recognize the important role that the United States has played, especially in the last several years, in trying to work toward—along with these international agencies—to work toward a situation in which the efforts that a country makes for itself are examined and carefully analyzed, and the aid that other countries and international agencies are prepared to make available to them is related to the self-help effort which they are willing to undertake. There has been really a very significant gain over the last several years, and the United States has played a very important part in it.

SENATOR CLARK: Now in terms of resentment incurred in the borrowing countries, do you notice any difference in your experience or in the experience of your agency between the resentment which is incurred toward the aid administrators as a result of these loans, and the international loans made by institutions whose governing board or executive officers are not sort of gringos?

Mr. Bell: I think there is no doubt that an international agency operates from a position where it can ask for a meeting of technical standards without carrying any particular political overtones, whereas the United States has a somewhat more delicate job.

We ask for the same technical standards to be met. It is possible for us to be accused of doing something for political reasons, or the political element may be brought in. In this sense I think Senator Fulbright's point, which he has made frequently, is a very sound point.

The international agencies certainly can operate from a nonpolitical setting, so to speak, and certainly we, the American program, operate under the leadership of the international agencies wherever we can. We strongly encourage the Bank and the Fund and others to take the lead, because there is less direct political risk.

On the other hand, it is quite possible for us, for the United States, and has been possible for many years, and in country after country, to handle the delicate relationship between aid giver and aid receiver without rancor, without difficulty.

Looking back, for example, during the Marshall Plan days, Bill Foster has told me how he had some very severe knockdown, drag-out fights in private, in which he said to one or another of the European countries:

"Look, you are a sovereign nation and you can adopt whatever economic policies you want, but we are also a sovereign nation. If we are going to make our aid available to you, we have to be satisfied that your economic policies make sense."

Now we are saying that today in private and quietly, and normally without any difficulty. You look around the world and the places where the large amounts of American aid are going, these are not the places where there is difficulty, where there is resentment, where there is argument. The places where there is a lot of controversy are cases where there is very little aid involved, where the real problem is not aid at all, but the political differences between ourselves and the country in question. I would be delighted to expand on this point in executive session. I think the point is perfectly obvious.

Let me state it in a slightly different way. We have found that it is possible to insist on very strong self-help standards in many countries under our bilateral aid program. It is easier to do that, and it is preferable to do that within a multilateral framework, within a consortium or within CIAP or in any way that provides participation by the country in question and a joint agreement on the technical standards that ought to be applied.

But we don't take a back seat to anybody in asserting that we have been able to apply very strong self-help standards under our bilateral program.

SENATOR CLARK: That leads me to my last question, Mr. Chairman. I am sure there is a wide difference of opinion in the membership of this committee.

My own view is that most of the problems confronting the world today are a result of the exaggeration of the nation state as the be-all and end-all of political organizations of society, far more so than the alleged struggle between communism and capitalism. Therefore I would like to see personally, and I know many of my colleagues would strongly disagree, a gradual development of these multilateral and even worldwide institutions, and a gradual phasing out of our bilateral and national aid programs and a lot of other programs also.

I take it from your close experience with this problem during the last 2 years that you would conclude that the time for that is not yet, although perhaps we can make some progress along that line.

MR. BELL: Oh, yes. I want to be perfectly clear. As the Secretary testified yesterday, we have strongly advocated and we strongly advocate today steady movement toward more funding through international agencies and more and better arrangements for multilateral coordination. We think those trends are in being and we agree with them and support them.

We think that there will continue to be the need for a bilateral aid program and a strong one for at least several years to come. . . .

VII

Executive-Legislative Relations
and Foreign Aid

The system of Constitutional checks and balances was designed to ensure a certain amount of tension in Executive-Legislative relations. It succeeded—as the makers of aid policy well know. With regard to aid, the tension is focused on two questions: How big is the program going to be? Who is going to run it?

As for the first question, Congress usually favors a smaller aid program than does the Executive. This debate over size is tied to the loan-grant controversy—those who favor curtailment of the program tend to advocate loans.

Both friends and foes of aid in Congress are especially sensitive on the question of Legislative control. Most Congressmen feel that they do not have enough control of the month-to-month development of aid policy. Although the standard techniques for controlling Executive administrators have been employed by Congress, some of these have not been effective. The techniques used are:

1. *Auditing government accounts after the money is spent.*—This method may improve the Executive Branch bookkeeping procedures, but it has little to do with actual uses of the money. It does not inform the auditors of the real impact of aid, because it fails to ask how the recipients' resources would have been allocated in the absence of aid.

2. *Appropriation of funds.*—This technique, used in conjunction with the threat not to appropriate funds, is the most effective means of control over aid available to Congress. By threatening to withhold next year's funds, Congress can influence this year's aid activities. Without appropriations, the Executive can do little, except through the Export-Import Bank, which borrows directly from the Treasury.

3. *Statutes.*—Although statutes do place wide limits on aid activities, the inevitable ambiguity of language always leaves room for the Executive so to "interpret" the statutes that they may be made to permit almost anything. The fact that the Executive often

fails to take advantage of this ambiguity does not necessarily mean that the statutes control Executive behavior; the Executive is more likely to be held back by its fear of Legislative reprisal in the form of cuts in future appropriations.

4. *Investigation.*—The effectiveness of this technique is difficult to assess. Congressional investigations have undoubtedly had an impact on the administration of the aid program, though it may not be acknowledged by the investigators. A Congressional investigation of "waste" in the aid program, however, is unlikely to result in more economical aid administration, but it may increase the "waste" by its demands on the time of aid administrators and its insistence on the adoption of cumbersome bookkeeping procedures. It may also prove that the investigators are using a faulty concept of "waste," but it is unlikely to prove that aid officials are intent on "stuffing money down a rat hole."

The following readings will highlight various aspects of the Executive-Legislative battle over the size and control of the aid program.

18. *The Congressional Politics of Foreign Aid*[1]

The profound changes that have taken place in United States foreign policy since 1945 have altered substantially the role of Congress in foreign affairs. These changes not only affect the relationship between the White House and Capitol Hill; they also affect the respective roles of the two Legislative bodies.

In the isolationist atmosphere of the prewar era, Congress took only a passive interest in foreign policy. This apathy was particularly evident in the House, which had no Constitutional right to participate in treaty-making, the Legislative Branch's principal foreign-policy function at that time.

But as the Cold War took shape, and more immediate foreign-policy concerns came to the fore, treaty-making took a back seat. The first order of business was the vast array of nonmilitary programs that stemmed, in one way or another, from the confrontation with Communism in every corner of the globe. As a consequence, the principal Legislative concern with foreign policy could now be boiled down to one word: appropriations.

[1] SOURCE: David A. Baldwin, "The Congressional Politics of Foreign Aid," *Challenge, The Magazine of Economic Affairs*, September–October, 1965, pp. 22–25. Reprinted with permission.

Since the Constitution requires both Houses to approve appropriations bills, and since custom dictates that such bills should originate in the House, the once-ignored lower chamber came to play a key role in foreign policy through its power over the public purse. For practical purposes, however, much of this power is concentrated in the subcommittees of the House Appropriations Committee that oversee the budgets of the State Department and the foreign-aid program. Their respective chairmen, John Rooney (D., New York) and Otto Passman (D., Louisiana), have thus become two of the most powerful men in Washington.

But Congress has not been particularly happy about its new responsibilities. And its continued grumbling about appropriating money to give—or loan—to foreigners has become a time-honored issue in American politics.

Various explanations for the Legislative hostility to foreign aid have been offered. Some say that this antagonism is based on legitimate objections to the way the program is run. If aid could be administered more efficiently, runs the argument, Congress would be more friendly. In February, 1964, however, this explanation was found wanting. Although the operational efficiency of the World Bank was unquestioned, the House of Representatives defeated an attempt to expand the resources of the IDA, a Bank affiliate. Apparently, fears of "mismanagement" are not the only source of Congressional ill will toward foreign aid.

Others have suggested that foreign aid's troubles on Capitol Hill can be explained by a "lack of understanding." What is needed, they say, is "education" of Congress regarding the nature and purposes of the aid program. After twenty years of being "educated," however, the average legislator does not seem to be much better disposed toward foreign aid. Otto Passman probably knows more about the aid program than most legislators; yet he opposes it. To know aid is not necessarily to like it.

When the gigantic defense-appropriation bill comes before Congress, it receives relatively superficial criticism compared with that given to the foreign-aid bill. In fact, the White House sometimes has to fend off Legislative attempts to appropriate more money than has been recommended. Why does a bill involving 10 per cent of the GNP encounter less opposition than one dealing with 1 per cent of GNP? Is it because Congress "understands" defense strategy better than foreign aid? Is it because the Defense Department is so efficiently managed? What about the fact that defense industries account for at least 10 per cent of the manufacturing employment in fifteen states? Does a Congressman from Oklahoma vote in favor of oil depletion allowances because of his superior "knowledge" of the oil industry? Attempts to explain legislative behavior purely in terms of the legislator's understanding of the problem can be highly misleading.

What, then, accounts for the Legislative antipathy toward foreign aid? Since re-election is the principal concern of most Congressmen, the opposition to foreign aid can be largely explained by its lack of a domestic "constituency." To put it bluntly, those who benefit most directly from foreign aid do not vote for Congressmen.

This absence of a domestic constituency gives Congress a strong bargaining position vis-à-vis the White House on foreign-aid questions. While on other bills, a strong President can bring pressure on a Congressman through his constituents; there is very little he can do in this regard when it comes to the foreign-aid bill. In such a situation, the White House has had to devise many strategies to push through the annual foreign-aid appropriations. The following are but some of the stratagems devised by four Presidents—Truman, Eisenhower, Kennedy, and Johnson—to push the perennial foreign-aid bill through a reluctant Congress.

Something for the voters.—The easiest way to get Congress to agree to a proposal is to suggest something which Congress likes. And Congressmen like things that make their constituents happy. The problem, then, is to find forms of aid that will benefit domestic groups in rather obvious ways. P.L. 480 is a good example. The desire of farmers and Congressmen to get rid of embarrassing agricultural surpluses coincides with the desire of the Executive Branch to transfer resources to less-developed countries. The White House has no trouble in securing renewal of P.L. 480 legislation. The Export-Import Bank also has a domestic clientele. The National Foreign Trade Convention regularly endorses its activities. Other ways to strengthen the domestic support for aid include tying aid to American exports, and requiring that goods, financed by aid, be shipped in American bottoms.

Minimum-requirements gambit.—This year's aid request was described by President Johnson as a "minimum request" which "reflects a determination to present to Congress the lowest aid budget consistent with the national interest." Similar statements have accompanied each foreign-aid request since 1945. The argument is always the same: perhaps there has been some fat in the past, but that has all been eliminated now. Representative Otto Passman can be relied upon to point out that he has heard that before. The minimum-requirements gambit is actually a common strategy in the politics of federal budgeting. It is considered wiser to ask for "what will go" rather than for what one really wants. The Johnson Administration's request, the lowest in fifteen years, must be understood in this light.

Study the problem.—The foreign-aid program has been studied numerous times. Witness the Gray Report (1950), Rockefeller Report (1951), Randall Commission Report (1954), Fairless Committee Report (1957), Johnston Report (1957), Draper Report (1959), and Clay Report (1963)—not to mention several studies initiated by Congress and by private groups. Although the alleged purpose of such studies is to advise the President, the real purpose is to help legitimize foreign aid in the eyes of Congress and the public. After each study, the Executive can go to Congress and say that on the basis of the report it is asking for X dollars. Since Congress usually suspects that such commissions have been packed in favor of aid, the trick is to appoint people who would not usually be friends of aid, but who can be won over. Thus a great many businessmen are selected for such positions. Everything goes well as long as the businessmen can be persuaded to endorse proposals favored by the White House. The danger is that these commissions sometimes actually try to advise the President. When that happens, as it did with the Clay Committee in 1963, chaos results.

"Militarize it."—One of the quickest ways to stifle opposition to a program is to describe it as "essential to national defense." The questions of "What sort of defense?" "Against what?" and "When?" are best left unasked. The labels attached to the programs of AID and its predecessors illustrate the executive's desire to emphasize the close ties between aid and national security—mutual security, international development and security, and mutual defense and development. By combining military and economic assistance in a single bill, the executive hopes to secure kinder treatment from Congress. It is an executive version of a "legislative rider."

Recently, however, the wisdom of this strategy has been called into question by the Chairman of the Senate Foreign Relations Committee. Senator J. W. Fulbright would like to see military aid inserted in the defense budget, and economic aid channeled increasingly through international organizations. Now Fulbright is neither a foe of aid nor politically naive. Why would he propose such a change? First, he is a foe of *military* aid, and would probably like to attack it more vigorously. For the same reason that police hesitate to shoot at a criminal clinging to a hostage, Fulbright has been frustrated in his desire to attack military aid. Second, he may really believe that economic aid will not suffer as much as others claim—and he may be right. The public image of the magnitude of foreign aid is based on the annual foreign-assistance bill. Without the military component, the Executive would be proposing a smaller foreign-aid program in the eyes of the public.

Representative Thomas Morgan (D., Pennsylvania), Chairman of the House Foreign Affairs Committee, is "violently opposed" to separation of military and economic aid. "As long as we have military assistance," he argues, "we should wrap it in the AID package. It has a strong influence in helping put the program through the House." Although Morgan is a friend of aid, he is hardly a disinterested one. His attitude toward the Fulbright proposal must be understood in terms of the potential effects on the prestige of his committee. The foreign-aid bill is about the only piece of important legislation that goes through the Foreign Affairs Committee. If military aid were to be transferred to the Armed Services Committee, Morgan's committee would have less to discuss. Fulbright's advocacy of more multilateral economic aid also threatens the power of the House Foreign Affairs Committee, since legislation pertaining to such aid is often given to the House Committee on Banking and Currency. It may well be that Morgan is right in saying that economic aid would suffer from separation, but his arguments are not those of an impartial observer.

"*What aid program?*"—A basic rule of military tactics is to keep the troops spread out when they are resting so that they will be less vulnerable to artillery fire. This applies to aid also. By disbursing aid through many channels, the Executive makes it harder for the Legislative foes of aid to get it in their sights. One day, they defend P.L. 480 before an agricultural committee; the next day, they defend a contribution to the IDA before a banking and currency committee; and the next, they defend "foreign assistance" before a committee on foreign affairs. The term "foreign assistance," as used by the Executive, excludes programs of the Export-Import Bank, the Peace Corps, P.L. 480, the IDB, and the International Bank and its affiliates. When Otto Passman and other "unfriendlies" try to discuss these activities, the Executive is quick to observe that "normally these are not considered as 'foreign aid.'" The vigor of Passman's objections to the multiplication of aid agencies is a good gauge of the effectiveness of this strategy. When the IDA expansion was being debated in 1964, he grumbled: "There are sixteen spigots by which these countries can, and do, draw off our resources, our wealth through foreign aid. . . . This is a way for the spenders to do some of the things that the Congress said last year would no longer be permitted through our foreign aid program."

Camouflage.—Euphemisms always abound in public debate of foreign aid. Two of the most useful from the viewpoint of the Executive have been "defense support" and "soft loan." Defense support was invented in the 1950's as a means of disguising economic aid in order to make it more palatable to Congress. Soft loan also came into its own around the same time. This term has been applied to dollar loans repayable in inconvertible currency and to loans carrying especially low interest rates or long repayment periods. By emphasizing the "loan" aspects of such transactions, the White House could pass them off as "sound" and "business-like"—not at all like giving money away. The Administration often refers to loans repayable in local or foreign currency, but it rarely uses the term "inconvertible currency" since this would call attention to the limited usefulness of such currency.

The obligation device.—Much of the money appropriated for foreign assistance each year reverts to the Federal Treasury if it is not obligated during the fiscal year for which it is earmarked. There is a device, however, which permits the Executive to carry over funds from one fiscal year to the next. Suppose that it is May and you are an aid official. The country of Ruritania submits a project proposal which is not well planned but which has possibilities. If there were no time limit on the use of your funds, you would probably delay a decision until Ruritania revised its proposal. Knowing, however, that time is running out, and knowing that you can always deobligate and reobligate if the project does not pan out, you may well go ahead and obligate the funds. David Bell, Director of AID, vehemently denies that funds are ever obligated just to carry them over. He is probably right in a sense because the desire to carry over is usually only one factor in deciding whether to obligate funds for a given project. Once again, we can measure the effectiveness of the obligation strategy by the vigor of Passman's denunciations of it.

"This too shall pass."—The reluctance of Congress to commit itself to a long-range (fifty-year) program of foreign aid tempts the Administration to emphasize the temporary aspects of aid. The

many occasions on which various Presidents yielded to this temptation in the past make it more difficult to deal with Congress today. Having been told that the end was in sight, many legislators feel betrayed. It would be bad manners to say to Congress: "Look, money has become a vital instrument of statecraft; and we want you to keep appropriating $3 billion or $4 billion for that purpose every year from now on." Instead, the Executive still holds out the hope of ending aid. The publicity given to the recent termination of aid to Taiwan was aimed at reassuring Congress on this point.

Solemn international obligation.—Although Congressional obstacles to passage of foreign aid are many, the most formidable is the House Appropriations Committee. Strategies which circumvent this committee are especially useful to the Executive. The "solemn international obligation" strategy is designed to take advantage of the two-step authorization-appropriation process through which aid bills must pass. It works like this: legislation authorizing contributions to international aid-giving organizations is submitted to relatively friendly Legislative committees. After securing authorization, the Executive then commits the United States to give X dollars to the organization. By the time the appropriations committees get into the act, the Executive Branch can bolster its case by frequent references to the "grave repercussions" of failure to "fulfill an international commitment." After all, we wouldn't want Uncle Sam to be known as an international deadbeat.

A good example of this strategy occurred in January, 1964. On January 22, 1964 a bill was passed which authorized the U.S. Governor of the IDB to vote for an increase in Bank resources and to "agree on behalf of the United States" to subscribe its share. On January 28, the U.S. Governor cast his vote. By the time the Passman subcommittee on appropriations opened hearings on March 17, the United States had a "solemn international obligation." Passman's complaint: "When the Congress authorizes that kind of program and makes the commitment, does this committee have any alternative other than to appropriate the money? What is the use to lock the door after the mule is out?". . .

Multiyear appropriations.—One way of bypassing Passman is to secure appropriations for several years at a time. Eisenhower and Kennedy both tried this strategy, but both suffered resounding defeats. The Export-Import Bank is probably the best example of successful use of the "back-door financing" strategy. It is authorized to borrow directly from the Treasury, and it can relend funds

which it receives in repayment. Other strategies for getting aid
through Congress may come and go, but the prospect of circum-
venting the annual authorization-appropriation process completely
will continue to fascinate Executive Branch officials as long as
there is an aid program and a Congress.

Share the burden.—If there is one proposal that is sure to catch
a legislator's attention, it is one to "share" the foreign-aid burden
with other nations. This argument has often been used to secure
Congressional support for contributions to multilateral-aid agencies. The IDA was originally presented to Congress as a means of
inducing Europe and Japan to enlarge their aid programs. In 1964,
when it was time to replenish the resources of IDA, the same argument was used. Passman complained: "These people espousing the
cause of IDA said, and I paraphrase, 'Look, we have talked these
people into putting up this much money and if we do not put up
this 41.6 per cent, or whatever the portion is, we will lose it. If we
don't put up ours, they won't give anything.'" When the next international aid agency is set up it is safe to predict that the "share
the burden" argument will again be heard.

New improved model.—Selling foreign aid to Congress is a little
like selling soap. Each year the product is about the same, but the
seller feels compelled to claim vast improvements. Although new
programs are usually harder to get through Congress than old ones,
this is not true of foreign aid. In 1960, the IDA was new and encountered relatively little opposition, but in 1964, it was a different story. Foreign aid yields few spectacular results which can be
cited in support of established ways of doing things. Congress
views the terms "waste" and "aid" as synonymous. It is easier to
fit the program to Congressional opinion than to change the opinion itself. Thus, instead of trying to convince Congress that aid is
really a success, the Executive often admits past failures and re-
vamps the program. The man in charge is fired—there have been
about a dozen aid directors—or the name of the agency is changed
—ECA, MSA, ICA, AID—or some other tinkering occurs. From
1947 to 1957, the Executive tended to favor grants as opposed to
loans, but Congress disagreed. Since 1957, the Executive has vigorously denounced grants and advocated loans. It would not have
been cricket [politic] to go to Congress in 1957 and say: "Look, we
would prefer grants, but since you won't give them to us, we will
take our second choice, which is loans." Instead, the Executive
must present each year's program as a new and improved model,
free from predecessors' defects.

Not all of the strategies discussed above are used every year; but all have been used and it is a safe guess that they will be again. Some readers may feel that the strategies are Machiavellian; they probably sympathize with Passman's lamentation that "the international giveaway artists seem to be winning the fight to hide the amount of money requested for foreign aid from the people and, yes, from the Congress." Others will feel that Passman has given the Executive Branch little choice.

In the final analysis, it is difficult to carp about the kind of political stratagems described above, for no matter how one feels about the particular issue of foreign aid, there is little doubt that such tactics are part of the warp and woof of the democratic process.

19. *Development Loan Fund*[2]

[EDITOR'S NOTE: *The Executive Branch has periodically sought to free itself from the requirement for annual authorizations and appropriations for foreign aid. The excerpt from the following memorandum sets forth the arguments used by the Executive Branch in 1957 in justifying a proposal for a development loan fund based on multiyear appropriations. Although Congress accepted the idea of the Development Loan Fund, it rejected the Executive's concept of long-term financing.*]

1. *The executive branch proposes that the development loan fund should be established as a new and more effective instrument of United States national policy.*

Our purpose is that it should provide financing in ways which will be effective—as the present development program cannot be— in two very important respects: (*a*) in encouraging the receiving countries to greater self-help; (*b*) in bringing about increased activity on the part of other financing sources—private investors, the World Bank, and the Export-Import Bank.

Only if it achieves these purposes will our development financing have the intended impact on prospects for economic growth of the less developed nations. The sums which the United States can put into this effort are necessarily too limited to be decisive when taken alone. To achieve our purpose, they must be used in

[2] SOURCE: *Mutual Security Act of 1957*, Hearings before the Senate Committee on Foreign Relations, 85th Cong., 1st sess. (Washington, D.C.: Government Printing Office, 1957), pp. 613–14.

such a way that they will have a maximum catalytic effect in bringing the resources both of the countries themselves and of other financing sources to bear more effectively on the development of the borrowing countries.

2. *To achieve this purpose the fund must operate through procedures altogether different from those under which development assistance is now provided.*

We must shift from the present practice of planned country programs, financed through year-to-year appropriations, to the more businesslike practices of the World Bank and Export-Import Bank. To this end, we believe that the fund should be able to: (*a*) place primary responsibility for the planning of development projects and proposals on the receiving country; (*b*) offer that country a convincing incentive to discharge this responsibility effectively, by creating the prospect that if—but only if—it comes forward with sound projects it can reasonably expect to quality [qualify?] for continuing U.S. financing; (*c*) work closely with other financing sources in joint or related activities, and to encourage them to undertake financing activities that would not be feasible in the absence of our own.

3. *In order for the fund to operate in this way it must have certain characteristics inherent in a financing institution: It must have the same assurance of continuing resources that any bank—public or private—needs in order to operate effectively.*

Only with this assurance will the receiving countries be moved: (*a*) to plan for the most effective long-term uses of our and their resources, e.g., by preparing needed long-term projects and programs, whose completion would require our continuing assistance; (*b*) to undertake complex negotiations concerning these projects with the fund, in order to insure that they meet—or can be altered to meet—the fund's criteria; (*c*) to embark on these long-term projects and programs with full vigor and confidence.

And only with this assurance will private investors, the World Bank, and the Export-Import Bank have sufficient confidence in the future scale of the fund's activity to feel safe in relating their plans to that activity. . . .

Without this assurance of continuity the fund could not achieve the purposes set forth . . . above.

Unless other countries, private investors, and public institutions can be offered convincing assurances of the availability of continuing financing, they will be as reluctant to work with the fund on a long-term basis as individuals would be to work with a commercial bank if they did not know from one year to another whether it would have adequate resources.

We do not believe that the necessary assurance would be provided by a general declaration in the law or even an authorization to be followed by annual appropriation. It is inherent in the legislative process that there could be no reasonable assurance as a result of either of these procedures that an adequate amount—or indeed any amount at all—would be added to the fund's capital in future years. Thus, for the purpose which the new concept is intended to achieve an appropriation to cover only 1 year's activity would be no better than the present system of annual appropriations. The essence of the assurance which is required to make the fund effective is the knowledge that specific sums will be available in future years; this assurance can only be conveyed by action which specifically sets these amounts aside and which indicates the times at which they are to become available under specified conditions. . . .

20. *Long-Term Financing on the New Frontier*[3]

[EDITOR's NOTE: *After its rebuff in 1957, the Eisenhower Administration was reluctant to continue pushing for multiyear appropriations. The Kennedy Administration, however, decided to renew the request to Congress for authority to borrow aid money from the Treasury. The newly installed President suffered his most resounding political defeat on this issue. He learned, as had the preceding administration, that the right to appropriate money is one of the Legislature's most jealously guarded prerogatives. The President's request was delivered to the Senate Foreign Relations Committee by Frank M. Coffin, Managing Director of the Development Loan Fund and Chairman of the Group on Program Presentation of the President's Task Force on Economic Assistance.*]

MR. COFFIN: The key log in the whole development lending structure is our request for permission to borrow from the Treasury and to use loan repayments in the total amount of $8.8 billion over the next half decade.

[3] SOURCE: *International Development and Security*, Hearings before the Senate Committee on Foreign Relations, 87th Cong., 1st sess. (Washington, D.C.: Government Printing Office, 1961), pp. 200–202.

Let me state with some precision what it is we are asking and why. We are asking for a presumptive or prima facie authority, not an absolute authority, because this authority is subject to revocation or modification. It will be a shifting of the burden of proof from the yearly proving of needs, which can never be precisely identified, to putting up to those who would limit or cancel access to our funds, the burden of proving that the funds are being badly used or not wisely used.

This has been called many times back-door financing. To me the back-door analogy connotes somebody unlawfully on the premises who should be ejected at the earliest possible opportunity.

I rather think the analogy is more appropriate of somebody on the premises with permission, a licensee, whose license is always subject to revocation for good and sufficient reason.

The Congress will have two kinds of control. They will have, first of all, control of knowledge, of assurance that their license is not being abused; and, secondly, they will have a control in the nature of several kinds of actions that can be taken.

In terms of the assurance that the license will not be abused, we have written into the law some of the criteria which have been in before, and have added some new emphasis, criteria which will govern lending.

There will be this interagency loan committee which will determine loan policies, and on some major or unprecedented loans will actually look into the proposal to be acted upon by the aid administrator.

Congress will have quarterly reports from the aid agency. The aid agency will have to operate within the annual availabilities, even though they do get borrowing authority and, of course, you have the investigative and hearing process available at any time.

In terms of action which Congress can take, the first kind of action is that by the authorizing committees in changing the basic legislation itself.

The Appropriations Committees will have the opportunity, if they wish, to limit even operating expenses—not just administrative expenses but even operating expenses—under the Government Corporations Control Act.

I would point out that the action that Congress would take or the Appropriations Committees, backed up by both Houses, in taking advantage of the opportunities under the Government Corporations Control Act, would not be subject to Presidential veto since we do not have item veto.

Finally, there is the very considerable power which Congress has to limit or qualify or modify its annual appropriation for administrative expenses.

Why is the shifting of this burden of proof important? Why, the question can fairly be asked, do we ask for this when our system of annual appropriations works so well when the Federal Government of the United States deals with State governments?

My answer to that is that annual appropriations in the foreign aid program would be satisfactory if all that we expected of our aid program was to put in money each year in certain countries for budgetary support, if all that we expected of our aid program was to fund programs of technical cooperation so far as funds were available on more or less an annual aid level basis; or if in the lending field our objective was simply to fund as many projects as we had funds available to do so with.

But we are not dealing with State governments which have smoothly functioning administrative mechanisms which are used to dealing with the Federal Government, used to the uncertainties of the annual appropriation system. We cannot, when we deal with State governments, exert any great leverage to bring about reform within State governments or structural change, and we certainly cannot, sitting here in Washington, gear our Federal-State grant system to the development efforts which States are willing to make.

But this is precisely what we propose to do in the field of development lending overseas with foreign governments.

If we talk to a foreign government and have any serious intention of obtaining a serious reaction by that government to overhauling its tax system or its administrative structure or its budgeting process or its rate structure or its fiscal policies or its foreign exchange rate policies, we have to do more than deal with that government on a project-by-project basis.

For example, if we were to say to Country X, "We will make available to you $10 million for the rehabilitation of some of your railway equipment," and then if we were to follow that up by saying, "We will do this if you revise your outmoded rate structure," that foreign government would be within bounds if it were to say to us, "Well, you loan on a project-by-project basis. So long as our project meets your criteria, and unless you discriminate against us, we shall expect to receive fair treatment just as you would give it to any other country which has submitted documented proof that its project will contribute to the economy of the country."

On the other hand, if we were to say to Country X, "We will give you $30 million on a long-term loan basis over a period of 3, 4, or 5 years, if you will undertake certain measures to improve the administrative functioning of your country," then we can annex that "if," that proviso, because we are giving something over a period of years which will constitute a base for that country's planning. That makes all the difference in the world.

It has been argued that the borrowing authority for development lending is to be financially irresponsible and I submit, Mr. Chairman, that the test of financial responsibility lies in our total approach to our own Government. We want to know what we are trying to accomplish with our funds. The test of responsibility is to make sure that these funds are likely to be used in the best possible, most fruitful way.

If we pass that test, then the other test of responsibility is whether our own house is in order, and whether we are raising the funds to meet all the needs of our Government in the best and most sound fiscal and economic way.

So the real question is what kind of an aid program do the American people feel it is in their interest to have, and we, who are speaking for this program, and I am sure I have no need to say this to you who have long proposed this kind of approach, we feel strongly that this kind of program that we have described is the only kind that has a substantial chance of success in the world in which we live.

21. *Attempts of Congress to Administer the Program*[4]

[EDITOR'S NOTE: *During the 1965 hearings on foreign aid, Senator J. W. Fulbright, Chairman of the Senate Foreign Relations Committee and a friend of foreign aid, attempted to anticipate some of the criticisms of the program by his fellow Congressmen through friendly questioning of Secretary of State Dean Rusk.*]

THE CHAIRMAN: This other question perhaps you shouldn't commit yourself on, but I want to raise it. The Congress attempting to move into the area of precise terms of administration causes great difficulty for the administration. It is perfectly obvious, of course, and natural, that the Congress has the complete power to have a program at all.

[4] SOURCE: *Foreign Assistance, 1965*, Hearings before the Senate Committee on Foreign Relations, 89th Cong., 1st sess. (Washington, D.C.: Government Printing Office, 1965), pp. 67–68.

It can stop the power this year if it wants to, but as long as it agrees to have an AID program, then it moves into the administration of it, by setting down precise requirements for loans and even going to the extent of forbidding you to negotiate or to have relations with specific countries. It seems to me you create an intolerable administrative problem for any program of this kind. Do you wish to comment?

SECRETARY RUSK: Yes, Senator, I would like to comment on that, because we have had a number of occasions to get into this issue in the course of the consideration of aid by the Congress. We do believe that the law can properly establish policy and criteria.

THE CHAIRMAN: Broad guidelines.

SECRETARY RUSK: Broad guidance, but we do feel that it puts manacles on us if administrative details are spelled out in the law, or if specific policy with respect to specific countries is made a matter of law.

The world situation moves far faster than the annual legislative cycle of the Congress, and we feel that there ought to be flexibility to deal with these matters as the interest of the United States require, on a week-by-week or month-to-month basis.

I know there are certain cases, and we have gone into this in executive session, where the general feeling of the Congress with respect to a particular country turns out to be the view of the administration, and is the way in which relationships are developed. But even there we would not want to see that in legislation because these matters can change. We would like to have the freedom of movement.

THE CHAIRMAN: The object of your program is to change them in many cases, isn't it?

SECRETARY RUSK: That is correct, sir.

THE CHAIRMAN: And you can't change them if this is put into the law.

SECRETARY RUSK: That is correct, sir.

THE CHAIRMAN: The Senator from Oregon[5] has gone, but anyway this is no secret—one of the main differences between us and one of the principal reasons why I feel the movement toward multilateralization of the program is so important, is the very fact that he and certain others, who share his view, are attempting more and more to restrict the administration.

[5] Wayne Morse.—ED.

To be perfectly frank, one of the main reasons why I think it is good and proper to move in this direction is to avoid further and further restriction upon your Administration. We have had several examples. One was the interest rate controversy.

There were certain people who wished to make very high interest rates on a program that the main excuse for it is its soft loans. When you approximate it, if you ran the AID program on the same basis as the International Bank, there would be no need to have the AID program, would there?

SECRETARY RUSK: Basically that is right as regards interest rates, sir.

THE CHAIRMAN: The same way with this Inter-American Bank. If you put requirements that it all must be paid back in dollars under certain conditions, then there is no need in having it. So if the Congress makes the decision to have a program—and with very broad guidelines—it seems to me it is an impossible situation to expect you to achieve anything.

Last year we had a controversy about whether or not you would be allowed to upgrade the quality of your personnel. This Committee and the Senate agreed to allow Mr. Bell certain limited selections, but in the process of the congressional control it was denied. Now this seems to me absolutely intolerable, if we are going to have a good administration.

SECRETARY RUSK: Well, we wanted the same privilege we had for the foreign service.

THE CHAIRMAN: I thought it was very reasonable. We had over 80 amendments to this bill offered last year. They were not all, fortunately, voted on, but a great many were. A few of them were relevant to the foreign aid program. Most of them were not.

But in any case, if we are going to have a program, it seems to me, and if it is going to make any sense in the future, it has to move more in the fashion of the OEEC, the Marshall Plan, the CIAP, and in other cases where appropriate you follow the same pattern.

It is in a sense distasteful to Members of Congress since we all have applicants in our own districts for a similar kind of aid. You understand that, I am sure.

SECRETARY RUSK: Yes, I do, Senator.

THE CHAIRMAN: If you are going to have a program, it seems to me it should be disassociated insofar as it can be from specific restrictions in the administration.

SECRETARY RUSK: We fully agree, sir.

22. *Congressional Control: 1965*[6]

[EDITOR'S NOTE: *In the course of the 1965 hearings on foreign aid, Senator Wayne Morse emerged as the leading exponent of greater Legislative control over the aid program. The following dialogue brings out the connection between the Executive-Legislative struggle for control of aid and the issue of multilateral vs. bilateral aid channels.*]

SENATOR MORSE: I think you should understand in this debate that many of us feel that you are developing a foreign aid program in which the legislative representatives, in fact and in effect, have less and less control of American taxpayers' money that is being spent in the foreign assistance program. That is what I think the public is eventually going to resent. When we are fighting to preserve these checks, we are really on the side of foreign aid, although we are labeled as a "neo-isolationist" and "anti-foreign-aiders," and so on, by writers who devote most of their time to reading their own writings.

But I want you to know that I am concerned about the comments in your statement this morning which seem to indicate that it is the plan of the Department to make greater and greater use of these multilateral agencies. There is not a whisper from you in your statement as to the imposition of any American checks in respect to the use to which a foreign body or organization can put American taxpayers' money.

I think we have to be reasonable about it, but I certainly think that it is reasonable to say that American money that goes into the International Monetary Fund or the World Bank, or any one of these so-called international multilateral organizations, should be subject to certain limitations imposed by the Congress. If they don't want to accept those limitations, just don't give them the money.

There is a great void of difference, I think, that exists between some on this Committee and the Department, if I read your testimony this morning right. Those of us who are concerned about a tendency in this country for the executive branch of Government to take over more and more basic legislative functions.

[6] SOURCE: *Foreign Assistance, 1965*, Hearings before the Senate Committee on Foreign Relations, 89th Cong., 1st. sess. (Washington, D.C.: Government Printing Office, 1965), pp. 40–41.

I am, as you know, greatly disturbed about it, and I think we have an example in these multilateral international agencies. We have an example of what I consider to be a most dangerous trend in this Republic: of the Congress delegating more and more authority and power and decision to you gentlemen, estimable as you are, in the executive branch of the Government. I think that breaks down our system of checks and balances.

I don't propose to give you a lecture here this morning, but, as counsel for the opposition, to tell you at least what some of our fears are, and why we are opposed to your program as you have presented it this morning.

SECRETARY RUSK: Senator, may I comment very briefly?

SENATOR MORSE: Oh, I would be delighted.

SECRETARY RUSK: I talked this morning about a balanced program: strong support for those international agencies that appear to be able to do an effective job, plus a strong and vigorous bilateral aid program.

In referring to the taxpayers, there is the possibility in many of these international agencies to multiply the dollars one and a half times straightaway through the matching, or more than matching from others, 40 percent as against 60 percent in the U.N. Special Fund, and 42 percent against 58 percent in IDA.

We participate in the management of those operations, and I think that we have felt that under men like Mr. Eugene Black, Mr. George Woods,[7] and others, that they have achieved a very high standard of managerial skill. It is a balanced program that we are talking about, where it can be effective through international bodies where we can mobilize additional funds, fine; where we need to do it on a bilateral basis, yes.

But I think I would have to say that when we elect to use an international body, there are some things which are not appropriate to the international rule. For example, we can't turn to an international body and tailor it exactly as the Congress might wish to tailor our own bilateral programs with respect to particular and special countries or highly sensitive situations.

That is one of the reasons for having a bilateral program as well as an international program. Congress would have to make its own judgment as to how best and in what combination to support both the multilateral as well as the bilateral program.

SENATOR MORSE: It is going to make its own judgments and lay

[7] George Woods is president of the IBRD; Eugene Black was his immediate predecessor.—ED.

down its own criteria as to the terms and conditions on which we will participate in such a body. If they don't want us to participate with those congressional checks retained, why then we just can't participate.

Let me very quickly say that is what bothers me so much about the soft currency funds. Those are American dollars that go into them. My feeling is that you will get much more careful administration given to your hard loan funds than to your soft loan funds, that you have to always be on guard about that.

You made an observation about the people that are involved representing our country on these international bodies. You see, I will never talk in terms of individuals. Let me be completely impersonal about it. I am going to talk about the fact that whoever the individual is, he is a human being. We have learned under our system of government, that you have to write in the procedures that protect the people from the administration by human beings to retain a government by law.

We talk about a government by law, but it is administered by human beings. You protect that government by law by getting the kind of restrictions and checks imposed upon your national policy that isn't going to permit any person, I care not how noted his name, from substituting himself and his judgment for what might be a better national policy.

And so we are in a field, as you can see, of abstract principles of representative government. I happen to feel that our foreign aid program more and more is breaking down those principles. That is why you are going to find me urging to tighten the congressional checks.

23. *Musical Chairs in the Foreign-Assistance Program*[8]

[EDITOR'S NOTE: *The constant Legislative dissatisfaction with the aid program tempts the Executive to revamp it often in order to show Congress that the alleged "mistakes" of the past are unlikely to recur. This frequent reorganization is a source of continual frustration for aid administrators. In November, 1962, D. A. Fitz-Gerald, who had been a senior aid administrator for many years, was about to retire from Federal service. He could thus speak both authoritatively and frankly of the effects of frequent tinkering with*

[8] SOURCE: D. A. FitzGerald, "Musical Chairs in the Foreign-Assistance Program" (press release; November 16, 1962). Reprinted with permission.

the program. This statement, released to the press on November 16, 1962, is that of an experienced aid official "getting it off his chest."]

It's time to stop this farcical game of musical chairs with the administration of the foreign-assistance program. Fowler Hamilton now has had his chair pulled out from under him. Even if he were not ideally suited for the job—few people are—after a year of painful experience, it is clear that he would do better than any new recruit who can be found.

Mr. Hamilton of course is not the first to be unchaired. Indeed one might say that he has a long line of "illustrious" predecessors. Since Paul Hoffman was appointed as the first Administrator of the Economic Cooperation Administration (Marshall Plan) in April, 1948, there have been ten administrators of U.S. foreign economic assistance programs, often with a several months' interregnum between the departure of one administrator and the accession of his successor. In addition, during this same period, the Point Four program had two administrators during the four years of its independent existence, and the Development Loan Fund had three managing directors during its four years of independent life. All told, this works out to one new administrator about every eighteen months. Here is a program, which for size, complexity, and difficulty of administration, is clearly in a class by itself. It dwarfs even the biggest businesses in the United States. Where would General Motors, or AT&T, or Standard of New Jersey be if these companies changed their chief executive officer once every year and a half and usually selected someone whose experience had been in an entirely different field. A university professor—for example.

Nor is this ridiculous game of musical chairs a monopoly of either the Democrats or the Republicans. Both of them have been equally adept—or should one say equally inadept. President Truman, from April, 1948, to 1952, had four directors: Paul Hoffman, William Foster, Richard Bissell, and Averell Harriman (though it can be said for this succession of appointees that they were experienced in the business) plus two more directors for the Point Four program. William Foster had been Deputy Special Representative in Europe and Deputy Administrator before he took over as Paul Hoffman's successor. Richard Bissell had been deputy to Mr. Foster. Mr. Averell Harriman was the first special representative in Europe until appointed director of the Mutual Security Program in 1952.

President Eisenhower did a little better but only as to length of service. In eight years, the aid program was headed successively by Harold E. Stassen, James Smith, John Hollister, and James Riddleberger, all of whom initially had to learn the business pretty much from scratch. Development Loan Fund, which came into being in 1958, was managed first by Dempster McIntosh who was succeeded by Vance Brand.

So far, President Kennedy has been most "successful" in this game of musical chairs—two directors, Henry Labouisse and Fowler Hamilton in less than two years plus Frank Coffin as Managing Director of the Development Loan Fund for about eight months until it and ICA were merged into AID! This is one instance in which the New Frontier has lived up to its promise to get moving!

A change in the senior officer and even in his immediate subordinates may be warranted when a new Administration ascends to power as the Eisenhower Administration in 1953 and the Kennedy Administration in 1961, even though both Republicans and Democrats have proclaimed that foreign assistance is a bipartisan or perhaps more correctly nonpartisan program. Some changes in direction and emphasis at these times are to be expected, though even these changes are not without some offsetting disadvantages in terms of lost motion and inefficiency.

Every new administrator, since he is a human being, has his own peculiarities and preferences. He has his own notions—some good, some bad, some preconceived—of the changes that should be made in foreign-aid policies, programming, and administration. Any program of the size of the foreign-aid program has what the physicist would call "momentary inertia." Substantial momentum is lost in the zigs and zags inevitably associated with each new administrator, particularly if he has no prior experience in this complicated business.

There used to be a rough rule of thumb in the International Cooperation Administration that it took a new country aid director at least three months to become even reasonably familiar with the foreign-aid program in the country to which he was assigned if he was transferred or promoted from within, and at least six months if he was recruited from the outside. The latter, no matter how competent, would become reasonably effective only after a year on the job training and would not reach the peak of his usefulness until after a lapse of two or three years. What is true of country mission directors is even more true of the aid administrator and his senior officers in Washington.

Successive administrations, both Republican and Democrat, not only have played a game of musical chairs with the administrators of the foreign-aid program but periodically have wrung in a new set of chairs, rearranged the music, and reorganized the game. The original Economic Cooperation Administration was followed by the Mutual Security Administration and a parallel Technical Cooperation Administration to manage the Point Four program. These in turn were merged into a Foreign Operations Administration. FOA was in turn reincarnated as the International Cooperation Administration and a year or two later by a companion Development Loan Fund. Now the Agency for International Development has replaced both ICA and DLF. Each reorganization has been accompanied by more or less serious delays in both programming and implementation, a lowering of employee morale, and a loss of confidence in the public eye.

The last of these reorganizations has been the most far-reaching, as it was accompanied by drastic internal changes which were dictated, not by any fundamental weaknesses in the existing organization, but by a mistaken belief that persistent and intractible problems of substance could be resolved by a radical change in the form of the organization. Employee morale has been at an all-time low for months and was undoubtedly dealt a further blow by the action of the Second Session of the Eighty-seventh Congress in sharply curtailing funds for the Agency's administrative expenses. Along with a serious loss of efficiency, the program has suffered from the inevitable delays that accompany a drastic reorganization and the lack of experience and savvy on the part of new top leadership.

In the last six or eight years, the program has suffered seriously from another practice indulged in by both Republicans and Democrats. This practice is to disparage programs and performances of the past and to advance a new set of titles and phrases which is supposed to reflect new concepts and vastly improve administrative efficiency. In 1961, the key word was "turnaround." Nothing, well almost nothing, that had been done in the past, or was then being done, was any good. Even titles were suspect. "Defense support" was wholly bad so it was retitled "supporting assistance" and described as a necessary evil if not quite "good." Technical assistance—Point Four—for which there is an enormous reservoir of good will and support in the country went down the drain—almost the baby as well as the bath water—to reappear as "development grants." The old program and its administration, it was alleged, was "soft," the new would be "hard."

Of course, there have been many soundly conceived changes in emphasis, in composition, and in geographical incidence. The Marshall Plan was obviously concentrated in Europe and on rehabilitation of physical resources. After the outbreak of the Korean War in 1950, emphasis shifted to military security, and geographically, to Asia. The FOA consolidated overseas economic and technical programs in one agency. During the existence of the International Cooperation Administration, many African problems came to the fore, and with the advent of AID, the headlines shifted to Latin America and the *Allianca para progresso*. But by and large, after the basic changes in response to the Communist aggression as demonstrated by the Korean War, the shifts have been in emphasis. No brand new principles have been discovered and put into effect. The importance of soundly conceived country programs, of priorities, of self-help, trained human resources, of contributions from other free world countries were clearly recognized and encouraged prior to the submission by the Kennedy Administration in 1961, of its "Program for the Decade of Development."

These periodic attempts to shuck off the old and don the new, can in the long-run, have only adverse consequences. First of all, it breeds a lack of confidence in the integrity of the program. The bold, new look in foreign aid, Republican- or Democrat-sponsored, is quickly revealed at least to the sophisticated as no more than a new model of the same old machine without the dents the old one had acquired, with a new color scheme and perhaps a dual carburetor system. It runs a little better, but not nearly as well as its sponsors have assured the public and the Congress that it would, and frequently develops unexpected "bugs" as a new and untested model often does. The Congress and the public become increasingly critical of the alleged inefficiency and ineffectiveness of the aid organization, an almost inevitable result since the new program was almost invariably . . . grossly "oversold." So then, another camouflage job is undertaken.

The United States foreign-assistance program is a difficult and complex one under the best of circumstances. It has a solid record of performance and its future should not be jeopardized by the fanciful contention that brilliant new policies, bright new administrators, and a brand new organization are going to vastly improve that performance. The policies will not be brilliant and new, but largely reflect a shift in emphasis. The administrator if new may indeed be bright, but lack for at least a year that vital ingredient of experience. The organization may be brand new, but will take a year or more to recover its morale and achieve the same degree of efficiency the old one had. These maneuvers may temporarily impress the uninitiated. They do not fool the experienced. And amongst the most experienced by now are those congressional committees and their staffs who over the years have handled United States foreign-assistance legislation—the Senate Foreign Relations Committee, the House Foreign Affairs Committee, the Subcommittee on Foreign Operations of the Committee on Appropriations, and the Senate Appropriations Committee. They maintain a continuity of membership and staff which the Executive Branch might well emulate. It is simply no contest when the brand new administrator meets up with these old pros—particularly if these old pros happen to be antiprogram! This is not to imply for the moment that the members of these committees are paragons of virtue and wisdom. On more than one occasion, it has been that they have pressed strongly for a bright, new, shiny, but unrealistic foreign-assistance package. When really substantive and constructive changes in the program are proposed, the Executive Branch should, of course, make haste to comply. But otherwise it should stand its ground. So:

1. Let's quit playing musical chairs with the administrator of the foreign-assistance program. Instead, let's find his successor quickly, preferably someone with experience, sign him up for the duration of the current administration at least, and give him the necessary authority, autonomy, and support.

2. Let's quit reorganizing the internal administrative structure for foreign assistance, thus mistaking form for substance and leading others into the same error.

3. Let's quit pretending periodically that we have discovered a brand new context to our foreign-aid program. Instead, let's build on old and proven principles and experience in order to improve future performance.

VIII

Military vs. Economic Aid

Since 1951, the annual foreign-aid bill has contained provisions for both military and economic aid. The latter is administered by the aid agency, and the Defense Department administers the former under the over-all "guidance" of the State Department. The two main issues relating to military and economic aid concern the relative emphasis which should be given to each form of aid and the appropriate strategies for securing Congressional approval of each.[1] Since Legislative-Executive relations were discussed in the preceding chapter, the following documents focus on the question of how much emphasis should be given to each type of aid.

24. *Military Aid to Dictators*[2]

[EDITOR'S NOTE: *One of the perennial problems connected with American military aid is the possibility that aid given to help deter external aggression will be used by a dictatorial regime to suppress legitimate internal dissent. This problem underscores a dilemma inherent in present-day American foreign policy. On the one hand, the United States wants foreign governments to be strong enough to repel invasion and to quell domestic Communist uprisings; on the other, the United States wants to stimulate the development of political systems in which governments rule by consent of the governed, instead of by military force. More than one dictator has used American military aid against domestic non-Communist protest groups. In the following excerpt from the 1962 hearings on foreign assistance, Secretary of Defense Robert S. McNamara defends the military assistance program.*]

SENATOR CARLSON [R., Kansas]: In your statement you refer to President Kennedy's recent Berkeley speeches and you quote him as stating:

[1] On this point, see Document 18, Chapter VII.

[2] SOURCE: *Foreign Assistance Act of 1962*, Hearings before the Senate Committee on Foreign Relations, 87th Cong., 2d sess. (Washington, D.C.: Government Printing Office, 1962), pp. 75–79, 420.

139

Our military policy must assist nations to protect the processes of democratic reform and development against disruption and intervention.

I ask you this question. In view of our military assistance programs to Latin America, how can we justify military assistance to the military dictatorship in Argentina?

SECRETARY MCNAMARA: The military assistance program to the Argentine is limited to training of personnel and is a very small program.

The military assistance programs for Latin America are designed to support internal security and provide a foundation for the economic development and the political developments which are essential to the long-range growth of those nations.

SENATOR CARLSON: By the information given, we hear that it is small, relatively speaking.

However, you are recommending, as I understand, in your program this year $77 million total for Latin America.

SECRETARY MCNAMARA: Seventy-seven million dollars, of which about $20 million is for training and $57 million for light equipment, small arms, transportation, and communications type equipment.

SENATOR CARLSON: The particular breakdown of expenditures I have here shows for Argentina, $3.317 million. I share the views of the President. I do not see how we, as a nation, can justify any program of expenditure that would continue in power military dictatorships. That is the reason it concerns me. I am sure we are going to have some discussions of that before we report, not only your section of this foreign aid bill, but others.

You are justifying it, of course, on the basis of training. Well, you are training them to continue a military dictatorship.

SECRETARY MCNAMARA: I think that the amount of training that we have provided and the military assistance we are planning to provide has little or no relationship to the participation by the military in recent events in Argentina.

I am sure that the action would have been the same whether or not we had provided the amount of training we are discussing.

SENATOR CARLSON: Let us go to Brazil.

There are rather substantial amounts, according to this information I have, that we contribute to Brazil. They have had a change of government, brought about by the military. What is our situation there?

SECRETARY MCNAMARA: Of course, it is not a military government in Brazil. The equipment supplied to Brazil was supplied in accordance with certain past agreements that I think you are familiar with.

There was a special situation there that led to those particular amounts.

SENATOR CARLSON: You state it is not a military government in Brazil. That is true, but was it not the military that changed the Government in Brazil recently?

SECRETARY MCNAMARA: I would think not.

I think you, rather than I, are the expert in this field, but I would say no.

SENATOR CARLSON: Is it not true that in many of the Latin American countries they are either military dictatorships or other dictatorships, and with our military assistance programs, and probably other programs, we maintain the governments in power, whether we agree with them or not.

What is our justification for that?

SECRETARY MCNAMARA: I think that the military organizations in countries passing through the stage of development analogous to that of the Latin American countries will always be one of the major power blocs in the nation. Our military assistance is not contributing to a nondemocratic orientation of that power bloc. Quite the contrary, the experience that we have had indicates that the exposure of the military officers of those nations to our schools acquaints them with democratic philosophies, democratic ways of thinking, which they, in turn, take back to their nations.

Beyond that, our assistance is very directly contributing to the economic growth and development of those nations.

Last Friday, I spent the day in Panama at the headquarters of our Caribbean Command with the Ambassadors and military chiefs of several of our missions in Latin America, discussing the ways in which we can further contribute through the civic action programs to the economic development of those nations.

In one particular instance there is a program being developed that will, for a very small amount of money, make it possible for approximately 10,000 man-years of work to be done on vitally needed roads, water sources, sanitation facilities, school buildings, and other foundations for economic growth and development.

SENATOR CARLSON: Mr. Secretary, with that last statement I agree thoroughly. I think that the military can play, and does play, an important part in not only Latin America, but underdeveloped countries, in sanitation, and roads and highways. I think that is a very fine part of the program.

I am concerned, however, about our nation, through military

assistance and Federal funds, maintaining governments that I do not believe would be classed as democratic or representative of the people. That is one of the concerns that I have.

SECRETARY McNAMARA: Senator Carlson, there will be about 18,000 men from these foreign nations schooled in U.S. military schools during the forthcoming year.

The great bulk of those will be actually in schools located in this country.

The remaining portion will be in attendance at schools operated by representatives of our Government in the foreign nations.

Each of these men will receive an exposure to democracy at work, to the traditions and philosophies of our Government, and I think he will go back to his nation with a far better understanding of democracy and its possible application to this particular nation than he had before he became a student in one of our schools.

In this sense, I think we contribute very directly to the furthering of democratic processes in those nations.

SENATOR CARLSON: With that last statement I am in thorough accord. I think that is a very fine program. I think the more people that have the benefit of our educational programs, as well as have the opportunity to observe the economy of this country and its social structure, the more helpful it will be. . . .

THE CHAIRMAN:[3] Mr. Secretary, before I call on another Senator, I wanted to clarify the exchange in the record with regard to military dictatorships. This is a very troublesome problem. Democracies are having difficulties in many parts of the world, particularly Korea, Pakistan, Sudan, Thailand, Taiwan.

You have different systems that can hardly be compared to ours, as far as representative democracy goes. This involves not just Argentina. You certainly cannot classify Brazil as a military dictatorship, is that right?

SECRETARY McNAMARA: I certainly would not classify Brazil as a military dictatorship.

THE CHAIRMAN: But even if it is not, it differs from our system. This is a troublesome problem, and it is hardly your decision, or responsibility, to judge whether or not you give military aid to one of these governments, is it?

SECRETARY McNAMARA: No.

The act is very clear on that specific point. It is section 622 that makes it quite clear that the military assistance to be provided to a foreign nation must be approved by the Secretary of State.

[3] Senator J. W. Fulbright.—ED.

THE CHAIRMAN: Some countries are having difficulty in making their self-government, or what we call democratic system, operate. Take Burma—this is the second time she has gone back to a military government, and, yet, we do not ostracize her. While we do not have a military program there, we are sympathetic to the country and seek to be of assistance, I think, in some ways, do we not?

SECRETARY McNAMARA: Exactly.

THE CHAIRMAN: We certainly do in Pakistan, although the head of that government, for whom I think we show great respect and interest, is clearly a military man. He stepped into a situation and we all approved of his actions—I mean, generally speaking, did we not?

SECRETARY McNAMARA: Yes.

I think it is quite clear on the record that the military assistance programs have not, in themselves, contributed to nondemocratic actions by the military personnel in the countries receiving those programs.

THE CHAIRMAN: If a country has to abandon its efforts at creating a democracy—we hope temporarily—and, yet, is still independent of foreign domination, we still are justified in trying to assist that country to maintain its independence, are we not?

SECRETARY McNAMARA: We are.

THE CHAIRMAN: That is the policy. We do not say that just because it has a military government we will not assist it. It has not been our policy.

Take Spain. No one has felt for years that that was a representative democracy but we poured millions of dollars, hundreds of millions, into Spain, have we not?

SECRETARY McNAMARA: Yes.

I think the test would be whether the aid itself contributed to counterdemocratic or to nondemocratic actions.

THE CHAIRMAN: And to maintain its independence from domination by the Communists?

SECRETARY McNAMARA: Exactly.

. . . .

SENATOR MORSE: . . . the presentation book uses precisely the same language in defining the primary objective of military assistance in all the Latin American countries:

Maintaining security against the Castro-Communist threat of violence in the cities, guerrilla warfare in rural areas, and the movement of armaments and men clandestinely across land, air, and sea borders for subversive purposes.

Is this really the chief purpose of military aid in every case? (The following information was subsequently furnished.)

Purpose of Military Aid in Latin America

In recognition of the fact that the principal threat faced in Latin America is Communist subversion and indirect attack, the primary emphasis of the military assistance program was changed from hemispheric defense to internal security in fiscal year 1962. The primary emphasis for the military assistance program in fiscal year 1963 continues to follow this concept. It is our firm conviction that the governments of Latin America will contribute most to hemispheric defense and to the security of the United States by maintaining internal security, which also is a basic prerequisite to national freedom and economic and social development.

The danger of internal subversion has not diminished since the need to change the emphasis of our assistance was recognized; rather, it has increased significantly. This threat is not peculiar to one or two or even a few of the Latin American countries. It exists in every country.

Latin American governments have themselves emphasized the need for increasing Latin American military capabilities to deal effectively with Communist subversion and violence. For example, the American governments at the Punta del Este Conference urged all OAS [Organization of American States] members, in Resolution 2, "to strengthen their capacity to counteract threats or acts of aggression, subversion, or other dangers to peace and security resulting from the continued intervention in this hemisphere of Sino-Soviet powers."

In order to assist the Latin American governments to speed economic and social development and meet the rising expectations and legitimate aims of their people, the President's Alliance for Progress was conceived. We have already seen attempts of extremists of both the right and left to impede the Alliance for Progress. And, as the Alliance achieves success, we can be assured that the extremists will use every means available to them—including subversion, terrorism, and civil war—to defeat it.

Therefore, if the Alliance for Progress is to have its chance, the governments must have the effective force required to cope with subversion, prevent terrorism, and deal with outbreaks of violence before they reach unmanageable proportions. Both the military and the police forces assume paramount importance in assuring that these governments will be able to cope with the internal threat and the movement of armaments and men clandestinely across land, sea, and air borders for subversive purposes.

It is for these reasons that the primary objective of military assistance in all Latin American countries is the development of a capability to maintain internal security.

25. *The Draper Report*[4]

[EDITOR'S NOTE: *In August, 1958, eight members of the Senate Foreign Relations Committee sent a public letter to the President complaining about alleged overemphasis on military assistance. In November of the same year, the President announced the appointment of a committee to study the problem. This nine-member committee included three former generals, an admiral, and a former Assistant Secretary of Defense. In its* Composite Report, *which is generally known as the Draper Report, the committee recommended small increases in economic aid and big increases in military aid.*

The Draper Report and subsequent interpretations thereof illustrate the need for the aid analyst to consider the political context of statements on aid. Some students of foreign aid have described the Draper Report as containing "a strong endorsement of economic assistance."[5] Does it? Or does this description fail to take into account the military orientation of the majority of committee members? Although the fact that most members had a military outlook proves nothing in itself, it should alert the student to the need to read between the lines.

The circumstances under which the Draper Committee was appointed are also relevant to the analyst's task. The eight Senators had argued that there was too much military and not enough economic aid. The appointment of the committee in November was interpreted by the press as a preliminary step toward increasing the emphasis given to economic, as opposed to military, aid. In a news conference, in November, 1958, Secretary of State Dulles confirmed this view:

---

[4] SOURCE: President's Committee to Study the United States Military Assistance Program, *Composite Report* (Washington, D.C., August 17, 1959), I, 146–56.

[5] Benjamin Higgins, *United Nations and U.S. Foreign Economic Policy* (Homewood, Ill.: Irwin, 1962), p. 76. A similar view is expressed by Richard P. Stebbins, *The United States in World Affairs, 1959* (New York: Harper, 1960), p. 96.

Q. Mr. Secretary, last August, eight members of the Foreign Relations Committee suggested in a letter to the President that military aid be cut back and economic aid increased. Does the appointment of the Draper Committee yesterday have any connection with this, or are we engaged in a re-evaluation of the relative merits of the military-economic aid?

A. I think that the appointment of the so-called Draper Committee is in part at least a response to that initiative taken by the Senators to whom you refer. There is always a very difficult problem in deciding how much emphasis to put on the military and how much to put on the economic. In my own judgment at least there is little doubt but what, as an abstract proposition, too much throughout the world is being spent on military and not enough on economic.[6]

It was expected by many, then, that the Draper Report would recommend an increase in the relative emphasis given to economic aid. Instead, it did precisely the opposite. The significance of its recommendation for placing even greater stress on military aid was obscured by its recommendation that both forms of aid be expanded. For fiscal year 1960, the committee recommended a $400 million increase in the Executive request for military aid but no increase on the economic side. For fiscal year 1961, it was proposed that both kinds of aid be increased. With regard to appropriations for fiscal year 1960, the report noted: "While the anticipated appropriations for economic assistance this year will not fully meet the requirements reflected in the appropriation requests made by the Executive Branch, which this committee has endorsed, our concern over the shortfall is not as great as in the case of military assistance."[7] Considered in its political context, the Draper Report's alleged "strong endorsement" of economic aid said, in effect: "Well, economic aid is not so bad; we should even increase it a little in a couple of years; but let me tell you about this military aid; that's what is really important; we have to increase that right away."]

Relative Emphasis Between Military and Economic Assistance

In your instructions you asked the Committee to give its:

. . . critical appraisal, after considering all relevant aspects of U.S. international security programs, of the relative emphasis which

[6] *The New York Times,* November 27, 1958, p. 18.
[7] *Composite Report,* I, 173.

should be given to military and economic programs, particularly in the less developed areas. . . .

In appraising this question, the Committee has found it necessary to consider the objectives and the interrelationships of military and economic assistance, the historical trends in amounts of funds provided for each, and what further shifts in objectives or amounts might be desirable and feasible in the United States interest. We have been concerned about the expansion of the communist drive through increased use of political, psychological, and economic weapons, and the need for countering it.

We have also taken into consideration the letter to you of August 25, 1958, from eight members of the Senate Foreign Relations Committee, questioning whether military assistance is being overemphasized, in which they said:

. . . with respect to the less developed countries there is a serious distortion in the present relative importance which is attached to military and related aid on the one hand and technical assistance and self-liquidating economic development assistance on the other.

It is necessary first to define the terms used. Military assistance, in its simplest terms, consists of weapons, equipment, supplies, and training furnished through our Department of Defense. Our economic assistance consists primarily of goods and services provided through the civilian agencies of our Government.

A. Continued Need for Military Assistance

We recognize a natural appeal for the increasing use of our aid in long-range investment for the economic well-being of the less developed countries. We have previously recommended a sizable increase in economic development assistance for fiscal year 1961, and stated that "lasting world peace will ultimately depend to a large degree upon more widely distributed economic progress . . ."

Many of those who advocate more emphasis on economic development aid, however, would propose to accomplish this by reducing military aid. On the basis of our studies, we feel this course would be dangerous.

The Committee believes that we must not allow military and economic assistance to become competitors for resources within preconceived limitations. It would be unfortunate if aid actually required on military grounds were reduced as being "nonproductive," in contrast to "more productive" economic aid. Both are "tools" for the achievement of our total objectives. Our analysis has convinced us that the needed increase in economic development assistance for the less developed countries must not be at the expense of a reduction in the needed military assistance either for these areas or for the NATO area.

The communist countries, in adding to their previous threats a strong military-economic assistance offensive, have not decreased their own direct military threat. Bloc forces adjacent to the boundaries of free world nations have not decreased in numbers and have been receiving intensive training and more modern weapons and equipment. Once communist military power is brought into action, either as a direct threat or in attack, it will then be too late to build the local forces required to meet it.

The Committee concludes that any marked decline in the level of general military aid deliveries at this time for less developed areas would represent a serious danger to the security of the free world.

It does not follow, however, that all of our military and economic aid programs must be continued indefinitely. We have, in our second and third interim reports, recommended changes in administrative arrangements for both military and economic aid which, if adopted, should result in greater selectivity of programs, better planning and more sensitivity of emphasis to changing needs.

B. The Relationship Between Military Assistance and U.S. Defense Expenditures

We believe that a real question of relative emphasis arises as between military assistance and our own defense expenditures.

Our security depends on strength at home and abroad, both of our own forces and those of our allies. Thus military assistance should be weighed against the funds provided for our own military establishment. This concept has already been recognized by the Congress in the Mutual Security Act of 1959, both by permitting the future inclusion of military assistance in the Defense budget and by the explicit provision that:

> Programs of military assistance . . . shall be budgeted so as to come into competition for financial support with other activities and programs of the Department of Defense.

Among the considerations to be taken into account in judging this competition are the relatively low cost per man of allied forces as compared with the costs of maintaining U.S. forces overseas;

the desirable build-up of forces in strategic positions where the maintenance of U.S. forces is neither practicable nor desirable; the more equitable sharing of the human and material burdens of free world defense; the increased confidence engendered within the countries concerned; the closer ties thus developed with the United States; and the increased unity and cohesiveness of purpose in the free world to which such a joint effort will contribute.

C. The Complementary Nature of Military and Economic Assistance

As we have studied the relationships between military and economic aid, we have been impressed with the wide variety of ways in which these two forms of aid complement each other. The most direct connection between the two is in the case of Defense Support, which is economic grant aid given to allies to enable them to maintain military forces important to the free world that are otherwise beyond their capacity to maintain. Since the scale of many countries' military effort is materially affected by the level of our military aid, so to a considerable extent in many cases is the amount needed by those countries for Defense Support.

Economic development aid is, however, for quite a different purpose. It represents an investment by our Government in the long-range economic future of the less developed countries and is independent of our Military Assistance Program. We make such investments both in countries where there is need for military assistance and where there is not.

Military assistance often is also a legitimate and useful instrument for more than purely military purposes. Social and economic benefits can, under some circumstances, be derived from assistance intended to support military forces. . . .

Economic assistance, by strengthening the local economy, permits it to bear a heavier military burden and increases the incentive to the country's people to sustain a military effort. Without internal security, and the general feeling of confidence engendered by adequate military forces, there is little hope for any economic progress. Nor does the maintenance of military strength in a less developed country, particularly when we cushion its impact with Defense Support, necessarily inhibit economic progress.

It should be noted that both military and economic assistance increase the total resources available to the recipient country. Within the practical bounds of flexibility in movement of these resources, a recipient country may shift internal resources from economic to military uses or vice versa in accordance with the local government's appraisal of their relative importance, which may not always be the same as our own.

D. *Changing Pattern of Assistance*

It is instructive to review the substantial changes in relative dollar amounts applied to military and economic assistance in the several geographic areas, which have been necessary in the past to respond to the constantly shifting threats, needs, and circumstances. . . .

The Mutual Security Program came into existence in 1951, incorporating most of the then existing programs in one program for legislative and appropriation purposes. At that time, under the impact of the Korean War, the balance in dollar expenditures for assistance was already moving from the heavy economic expenditures for European recovery to greater military expenditures, primarily to rearm our NATO allies.

In the years following 1951, the communist thrust turned toward the less developed countries resulting in a geographical shift of United States military and economic assistance toward these areas. . . . Today, practically no economic grant assistance goes to industrialized Western Europe, now recovered and increasingly prosperous. On the other hand, we have been expanding our contributions to the economic development of the less developed countries, while continuing to provide military assistance to NATO and to those countries with borders, or unresolved conflicts, with the communist bloc.

We have made a further analysis . . . of relative amounts devoted to military and economic aid on the basis of the following groupings: The NATO European countries other than Greece and Turkey; the 12 less developed countries which are currently receiving Defense Support as well as other forms of aid; Latin America, and all less developed recipient countries (i.e., the 12 Defense Support countries plus Latin America plus other less developed aid recipients).

. . . the approximately $6 billion of total United States assistance to both developed and less developed nations in fiscal year 1959 was about 40 percent military and 60 percent economic. The proportions vary widely by grouping, however, from 75 percent military and 25 percent economic—the latter being principally Export-Import Bank loans and Public Law 480 agricultural surplus transactions—in European NATO countries to 13 percent military and 87 percent economic in Latin America. . . .

E. Military-Economic Assistance Comparisons Should Consider All Sources of Aid

In measuring the relative amounts of the two types of assistance, *all* relevant sources and programs should be considered. Restricting the comparison of economic and military aid to the amounts within the Mutual Security Program, or even to the amounts encompassed within the total of *all* United States programs, would give a distorted picture. For example, the United States is the only free world country providing significant supplies of military equipment. This gives us special responsibilities and necessarily enlarges the percentage of our aid going for military purposes.[8]

On the other hand, the total economic assistance available to less developed countries is obviously not alone that provided by the Mutual Security and other United States programs. It also includes assistance from other developed free world countries; international agencies such as the International Bank for Reconstruction and Development; other multilateral arrangements in most of which we participate; and by private investment from the United States and other countries.

Figure 16[9] shows how the proportion of military as compared with economic assistance shifts when multilateral and other free world economic aid programs are included. Since private investment and some multilateral programs are not included in these charts, the over-all transfer of resources from developed to less developed countries for economic purposes is somewhat larger than the charts indicate.

In considering relative emphasis, it would be misleading to focus undue attention on the dollar ratios between the amounts devoted to economic and military assistance. They are derived quantities arising from analyses of the levels of resources needed to achieve different, though related, objectives. The vital consideration is whether needs of comparable importance have been met in all categories of aid. The pattern of this relationship, the "mix," is necessarily built and varies greatly country by country.

It should also be noted that some of the important objectives such as those of training can be achieved at comparatively low dollar cost; others, of comparable priority, are more expensive.

F. Conclusions on Relative Emphasis

The Committee does not believe any continuing formula can

[8] Does this necessarily follow?—Ed.
[9] Not reproduced here.—Ed.

be found that would satisfactorily determine the relative emphasis to be placed upon our economic or military assistance program whether over-all or in respect to any particular country.

The Committee believes that the impression held in some quarters to the effect that our Military Assistance Program is too great in relation to the economic development assistance program is not justified. From the standpoint of U.S. interests, we do not see any competitive relationship between the two. It may be argued that certain less developed countries have larger military programs than appear to be necessary. In such cases, we should make every effort to assist the country concerned to make appropriate reductions. However, there are other countries in which the military programs are not adequately supported. Our hearings and presentations have convinced us that the over-all present reductions in the level of appropriations for military assistance will result in an impairment of the security of the United States.

IX

Private Investment and Foreign Aid

Reduced to an elementary form, an aid transaction involves the transfer of scarce resources from one nation to another. Intergovernmental aid, however, is not the only means by which this can be accomplished. Private foreign investment also involves moving scarce resources from nation to nation. Thus, private foreign investment and governmental foreign aid are, to some extent, alternative techniques of reaching the same goal. Since 1945, spokesmen for the U.S. Government have continually reminded the underdeveloped countries of this fact. When confronted with requests for more foreign aid, American policy-makers have replied that other countries would not need so much aid if they would take the steps necessary to "attract" private investment.

The U.S. Government has actively sought to stimulate private investment abroad in several ways. (1) By reducing American trade barriers, the government has made it easier for goods produced abroad to be sold in the American market. This has increased the profitability of foreign production, which has thus become more attractive to American private investors. (2) Under its investment-guaranty program, the government has protected American private investors from some of the risks of foreign investment. (3) Treaties have been negotiated in order to ensure "fair" treatment of American investors by foreign governments. (4) Foreign governments have been advised regarding the advantages of reliance on private investment. (5) American economic-aid programs have been kept relatively small in order to minimize competition with private sources of capital. By using all of these means, the United States has tried to reduce the need for governmental foreign aid.

26. *Private Enterprise in Developing Countries*[1]

[EDITOR'S NOTE: *In 1959, the State Department received a report from Ralph I. Straus, who had been requested by that department*

[1] SOURCE: Ralph I. Straus, *Expanding Private Investment for Free World Economic Growth*, Special report prepared at the request of the Department of State (Washington, D.C.: Department of State, April, 1959), pp. 5–8.

to study the problem of how to expand American private foreign investment. Straus was then Special Consultant to the Under Secretary of State for Economic Affairs. In connection with the study, the Department of Commerce sent a questionnaire to nearly a thousand businessmen requesting their opinions on stimulating investment abroad. Some basic elements of the problem as seen by businessmen are discussed in this excerpt from the "Straus report."]

The Background

The nature and rate of economic growth in the developing countries, as well as the encouragement of private enterprise, depend primarily on the efforts and decisions of the leaders and citizens of those countries. Capital and know-how from outside sources— public or private—can help but cannot substitute for those efforts.

As governments succeed in meeting initial needs for public works and other facilities, they will be faced with a steady growth in the number and complexity of needed economic activities which are less susceptible to central planning. The hundreds of varied enterprises upon which economic growth depends and the thousands of decisions that go into establishing and operating them call for a vigorous and growing private business community.

It is significant that the impediments which tend to inhibit private initiative are frequently the same as those inhibiting economic development.

Private investment cannot flourish nor can development be accelerated where the attitudes toward the treatment of private enterprises are hostile, where there is internal or external insecurity, or where chronic foreign exchange shortages accompany chronic monetary instability. In addition, both governments and local businesses are also handicapped by weak banking systems, inadequate government services, and ineffectual legal frameworks for business activity.

Most of these conditions can be changed, however, where there is a will to change them.

Most governments in the developing countries are already attacking the deficiencies in the physical base on which private economic activity must rely—the highways and the railroads, the ports, the communications, the power grids, and the irrigation systems. Foreign assistance has been and continues to be made available to governments and to public utility enterprises for these purposes.

Foreign assistance has also in some cases helped to provide the financial stability necessary for development activity. Likewise, technical assistance and equipment have been furnished to improve health, agriculture, education, public administration, and other services vital to the development process. In this sense, government-to-government economic programs are basic to the encouragement of private enterprise.

Within the framework of U.S. assistance programs, projects have been established or are being planned to provide managerial training, industrial development centers, development banks, labor education, industrial research, industrial zones or districts, and assistance in developing laws and legal institutions conducive to effective business operations. In recognition of the need for increased private economic activity for the accomplishment of their development objectives, a number of countries have proceeded independently to adopt programs to encourage private enterprise. There is reason to believe, on the basis of what is already being done, that many of the developing countries are prepared to move more rapidly in this direction.

This is a significant area where the coincidence of interest of the United States Government, of U.S. business, and of the developing countries can be identified and enlarged. The private sector of the United States can promote the foreign policy of the United States by stimulating the growth of the private sector in the less developed countries. At the same time, foreign capital will be attracted by an energetic and successful class of local investors.

Where developing countries demonstrate an interest in receiving help for making the best use of the private potential in their own countries, the United States Government and U.S. business should be ready to respond quickly, systematically, and effectively.

U.S. Government Cooperation with Local Efforts

The United States Government has instruments to assist governments where they want to stimulate local private enterprise and attract private foreign investment. Assistance of this kind coupled with the measures recommended later in this study relating directly to American private investment can help to develop links between local and American investors which strengthen the concept of a partnership approach to economic development.

We recommend that projects designed to develop private enterprise in the participating countries be made an integral part of foreign assistance programs. This will require clear-cut policy decisions and the assignment of specific responsibilities to competent,

specialized U.S. staff, both in Washington and in the field, to secure as great an organized concentration upon the private sector
as has heretofore been accorded to agriculture, health and public
works programs. . . .

American Business and Local Efforts

American private investment has brought and can increasingly
bring to foreign nations not only the direct benefits of investment
but also many indirect benefits. One of the chief virtues of this
aspect of private investment is the natural, informal, and day-to-
day manner in which it achieves secondary benefits in the normal
course of business. Each U.S. enterprise abroad is inevitably a
source of technical assistance and a training center for personnel,
contributing significantly to the total quantity of skills available in
the country. Each tends to be a focal point of capital accumulation
for further useful investment, particularly in service and supply
industries, e.g., stores, production of components, transportation,
and housing.

Some American companies operating abroad have followed a
deliberate policy of helping in the development of locally owned
enterprises to which they have provided financial and technical
assistance in order to generate local sources of supply. This is a
type of developmental assistance impossible to duplicate in any
government assistance program. For example, American companies
operating in Latin America spent locally more than $4 billion in
1955, of which $1.8 billion was for local purchases—materials, serv-
ices, and equipment—and the balance for wages, salaries, and taxes.
During the same period, they employed 625,000 persons of which
only 9,000 were sent from the United States.

Business Behavior and Technical Assistance

American companies can increasingly help create a favorable
climate for private business by careful effort in harmonizing their
own interests with those of the people and governments of the
countries in which they operate. They can improve their relations
abroad by careful selection, orientation, and language training of
their American personnel. They can—as some have already done
on an extensive scale—assist directly in programs for the better-
ment of health, education, and social welfare. They can set up
—and this, again, is being done by some companies—specific training programs to teach industrial, commercial, and financial skills,

thereby making a direct contribution to development. Their research facilities can be focused on the solution of local technical problems, including additional uses of local products. Establishment of quality standards for products and the introduction of modern management-worker relationships can exercise a beneficial influence on local business.

American business and professional associations can promote and sponsor international business conferences and exchanges of study groups. Particular attention could usefully be devoted to establishing contacts and the flow of information between American organizations and such local institutions as development banks and industrial development centers. Private American business organizations are in a position to help provide or recruit specialized technical and managerial talent for employment by local business, banks, and promotional organizations. The creation of links of this kind provides an important source outside governments for local entrepreneurs or investment institutions to seek advice, partners, capital, and know-how.

There may also be possibilities of pooling the talent of a wide range of American firms in a private cooperative effort to provide technical assistance to one or more developing countries. It is difficult for government personnel to transmit U.S. business procedures and to assist in the establishment of credit and other institutions abroad as effectively as could be done by personnel drawn directly from business.

The Challenge to U.S. Business

Private business itself is increasingly aware of its own self-interest in the growth of the less developed countries. Even if business practices and expectations must in many respects become adapted to conditions abroad which would be unpalatable at home, the business stakes in the economic success of these countries are great enough to warrant such accommodation.

Business, of course, shares the national political, economic, and humanitarian interest in the world's economic growth. But private business in particular has a stake in demonstrating that private management and private capital offer a prospect of economic development no less promising than the offers of the propagandists of ruthless regimentation. Disillusioned rejection of the potentialities of private enterprise by large segments of the developing world is bound to mean a shrinkage of private commercial freedom everywhere. Failure to invest in world economic development carries with it the prospect of losses no less real than the risks of investment. . . .

27. *Private Enterprise and Foreign Aid*[2]

[EDITOR'S NOTE: *The Advisory Committee on Private Enterprise in Foreign Aid was authorized by an amendment to the Foreign Assistance Act of 1963. This amendment called for establishment of a nine-member group to "carry out studies and make recommendations for achieving the most effective utilization of the private enterprise provisions of this Act." In July, 1965, the committee, headed by the Chairman of IBM, Arthur K. Watson, issued its first report.*]

LETTER OF TRANSMITTAL

The Honorable David E. Bell, Administrator
Agency for International Development
Department of State

DEAR MR. BELL:

In submitting, herewith, the Report of the Advisory Committee on Private Enterprise in Foreign Aid, there is one principle I would especially like to emphasize. Over the past months, as we worked to relate foreign aid and private initiative, we came to believe that no matter how carefully our aid dollars are invested and no matter how wise and energetic AID's personnel may be, there is still not enough money nor people to accomplish the vast task the U.S. has undertaken.

To put this into perspective, our government is today putting over two billion dollars each year into the economies of 72 countries. Yet this considerable sum, divided among their populations, comes to but $1.44 per person. Even in Latin America, where the effort is most intense, the amount is only $2.73 per person each year. Clearly there are limits to what we can hope to achieve.

It is this realization, more than the original mandate of our Committee, which finally leads us to urge that the Agency for International Development put increasing stress on its role as catalyst and energizer for private effort. It is only through private resources, our own and those of the developing countries themselves, where the

[2] SOURCE: Agency for International Development, Advisory Committee on Private Enterprise in Foreign Aid, *Foreign Aid Through Private Initiative* (Washington, D.C.: Department of State, July, 1965), pp. 1–12.

additional resources are potentially adequate to meet the challenge. That is the basis of our recommendations. . . .

Respectfully submitted,
ARTHUR K. WATSON, *Chairman*
July 30, 1965

SECTION 1: PRIVATE ENTERPRISE AND FOREIGN AID

This report explores methods for harnessing the vast nongovernmental sector of the United States to the task of accelerating economic growth in the less developed countries.

In broadest terms, the Advisory Committee on Private Enterprise in Foreign Aid believes that nongovernment resources not only can do more, they must. Otherwise, foreign aid would be doomed to become a costly palliative of indefinite duration. The Committee concludes that business, labor organizations, agricultural groups, professional societies, educational institutions, foundations, and many other resources, if encouraged, are ready and willing to assume a broader role in international development.

Twenty years have gone by since the United States launched its first postwar program of foreign aid. In that time, some $40 billion of economic aid has been appropriated by the United States Congress; first, to help our friends in Western Europe recover from the destruction of World War II; then, to help the lagging countries of Africa, Asia, and Latin America in their long climb out of the depths of poverty.

By and large, foreign aid has achieved a great deal. Yet as one looks back on those 20 years, the programs seem to have presented an uninterrupted series of crises. In the annual Congressional reviews, the program's many remarkable accomplishments often have seemed swamped by accounts of its shortcomings and failures. It is hardly surprising that there is now a widespread desire to question what the United States has achieved for its time and money.

In the perspective of history, however, both the time and the money will seem modest. Twenty years is hardly long enough for a single generation to grow out of a deprived and ignorant childhood. The $40 billion is less than one-half of one percent of the wealth produced by the United States during the period.

The efforts of advanced countries to help less developed nations toward economic growth and political maturity will go on. From time to time, there will be doubts and misgivings about the wisdom or the effectiveness of the effort. Nevertheless, most Americans understand very well that the effort should continue and our political and economic interests are best served by building up the productive capabilities and democratic institutions of the less developed countries. What Americans do demand, and what they are entitled to have, is the assurance that their resources and support are applied with intelligence, skill and dedication.

The Resource Gap

If the less developed countries are to grow at tolerable rates, they will need a great infusion of capital and human skills from the advanced world.

As matters now stand, there is a huge gap between what the less developed countries need for a tolerable rate of growth, and what they are likely to get. As far as their capital needs are concerned, the gap has been measured by various United States and international agencies. Each of these measures is based on somewhat different assumptions and none can be entirely precise. Yet all of them suggest that the size of the gap is staggering—between $5 billion and $20 billion annually.

Part of the reason for this great gap lies in the underdeveloped areas themselves. They are simply unable to absorb large quantities of capital efficiently. For the most part, this is because of a second gap—the gap in human resources. This need is more subtle and, in many ways, more profoundly disturbing than the gap in capital. The less developed countries are critically short of the skills, traditions, and organizations that are part and parcel of a modern industrial society. These lacks run from skills in factory layout to skills in the conduct of management labor relations; from knowledge about plant breeding and animal raising to knowledge about flood control and weather forecasting; from skills in the mobilization of savings to skills in the distribution of foodstuffs.

The less developed countries lack also the men and institutions to ensure that the fruits of their growth will be fairly distributed. They lack union officials who are capable of bargaining responsibly with management, and tax collectors who are capable of enforcing objectively the tax laws of their countries. In short, most of the complex social and cultural infrastructure which we in the advanced countries take for granted has to be put in place brick by brick. Money alone will not do the job.

In surveying the size and nature of the problem, this Committee has come to three basic conclusions:

First, added capital cannot be expected to come from government sources in quantities sufficient to fill the gap. The nongovernment resources of the United States and other advanced countries must, therefore, play a much greater part.

Second, the skills and other human resources which the less developed countries need must also come largely from nongovernment sources. Governments simply do not have command over most of the human resources that are needed.

Third, the role of the nongovernment groups—of business enterprises, labor unions, professional societies, and all the rest—must be greatly expanded. Otherwise the economic development we do achieve will not provide the pluralism, the democratic balance, and the diffusion of benefits which are its final purpose.

The Means of Assistance

In the course of nearly two centuries of national existence, we Americans have managed to develop a social system which is unique in human history. We have built the world's most powerful economy and, in the course of this growth, have developed institutions on a giant scale. We have the largest enterprises in the world, the biggest labor organizations, the biggest governments, the largest farm complexes, the greatest universities, the largest private charitable and benevolent organizations. At the same time, we have maintained an open society in which economic and political power is widely diffused, in which initiative and innovation can spring up from many levels, and in which barriers between social and economic groups are as insignificant as man has so far been able to devise.

Most Americans see this great diffusion of power and this unparalleled measure of social and economic mobility as prime sources of this country's strength. Yet, from time to time, we feel a sense of impotence and inadequacy as we confront the monolithic discipline of the Communist societies, with their apparent capacity to mobilize all their men, all their technology and all their capital to some single purpose. From time to time, too, we feel at a disadvantage in the face of seemingly coordinated and disciplined actions of other advanced nations in Europe and Japan, which appear to have found a way for the public and the private sectors to move in close harness. As we see other nations face up swiftly to some crisis or some opportunity in international affairs, we sometimes wonder if the United States has yet found the formula for effective operation in the international area.

In theory, the American constitutional system puts the conduct of foreign affairs firmly in the President's hands, yet the economic resources which give him strength are not easily mobilized. In contrast to the monolithic reach of totalitarian states, our own Federal Government accounts for about 10 percent of the purchases of goods and services while state and local governments account for another 10 percent. The control of the rest is distributed among millions of farms, hundreds of thousands of business enterprises, and great numbers of nonprofit organizations.

U.S. interests abroad are almost as greatly dispersed. An estimated 3,000 U.S. businesses have facilities abroad. More than 500 educational, labor, charitable, and religious organizations have programs or facilities overseas. Each of these in its own special way represents a part of our American system; but few of them are responsive to any common purpose or common strategy.

As it turns out, some of the resources that are needed by the less developed countries lie within the ambit of the Federal Government; but a critical part of those resources lie beyond government's reach. The Federal Government may be able to provide some of the capital funds; but it needs the participation of other sectors of the American economy in providing the skills to design a plant, organize a market, train a work force, raise a crop, or distribute a commodity. The Federal Government has no command authority over the skills of a university, a foundation, or a labor union. Accordingly, a well-balanced strategy of assistance to less developed nations must contemplate that there will be a role for all sectors of the U.S. economy. If the environment is right, some of these sectors will move into such activities as a normal part of their own operations. Many already have. Others, however, will have to be encouraged, persuaded, or assisted to extend their activities to the less developed countries.

In sorting out the respective roles of the private and the public sectors in providing the resources for the aid program, this Committee believes that there are a few basic guidelines to be followed, guidelines which are derived from the experience and the convictions of the American people.

In the first place, private organizations are generally capable of greater speed, flexibility, and incisiveness than government agencies. Freed from government procedures, permitted to find their own ways of performing the tasks which are necessary for economic growth, private organizations can outperform official agencies. The comparative strengths are no reflection upon the men and women who man our government posts; on the contrary, our experience as members of the Committee has left strong, favorable impressions of the energy, dedication, and good sense of the AID leadership.

In part, the limitations of AID are due to the fact that it represents simply one part of a complex government machine which has many objectives apart from development. In individual cases, therefore, the development objectives may be pitted against conflicting government aims. In part, too, the limitations of AID simply derive from the fact that, under the U.S. system of public checks and balances, the program is subject to continuous scrutiny from many directions: from the press, from Congress, from other government agencies. The result is sometimes deeply frustrating. It usually takes many months for AID to comply with the statutory requirements for employing technicians or consultants, or for processing contracts, loans, or guaranties. There are exceptional cases. An emergency can generate faster action through extraordinary channels. But the use of extraordinary channels carries extraordinary risks for the government agency involved.

The Committee has been guided by a *second general point*, which also favors the more extended use of nongovernment channels in the aid program. There is always a risk that government-to-government aid may be mishandled. When this happens, both governments are exposed to special political risks. Such aid at times can generate a backwash of bitterness and resentment. Aid through private channels carries fewer risks of this sort.

A *third general guideline* by which this Committee has been influenced relates to the limitations of American private organizations. Though private entities may be free to react more quickly and flexibly, they operate with certain constraints of their own. Like all American institutions, they should be expected to make sacrifices to common national objectives. But there are limitations on the extent to which most private organizations can take on extraordinary financial risks. The existence of such organizations depends upon their ability to remain strong. This overriding fact cannot be disregarded by their managers.

There is still *a fourth guideline* which the Committee has found useful in its deliberations. Much of the work to be pursued under the foreign aid program, as we noted earlier, is intended to train people, to speed changes in institutions and values. Tasks of this sort take time, a great deal of time. They require prolonged, continuous contact from the aid-giving end. Yet without fixity of purpose and involvement of vital self-interest, such continuity is usually in constant peril. In its application, this fourth guideline can mean different things for different programs. In many cases, it argues for a transfer into private hands of activities now performed by government agencies. Pushed and hauled by the vagaries of public and Congressional sentiment, by the limitations of the annual appropriation process, and by the changing tactical concepts of successive administrations, government aid agencies cannot be expected to demonstrate constancy of purpose as their outstanding attribute. Accordingly, competent and stable private institutions may be far more effective instruments of national policy in some situations than government institutions.

A *fifth guideline* which has influenced the Committee's conclusions is the principle that public resources wisely used can attract private resources in even greater quantities. There are many illustrations in our national life in which public resources have been used as catalysts and energizers of the much greater sources available to the private sector. By providing such indispensably basic facilities as transportation and education, by clearing away obstructing bottlenecks, by reducing the risk and uncertainty of the political and economic environment, by providing some element in an undertaking which the private sector is unable by its own efforts to provide, a public foreign aid program can "leverage" its total impact many times.

The Means of Receiving

We in the United States see our nation as a symbol of the vitality and creativeness of a pluralistic society. We have not yet stamped out the last traces of poverty and prejudice in our economy. But what has been achieved so far gives Americans every reason to champion the role of private initiative and stress the importance of freedom of opportunity.

True to its history, the United States has urged the less developed countries to strengthen and extend their own private sectors and to build up many of the other institutions of a pluralistic society, such as trade associations, labor unions, family farms, cooperatives and foundations, as a critical step in the achievement of economic and political maturity. At the same time, we have come to learn that there are fundamental cultural and historical differences and important differences in priorities which distinguish the advanced countries from those in the less developed world.

The extent of some of the differences that have to be bridged is indicated by the reaction of some countries to the concept of private enterprise. To the countries of Asia and Africa which are just emerging from centuries of colonial rule, the words "private enterprise" conjure up a series of images and associations which are as different from the familiar U.S. connotation as night is from day. The outstanding examples of "private enterprise" in the colonial economies were usually enterprises controlled from the mother country, often with privileged status. In the heat and tension of the struggle for freedom, therefore, "private enterprise" is seen by many Asians and Africans as part and parcel of a system of domination from without; and the U.S. espousal of "private enterprise," especially foreign-owned private enterprise, is seen by many as a Trojan horse intended to impose a new form of political and economic bondage upon them. Although colonialism has long ceased to be a problem in most of Latin America, many nations in that area of the world tend to echo the reactions of the Asians and the Africans.

In addition, all underdeveloped countries express concern over other aspects of foreign private investment. Rightly or wrongly, they worry about the balance of payments impact of servicing a growing foreign interest. And they want to know how they can remain masters of their own house if foreigners control their principal means of production.

In most parts of the less developed world, therefore, local sentiment is torn between two conflicting views. On the one hand, they recognize that private enterprise can make great contributions to the development process. On the other hand, there is a fear of its bigness and of dominance by such enterprise. Of course, one would expect those local groups which are politically hostile to the private enterprise system to be hostile to foreign-owned business. But the same antagonistic reaction is also found among those who have a stake in the private system. In many countries, local businessmen see foreign-owned business as a giant "unfair" competitor, not as a helpful ideological ally.

The United States, therefore, confronts a less developed world in which private enterprise is often on the defensive. Indeed, it faces a world in which some nations profess to be evolving toward one form or another of socialism. Nevertheless, paradoxically, the future of the private sector in the less developed world is far from discouraging.

The experience of India is illustrative. In the execution of each of the three Indian Five Year Plans since 1951, the private sector has responded more dynamically and the public sector less dynamically than the Plan had projected. As a result, each successive Plan has assigned a larger role to the private sector than its predecessor Plan. In the process, doctrinaire Indian declarations on the subject of state socialism have given way to more balanced and more pragmatic evaluations of the respective roles of the private and public sectors.

The trend in other countries, such as Mexico and Pakistan, has been in a similar direction. In these countries, and in many others, a modern, dynamic private sector has evolved with unexpected speed. While the old cliches about "exploitation" continue to have great currency in these countries, there is at the same time a widespread recognition that many of the new entrepreneurs simply do not fit the old patterns. As a result, government servants are more disposed to accept the desirability of linking the freedom and flexibility of the private sector with the power and purpose of the public sector. At the same time, noting some of the unhappy consequences of state ownership in Egypt, Guinea, Ghana, and other countries, various governments in Africa, Latin America, and Asia have felt even more strongly the need to modify their doctrinaire socialist views.

In some ways, the experience of the less developed countries in the field of agriculture has also suggested a bigger role in the future for the private sector. The problems of agriculture have been more perplexing, and more threatening to the aspirations of the less developed countries than the problems of industry. In many cases, these countries have been unable to raise their farm output to match the increase in their population. The reasons have been complex and they have differed from country to country. Sometimes, the problems have been rooted in predatory forms of land tenancy, money lending, and monopoly marketing which have deprived farmers of any incentive to increase output. Sometimes there has been a need for greater public investment in roads, drainage, water, or power. Sometimes, the need has been for new seed and technology.

The first response of governments in the less developed countries, notably in India and Pakistan, had been to assume that the government itself would solve the problem through a combination of investment, coercion, and regulation. Today, however, it is rapidly beginning to be clear that the problem can only be met if it also engages the energies of many nongovernmental institutions —of private producers and sellers of seed and insecticide, producing and marketing cooperatives, banks, credit unions, and research institutes and testing stations. We begin to see new hope that these countries, by drawing on all their energy and resources, may yet solve the stubborn problem of agriculture.

Nevertheless, as matters stand today, the question of the future roles of the public and the private sectors in less developed countries is uncertain and undecided. Thus far, private enterprise is the dominant form in most less developed countries, including many which profess to some form of socialism. Indeed, in most of these countries, the revenues and expenditures of the public sector are far less important in relation to the nation's income than the levels that typically prevail in Western Europe and North America.

In due course, the less developed nations will generate their own patterns of public-private relationships. When they do, these patterns will bear the stamp of their own history and aspirations. In most less developed countries, the role of national planning will be a good deal stronger than the role to which we in the United States are accustomed. Most of these countries will be less disposed than the United States to acknowledge the innate desirability of private over public enterprise. Mixed private-public enterprise will no doubt be much more common than in our own experience. In many of these countries, the public regulation of private enterprise will continue long traditions, so contrary to our own, of being pervasive, detailed, and of leaving large areas of discretion in the hands of government officials.

We Americans are not without influence in affecting these attitudes. In fact, our influence is often far greater than we suppose. True to our own convictions, we should use our influence as we can. At every opportunity, we ought to broaden and strengthen the private sector. But we must be prepared to accept the fact that the most effective pressures are often achieved through quiet diplomacy rather than through stentorian ultimatums. Indeed, the most effective pressure of all, in the end, is to help increase the resources and capabilities of the private sector so that it may provide its own justification for an expanded role.

One final point. Even a society in which private enterprise is dominant, in which economic power is diffused, and in which checks and balances are basic to the system will need a public sector which has foresight, rationality, and planning capacity. In a nation trying to grow under forced draft, that need will be particularly great. To be sure, an economy based on diffused initiative cannot be either highly disciplined or readily predictable. In such a society, it is the function of many institutions to take on new initiatives that may not be according to plan, and to resist the efforts of others which may run counter to their interests. Economies of this sort, when they are successful, grow partly out of the foresight and planning and partly out of the competition and conciliation of the institutions that make them up.

In our efforts to achieve societies of this sort abroad, therefore, we must be prepared to accept the appearance of certain seeming contradictions in our efforts. We must be prepared not only to encourage the growth of private enterprise but also to encourage other institutions with which such enterprise will sometimes cooperate, sometimes clash, for example: an effective structure of government organizations, a creative and responsible structure for the conduct of labor relations, an efficient system of cooperative organizations where such organizations are appropriate, and a series of institutions devoted to educational, philanthropic, and other nonprofit activities. It is out of such a ferment that economic growth and the democratic process may be expected to appear.

Section 2: The Flow of Direct Investment

Of the many roles that United States private enterprise is equipped to play in the less developed countries of the world, that of investing in and managing branches, subsidiaries, or affiliate companies is the most obvious. U.S. business already has large investments of this sort outstanding in the less developed countries. By early 1964, its direct investment in these areas was $13.3 billion; of this total, $2.5 billion was in manufacturing, $7.5 billion in petroleum and mining, and $3.3 billion in other branches of business activity.

Compared with the needs and possibilities of the developing nations, however, the rate of increase in such investment has been insignificant. Here and there, to be sure, some special circumstance has generated a spurt of investment by U.S. enterprises. But the total increase of all direct investment by U.S. enterprises in the less developed areas was only $522 million for 1964. This contrasts sharply with the $5–$20 billion annual gap cited earlier. Most of this increase in direct investment was in the more advanced parts of the less developed world, especially in Latin America; and roughly 20 percent was financed by ploughing back profits previously generated in the less developed countries rather than by a fresh flow of resources from the United States.

The Problem of Climate

Why is so little private investment moving into the less developed countries? Businessmen would answer the question in different terms, but their answers would add [up?] to misgivings about "climate."

"Climate" seems a vague word. But it suggests the nature of the concern well enough. U.S. businessmen are accustomed to evaluating and accepting normal business risks. Not many of them are accustomed to evaluating and accepting political instability, threats and rumors of expropriation, systems of pervasive discretionary regulation, prospects of rapid inflation and devaluation, and other novel features of overseas investment.

Accordingly, the characteristic reaction of businessmen who have sensed the unfamiliar risks posed by the less developed world has been to turn elsewhere for opportunities. This is not to imply that once the climate were improved, all the conditions to attract foreign direct investment would be satisfied. A favorable climate must be thought of as being a necessary, but not a sufficient, condition for attracting foreign investment. The improvement of climate therefore, is only a first step in persuading businessmen to investigate the many opportunities in the less developed world.

Just as the word climate itself is vague in this context, so the means for its improvement in any country are also ill defined. If the threats of inflation and devaluation could be reduced, if the uncertainties of political life could be contained, if the latent and active hostility against foreign-owned enterprise could be held in check, climate would be improved. But these are symptoms of the basic problems of underdevelopment itself.

There are no simple nostrums for the improvement of a country's climate. Confidence cannot be guaranteed, for instance, simply by extracting a declaration in favor of private foreign investment from an aid-receiving country, if any duress is involved in the process. On the contrary, in some cases, commitments of this sort when extracted as a condition of foreign aid, may imperil a friendly government and expose foreign investment to needless risk.

Though the measures needed to improve a nation's climate may not be crystal clear, it is clear that in any such effort nothing succeeds quite like success. If a less developed country succeeds by its policies in attracting some capital, this in itself is the largest single step that the country can take to attract more capital. The stimulating effect of capital at work bolsters confidence and expectation.

There are countries, however, which are on dead center in this regard. With confidence impaired, the question is how to build back the climate to a point at which businessmen will be prepared to consider opportunities in such countries again. In a succeeding part of this section, we shall have various proposals to that end, including tax and guaranty proposals. But some general measures may be helpful.

AID has been supporting a number of programs aimed at increasing the degree of local understanding of a privately oriented economy. In some cases, AID is using its influence to point out that existing legal and regulatory structures are unnecessarily discouraging to business, both local and foreign. In other cases, schools of business administration receive support; in others, systematic contacts between private organizations are being financed; and in still others, selected individuals visit the United States to see for themselves how a complex privately oriented system such as the United States actually works.

As the Committee observed in Section 1, the climate for operations by foreign and local private organizations has improved recently in a number of major countries of the less developed world, such as India and Brazil. There remain many opportunities to link AID's work on the improvement of climate with the thoughtful and imaginative work which various business groups and foundations are undertaking on their own initiative. Recent programs sponsored by private groups in Turkey, Mexico, India, and other countries afford businessmen and government officials unprecedented opportunities to explore their common interests and reconcile their conflicts. More effective coordination of AID and nongovernmental efforts of this sort could increase their total effectiveness. Accordingly:

> We recommend that AID select a number of key aid-receiving countries for intensive study of factors which may improve the investment climate; that such studies enlist the help and advice of the appropriate business communities concerned; that an explicit program be developed for the improvement of the climate in those countries studied; and that, wherever the foreign aid program offers some effective opportunity for the improvement of such climate, the opportunity be used to the full.

Even as it makes this recommendation, the Committee is aware that AID's capacity to use the foreign aid program as leverage is limited in many ways. International agencies, such as the World Bank or the International Monetary Fund can, at times, be much less inhibited in trying to induce constructive change. To be sure, the fact that the United States is ready to provide added resources to a country which has made its peace with the international agencies may be an important reason for the influence of those agencies; but the fact remains that such agencies are at times in a better position to induce change. Accordingly, the Committee is pleased to note that international organizations such as the Organization for Economic Cooperation and Development (OECD) and the World Bank are developing various proposals which could improve the treatment of foreign private investors. . . .

X

Trade and Foreign Aid

As a means to achieve foreign-policy goals such as economic development, private investment is an alternative to aid. Trade is another technique of statecraft that can sometimes be substituted for aid. Most of the time, of course, American policy-makers use all three techniques—private investment, trade, and aid—with varying emphasis on each.

The basic economic function of foreign aid is to increase the recipient nation's access to imports. Since a nation must pay for imports with foreign exchange (or gold), the problem of gaining access to more imports is one of acquiring more foreign exchange (or gold). Assuming that a nation has no gold mines, it can get more foreign exchange in two ways: (1) By gifts or loans from other nations, and (2) by selling its goods and services to other nations. We call the first method foreign aid (or private investment), and the second, international trade. That trade is, to some extent, an alternative way to perform one of the functions of aid was underscored by a slogan popular in Europe in the 1950's— "Trade Not Aid." The slogan implied that Europe wanted imports from the United States, that Europe would prefer to sell goods to the United States in order to earn dollars with which to pay for these imports, but that the United States would not let in enough foreign goods and was therefore compelled to give Europe dollars with which to pay for American imports.

Since 1945, the policy-makers in the Executive Branch have considered trade and aid to be alternative techniques of statecraft. They have told Congress again and again that less aid would be required if American trade barriers were lowered. Congress, however, has been unreceptive to the argument. Tariff legislation has traditionally been considered a "domestic question" by Congress and has therefore been channeled through the House Ways and Means Committee and the Senate Finance Committee. Since aid legislation goes through other committees, it is difficult for the Executive Branch to demonstrate the intimate relation that exists between aid and trade policies.

172

By ignoring this relation, Congress has saddled the Executive with two conflicting lines of policy. On the one hand, Congress has resisted attempts to lower American trade barriers and thus to help foreigners to earn dollars; on the other, Congress has insisted on increasing foreign aid in the form of loans. The question then becomes: "How are foreigners going to acquire dollars to repay U.S. loans?"

28. Economic Policy and the ITO Charter[1]

[EDITOR's NOTE: *Trade liberalization has been an important factor in the planning of American aid policy since 1943. The establishment of the ITO was supposed to ensure rapid progress toward elimination of trade barriers. The history of the ITO, however, turned out to be much like that of the League of Nations; although the United States initiated the proposal, it would not join. The following speech was delivered by Secretary of State Dean Acheson to a meeting of American businessmen on May 3, 1949.*]

There is a character in one of Molière's plays who wondered what prose was and then was surprised and delighted to learn that he had been speaking it all his life.

The process of change in human relations is much like the speaking of prose. All of us are principals in the process of social change, but we seldom see ourselves in this flattering light. Lacking the detached perspective of the historian and preoccupied as we are with the affairs of each day, we are often quite unaware of how different is the way we think, act, and react today from the way we did a few years ago.

All of us in this country are aware, I think, that the conceptions and convictions that underlie our foreign policies have undergone a momentous transformation in the last decade. Certainly we have had to cast our economic thinking in a new perspective and to see the economic, political, and social factors in relation to the whole pattern of international life.

We have come to realize more clearly than ever before that foreign economic policy is not made in a political vacuum. It is hardly possible any longer to draw a sharp dividing line between economic affairs and political affairs. They are related and inter-

[1] SOURCE: Dean Acheson, "Economic Policy and the ITO Charter," *Department of State Bulletin*, XX, No. 515 (May 15, 1949), 623–27.

acting. Each complements and supplements the other. They must be combined in a single unified and rounded policy designed to serve and advance the national interest.

As businessmen, you are naturally most interested in those aspects of foreign policy that affect business conditions. Therefore I shall speak chiefly of some of the major elements of our foreign economic policy. I also shall necessarily refer, rather briefly, to some of our essential political objectives. They have a definite and obvious connection with the European Recovery Program, for example. All are closely related to the other elements of our foreign policy. All are parts of an integrated whole. Each is vital.

Our course of action in the last decade has been based on two perceptions growing out of the tragic events which have shaken and bled the world in our generation. We saw, first, that freedom and aggression do not mix; that where a ruler would enslave his neighbors, he must first enslave his own people; and, accordingly, that the cause of peace is served by the defense of popular governments and the institutions of freedom. Secondly, we learned the bitter lesson that freedom does not thrive and may even wither and die under the stress of economic privation and crisis, especially where its roots are shallow.

We sought an answer to both those problems in the United Nations. The charter pledges the member nations to strive to secure their people against both the scourge of war and the curse of material want. The Security Council has the primary responsibility for maintaining the peace. The improvement of the living conditions of the world's peoples is the task of the Economic and Social Council and the specialized agencies.

The obstruction of the Soviet Union, the aggressive conspiracy of the communists of all countries, and the unexpectedly serious difficulties of reconstruction prompted the United States to take additional measures. We went directly to the aid of Greece and Turkey. We undertook the European Recovery Program.

Developments in Europe since the end of hostilities provide a classic example of the interrelation of economics and politics. The free nations of Europe had to regain their economic health in order to resist the encroachments of communism. Yet the gathering momentum of recovery, given impetus by American aid, was endangered by the mounting sense of insecurity against armed attack. The North Atlantic Treaty would allay that fear and free the people of Western Europe to devote their full thought and energy to the valiant effort to achieve recovery. The security value of the treaty would be measurably increased by the provision of American military assistance to build up the security forces of Western Europe. Yet this military assistance must be provided in such a way that it will not detract from the progress of economic recovery.

I think the forces of freedom and democracy are entitled to draw encouragement from the recent trend of events in Western Europe. Since the beginning of the European Recovery Program, totalitarianism in Western Europe has made no advance. In every important election in this area, the people have clearly manifested their support of constitutional government. Communist efforts to impede recovery have been defeated by vigorous governmental action, notably in France and Italy. Labor has become increasingly aware of the dangers of communist agitation. Increased production and financial stability have been stimulated by renewed hope and confidence in the future. Hope and confidence in turn have been augmented by economic recovery. The effects of this marked improvement, both in morale and in actual living conditions, are being felt throughout Western Europe, and beyond.

Yet it would not be prudent to content ourselves merely with the success achieved thus far. We must press forward vigorously to the realization of our immediate objectives. We must go further and devise means for consolidating the gains now being made and for extending them into the future.

It is not enough merely to perpetuate the free institutions of the western world. They must be increasingly developed and made to yield greater benefits for all the members of the human society they are designed to serve. It is not enough to increase the productivity of the individual economic systems of the countries that make up the western community of nations. Means must be found to assure the adequate and equitable distribution of the material things that make for a better life, so that the peoples of this community and the world can share in the benefits that accrue from the common effort.

The fabric of the world economy, of industry, finance, and commerce must be restored. But even that is not enough. We know that at its prewar best, world production and world trade were not adequate to meet the basic needs of human society. We can be sure that the masses of people will no longer be satisfied with half a loaf.

An affirmative approach to the solution of world economic problems is an imperative need of our times. The United States Government has taken the lead in developing such an approach.

While providing the necessary emergency aid, we have persistently pursued a long-range international economic program. We look forward to the day when the differences between doing business abroad and doing business at home will be much less than at present—when currencies will be generally stable and convertible, trade and travel subject to only moderate restraints, and investment subject to fewer risks. To these ends we have been promoting currency stabilization; we have been negotiating trade-barrier reductions; we have been negotiating simplification of travel arrangements; we have been negotiating treaties and agreements covering investments, commerce, transport, and communications; we have been working on a plan to increase the flow of technology, and we have been working in the United Nations and its specialized agencies in a wide variety of fields. Most particularly, we have been working in that oldest and most important field of economic relations among nations—trade.

We have continued our established and effective policy embodied in the Reciprocal Trade Agreements Act. The usefulness of this principle was greatly extended by means of the General Agreement on Tariffs and Trade concluded by 23 of the world's leading trading nations, in 1947. A further extension is expected to result from the negotiations now in progress at Annecy, France, between these countries and 11 others.

The capstone of the economic structure we are seeking to erect is the charter of the International Trade Organization, which President Truman submitted to the Congress last week for ratification. I should like to talk with you about the purposes and principles of the charter.

The ITO charter was drawn up by more than 50 nations which were represented at the United Nations Conference on Trade and Employment at Habana [Havana], in the winter of 1947/48. The Habana conference was the culmination of at least five years of active planning and preparation by our government and the governments of many other countries. When the Conference adjourned, it had produced the most comprehensive international economic agreement ever negotiated.

The goal of the ITO charter is the realization of higher levels of material well-being through the expansion of international trade. For most countries in the modern world, the existence of an efficient trade mechanism is virtually an indispensable condition to economic advancement and the achievement of tolerable standards of living. It is only through such a mechanism that each country is able to specialize in the production of the goods which it can make most effectively and to exchange its output for the goods which other countries are better equipped to make. Where no such mechanism exists, or where it functions erratically and unevenly, the inevitable result is the partial breakdown of specialization, the reduction of the world's output, and the growth of economic discontent. An efficient world trading system is thus a powerful device for helping others, and ourselves as well, to acquire the material means to a better life.

The ITO charter seeks in two ways to create an efficient and expanding world trading system. First, it lays down a detailed code of rules of fair practice to govern the foreign trade policies of member nations. The main objectives of these rules are the elimination or reduction of a wide variety of trade barriers, imposed mainly by governments, and the taking of positive action to deal with difficult problems. Second, it provides for the establishment of an International Trade Organization within the United Nations family, to administer the detailed rules of the charter and to serve as a forum for the international consideration and solution of trade policy problems. . . .

A few years hence, the world will be faced with trade policy problems which cannot even be foreseen, let alone dealt with, today. But the existence of a permanent international forum and a body of tested rules will assure that nations will act with full knowledge of the views and probable reactions of their neighbors. In these circumstances, it seems to me much more than a wistful hope that conciliation and compromise will supplant the economic artillery duels which characterized trade relations in the 1930's.

The charter of the International Trade Organization is thus the beginning of law in the realm of world commerce and the vehicle for the growth of a spirit of mutuality and interdependence in trade relations. I know of no other road to the development of the kind of world trading system in which the world's productive energies can be transformed into the highest level of material wellbeing.

The charter of the International Trade Organization is worthy of the support of all those who believe that peace and progress may be pursued by enabling the people of the world to secure the means to a better life.

29. *The President's Trade Program—Key to the Grand Design*[2]

[EDITOR'S NOTE: *During the 1950's, the Eisenhower Administration had to fight hard merely to get the existing trade legislation renewed—it was renewed in 1953, 1954, 1955, and 1958. President Kennedy succeeded in replacing the Reciprocal Trade Agreements Act with the Trade Expansion Act of 1962. In the following speech, delivered on January 31, 1962, the Under Secretary of State for Political Affairs, George C. McGhee, describes how the trade program fits into the over-all framework of American foreign policy.*]

To some of you it may seem odd that I, the Under Secretary for Political Affairs, should be asked to discuss the background and implications of President Kennedy's proposals for new trade legislation. To others of you, I am sure, this will not seem odd at all. The origins of our present trade problems are political as well as economic. The trade policies of this nation have both political and economic implications, domestically and internationally.

In fact the new trade legislation proposed by the President has far-reaching implications of many kinds. The decision on this proposal will deeply affect our domestic economic life for years to come. This decision will also vitally affect almost every aspect of our international relations—political, economic, military, psychological, and so forth. I will try to illustrate these implications later.

A good place to begin, I suppose, is at the beginning—the beginning of the United States of America. One of the most important elements in the decision of the thirteen original colonies to form a federation under the American Constitution was their determination to eliminate artificial trade barriers among the individual colonies and to permit a free flow of trade across state lines.

This determination has been a major factor ever since in maintaining the political unity and integrity of the United States. It has played an even greater role in making the United States the richest and most economically powerful country in the world today.

For the first 150 years of our national history, our international

[2] SOURCE: George C. McGhee, "The President's Trade Program—Key to the Grand Design," *Department of State Bulletin*, XLVI, No. 1182 (February 19, 1962), 289–93.

trade was a constant source of controversy in our domestic politics —sometimes the only major source of controversy. At first the issues were relatively simple. The infant industries, primarily in the Northeast, wanted tariff protection against the competition of the older and more efficient industries of Great Britain and other nations of Western Europe. The consumers, including some of the industrial producers themselves, wanted to buy goods as cheaply as possible. Most manufactured goods came from abroad. The farmers, especially in the South and West, wanted to sell their surpluses abroad, such as cotton and tobacco. From the administration of Andrew Jackson to the Civil War, the South and West usually controlled our trade and tariff policies.

After that the basic issues did not change, but both the political and economic aspects of our tariff policies became much more complicated because of the reconstruction period, the rapid growth of American industrial power, and our westward expansion. Although some industries and areas were directly affected, it became increasingly difficult for the average citizen to determine where his real interests lay. Today this difficulty has been compounded many times, partly because of the complexity of American economic life and partly because of the diversification of our international interests.

In our efforts to climb out of the great depression one of the most important and far-reaching measures adopted was the repeal of the existing restrictive tariff legislation and the adoption of the Trade Act of 1934, sponsored by Secretary of State Cordell Hull. This legislation, which has been extended and improved several times, has served American interests very well. However, even this legislation has now become obsolete for a variety of reasons, including the following:

First, the emergence of the European Common Market and the prospective enlargement of this market by the adherence of the United Kingdom is creating an entirely new trading world. Under present legislation we are unable to adapt ourselves to this new trading world.

The President does not now have nearly enough bargaining authority to negotiate on behalf of the American people with the expanding Common Market, a market larger than our own in population and potentially larger in purchasing power. Because of our most-favored-nation treaties, the effects of such a negotiation would involve many other nations. The President also lacks authority to negotiate directly with these other nations—with such rising industrial nations as Japan, with the partly industrial members of the British Commonwealth, with our neighbors in Latin America, and with the lesser developed countries of Asia and Africa.

Present legislation permits the President to reduce tariffs only by a very limited amount, and it also requires him to negotiate such reductions on a reciprocal, item-by-item basis. Many nations do not like to negotiate in this manner, and the new European Common Market will eventually become incapable of negotiating in this manner.

Therefore, unless the President is given broader and more flexible bargaining authority, we will be denied full access to the new trading world. We can continue to restrict imports into this country, but we can do little to provide increased opportunities for American industrial and agricultural exports.

Second, in the period since 1934 the United States has been catapulted from a position of political isolation and relative economic isolation to a role involving major political and economic responsibilities.

To give one example, we have assumed responsibility for helping a great many less developed countries to maintain their political independence and to achieve economic and social advancement. We are spending a great deal of money for this purpose, in various kinds of loans and grants. However, a large part of this money may be wasted unless we are able to help the less developed countries to establish a mutually beneficial trading relationship with the rest of the world.

It does very little good to provide aid to a country for the purpose of increasing its production of a basic commodity which is already a glut in world markets. It does very little good to help a less developed country establish new industries unless these countries have a reasonable prospect of selling their surplus industrial products abroad at some future date.

It does very little good to build up a new nation's economy unless that nation has a reasonable assurance of being able to import the goods it will need to sustain its economy. Finally, it does very little good for us to support the political independence of new nations if we are willing to let them become economically dependent upon the Communist bloc.

In all these ways our major role in the world will be undermined unless we are able to develop trade policies that are consistent with that role.

Third, this nation and other free nations have been engaged for many years in an unprecedented struggle for national survival—a kind of world civil war that is sometimes called the "cold war." This struggle has many different facets, and it is easy to concentrate almost exclusively upon one or two facets and to ignore the others.

Thus far, this struggle has involved the threat of devastating military force, as well as the occasional application of limited military force, both overtly and covertly. For the most part, however, the struggle is being fought by a wide variety of nonmilitary techniques—political, economic, diplomatic, psychological, and so forth.

The economic component of this struggle is a very important one. The Sino-Soviet bloc seems determined to make as many free nations as possible, especially the less developed nations, economic dependencies of the Communist empire through various aid and trade arrangements. The bloc also seems determined to subject the Western industrial world to ruinous competition wherever it can. The bloc is also eager to acquire strategic goods—manufactured goods and raw materials—which it does not possess in adequate quantity or quality.

Finally, of course, the Sino-Soviet rulers are determined to prove to the entire world the superiority and invincibility of the Communist political and economic system, to prove that the industrial nations cannot survive with their systems of political democracy and private enterprise, and to prove that the less developed nations can fulfill their aspirations only by adopting a Communist-type political and economic discipline.

Our present trade legislation does not give the United States the tools needed to meet this multipronged Communist threat. We cannot protect our own national security adequately, nor can we adequately help to protect the independence of other free nations.

I turn now to the last, but not the least, reason why present trade legislation is inadequate. We have a domestic economic interest in accelerating growth, preventing inflation, and maintaining a sound balance in our international payments. A long-term solution to these problems can be achieved only if we are able to develop and maintain the full potential of our trading relationships with Western Europe and the rest of the world. For example, we may need to increase our imports considerably, and it is equally clear that we will need to expand our exports to an even greater extent. We simply cannot do these things under existing trade legislation. . . .

Our ultimate political goal is strength and unity in the free world —the creation of what the President has called a community of free world nations. In the long run unity among free nations cannot be assured by force, by psychological strategy, or even by diplomacy. Unity will ultimately depend upon the development of a real community of interests, involving all of the varied activities and aspirations of man. Trade is the warp and woof of such a community.

Trade is the one most universal common denominator among the pursuits of man. Trade provides strength through independence. The attraction to free world nations of participation in the trade of the free world, which aggregates $115 billion a year, dwarfs the opportunities offered by the $4-billion trade between the free world and the bloc.

The adoption of the new trade legislation can have a tremendous psychological impact throughout the world. It will demonstrate that the American people are prepared to practice the principles of free competitive enterprise that we have preached for so many years. It will demonstrate that the empirical mixture of public and private enterprise developed by Western societies is superior to totalitarian systems.

It will also demonstrate the ancient fallacies of Communist theory and strategy. The Communists have always maintained that the conflicts among the nations of the so-called capitalist world—and the conflicts among special interests within these nations—will eventually bring Western civilization to a state of disintegration and decadence.

The European Common Market, with its high rate of economic growth, is already confounding the Communist theories. We can join in confounding Communist theory still more. We can prove conclusively that communism is neither desirable nor inevitable. We can prove that it is not even an economic system fathered by Marx and Lenin but is rather a new form of feudalism dressed up in the psychology of Pavlov and the technology of the Western industrial revolution.

All that I have said adds up to one fact. The enactment of the new trade legislation proposed by President Kennedy will enable the Government and people of the United States to take a powerful new initiative in domestic and international affairs. For many years, under various administrations, the American people have worried about specific and dangerous crises—in China, Korea, Berlin, Hungary, Suez, Lebanon, Cuba, Laos, the Congo, and Vietnam. For years they have demanded the United States "seize the initiative."

And this is, however, not always easy to do. The peaceful house-holder is rarely able to take the initiative against the burglar. But we now have an opportunity. We can and must take advantage of it to seize the initiative. By doing so, we can accomplish a combination of results that will far overshadow the significance of particular crises and will help us to reduce the number and diminish the proportions of future crises.

I do not want to imply that the new trade legislation will automatically solve the problems of American domestic life nor all of the problems of our international relations. This is not a panacea. It is merely a set of tools. But it is a set of tools that we cannot afford to do without.

We have a world to gain—not for ourselves alone but for the cause of peace and freedom, for the things that gave this nation birth and nurtured it. Our ultimate goal, as stated by President Wilson when we entered the First World War, is a universal concert of free peoples that shall encircle the globe and "make the world itself at last free." As President Wilson also said on that occasion, God helping us, we can do no other.

30. *Aid and Trade*[3]

[EDITOR'S NOTE: *In the hearings on the Mutual Security Act of 1953, Senator J. W. Fulbright questioned Mutual Security Agency Director Harold E. Stassen on the relationship between aid and trade.*]

SENATOR FULBRIGHT: Are these estimates that you have made based upon no change in our trade policies of this country?

MR. STASSEN: Yes, they are based on the estimate that the reciprocal trade legislation be extended as it is for 1 year, and that a study proceed of the whole over-all trade picture and economic picture.

SENATOR FULBRIGHT: If Congress should increase the obstacles to the importation of goods would that not affect the estimates that you have made?

MR. STASSEN: Yes, it would. It would create an increased requirement for aid, or produce more serious consequences overseas if aid were not increased.

[3] SOURCE: *Mutual Security Act of 1953*, Hearings before the Senate Committee on Foreign Relations, 83d Cong., 1st sess. (Washington, D.C.: Government Printing Office, 1953), pp. 71–72.

Senator Fulbright: Well, assuming your estimates of what are needed are correct, which I think we ought to assume, then it would necessarily follow that if we cut off the importation of the goods which you represented here in your chart a moment ago, and if you were to achieve the objective, you would have to increase the amount appropriated under this bill, would you not?

Mr. Stassen: That is a fair conclusion, but that would not be the most serious consequence. If you stopped any appreciable amount of imports from their present level, you would also cut back on the export side, and then you would start internal economic effects in the United States that could be very, very serious.

In other words, as I testified to another committee yesterday, the year in which our imports were at an all-time low was 1933. At that time we also had very serious unemployment inside the United States, we had losses in business, and we had very low agricultural income; in other words, you had a whole series of interrelated adverse internal economic factors come to bear.

Now, it is never possible to say which one of these causes the other, but you can see a pattern of them all fitting together in a bad picture when you chop down to an inordinately low amount the imports and, consequently, reflect back by chopping off exports, and you fit into a descending economic situation.

Senator Fulbright: Well, with regard to the question asked you by Senator Smith about how long this aid program would last, is it not very closely associated with the idea of when the balance of payments may be reached under normal trade policies? If we could increase our imports to balance our exports, that in itself would end the necessity for much of this aid outside of specific military matters, would it not?

Mr. Stassen: Outside of strictly military matters and outside of some comparatively minor, but important, amounts for the technical assistance and mutual development in the less developed countries.

Senator Fulbright: Yes. I mean is it not true that the only— well, I do not like to say only—but the logical way to end the necessity for aid is to balance our payments in the economic field, that is, we ought to import as much as we sell—buy as much as we sell—is that not really the principle involved?

Mr. Stassen: Well, of course, you have to study the internal effect of increased imports, and there are problems, too, there, affecting special industries and special labor and agricultural situations.

That is why I feel the President's recommendation for a new and intensive study for a year is highly desirable.

SENATOR FULBRIGHT: I could not agree with you more. I agree it is highly desirable, but from what we know now, unless we can balance those imports, the people that we consider to be our friends will have to make a drastic reduction in their standard of living or we shall have to make it up by gifts. Isn't it true that they must either change their standard of living by a very substantial amount or we must make up the balance? Have we not been making up that balance in grants for a number of years?

MR. STASSEN: Yes, if you further qualify it with the defense matériel side, which is not quite met by that picture, and the fact that there are other economic effects that occur in an adverse way under those circumstances, I would say that you are correctly describing the sort of general relationship of these factors.

SENATOR FULBRIGHT: I do think it is important. As you have said, these estimates are based on an assumption that there certainly would not be any obstacles to trade—that it would remain as it is. It indicates, therefore, that there is a close relationship between our trade policies and this program, and they should be considered together.

MR. STASSEN: There is a close relationship; yes. . . .

XI

The American Economy
and Foreign Aid

Foreign aid, like defense spending and other techniques of state-craft, has an impact on the American economy. Since this fact is, for policy-makers, a basic assumption in the planning of the aid program, the aid analyst should be aware of just what effects the program has on the economy and of the political attitudes toward these effects.

31. *Goldwater on Foreign Aid and the Balance of Payments*[1]

[EDITOR'S NOTE: *Barry Goldwater, the 1964 Republican nominee for President, analyzes the relationship between aid and the balance of payments in the excerpt below. The following points should be noted: (1) Goldwater is wrong in saying that the balance of trade includes the amount of money Americans invest overseas. On the contrary, the balance of trade includes only imports and exports and excludes international capital movements. (2) It is misleading for Goldwater to attach significance to the fact that the balance-of-payments deficit and the foreign-aid outlay both were approximately $4 billion. The fact that both figures approached $4 billion does not indicate a direct causal relationship. (3) It is also misleading for Goldwater to imply that if exports exceed imports, dollars spent on imports do not "cause" balance-of-payments difficulties. In balance-of-payments statistics, each dollar paid to a foreigner—whether for imports or as aid—is valued equally.*]

Two important developments were reported recently on the same day by the nation's press and other news media.

[1] SOURCE: Barry Goldwater, "Foreign Aid and the Balance of Payments," *Los Angeles Times*, September 12, 1963. Copyright 1963, *Los Angeles Times*. Reprinted with permission.

186

These developments were reported in separate stories; their significance, however, would have been much more evident had they been contained in a single article.

The first story was headlined "U.S. Gold Outgo Tops $1 Billion," while the second one was headlined "McNamara, Rusk Appeal for Aid Bill."

At first glance, the United States balance-of-payments problem and the Kennedy Administration's efforts to continue our huge foreign-aid program may not seem related in any way. The fact is that foreign aid and the loss of our gold are intimately connected; in fact, one is the partial cause of the other.

The much discussed balance-of-payments situation is made up of two distinct elements. The first is America's commercial trade balance; whether we export more goods and services to other countries or import more into the United States determines this balance. This balance of trade also includes the amount of money Americans invest overseas as compared with the amount foreigners invest in our country.

The other element in the balance-of-payments problem is the spending by the United States Government in foreign nations. This spending is largely in the area of grants and loans to other countries—in short, the foreign aid spending which has continued since World War II.

The United States has been burdened with a substantial deficit in its over-all balance of payments for several years. This deficit reached crisis proportions in 1960, when $3.9 billion was lost to the United States.

The Kennedy Administration has attempted to stem this outflow of gold by several means. Last year, the so-called Trade Expansion Act was passed in an effort to improve our trade balance. More recently, restrictions were placed upon American investments in foreign securities.

It is ironic to note that these Kennedy moves to prevent devaluation of the dollar and to forestall runaway inflation have been directed at the trade balance only. This is ironic, because the United States has a favorable trade balance; we export more than we import.

I suggest that these efforts by the administration are misdirected. The cause of the weakening position of the dollar lies elsewhere, specifically in the government's spending overseas.

The Commerce Department has projected a $4.2 billion deficit for 1963, a new record. Nevertheless, we find President Kennedy and his lieutenants, Secretary of Defense Robert McNamara and Secretary of State Dean Rusk, urging that the United States spend more than $4 billion on foreign aid.

It doesn't take a mathematical genius to figure out that our wasteful foreign-aid payments are the direct cause of our balance of payments crisis. I suggest that this self-induced undercutting of our own currency and possibly of our own economy is ludicrous.

It's about time we woke up. The United States can't go on carrying the world on its shoulders if its currency is fatally weakened. In its own best interests, the administration should be slashing its own recommendations to Congress in the field of economic aid.

I suggest that it is the failure of the New Frontier to take a hard-headed, realistic approach to the foreign-aid problem that not only is aggravating the balance-of-payments problem, but also undermining the faith of foreign nations in the U.S. dollar.

32. The Impact of Foreign Aid on the American Economy[2]

[EDITOR'S NOTE: David E. Bell, the Administrator of AID, discussed the relation between aid and the domestic economy in the following speech, which he delivered in Pittsburgh on October 23, 1963.]

It is not yet as widely understood as it should be that since late 1959 a drastic change in procurement policy has taken place regarding the expenditure of our foreign aid funds. With few—and diminishing—exceptions, we now limit the use of our foreign aid appropriations to the procurement of United States goods and services. This change was made to minimize the impact of the foreign assistance program on the U.S. balance-of-payments deficit.

The resulting figures speak for themselves. Of the $2.4 billion of economic aid committed in fiscal year 1963, $1.9 billion, 80 percent of the total, will be spent directly in the United States for U.S. goods and services.

With respect to individual commodities the effect of the changed policy is very plain. For example, in 1960, before the new policy took effect, only 11 percent of the iron and steel products financed

2 SOURCE: David E. Bell, "The Impact of Foreign Aid on the American Economy," Department of State Bulletin, XLIX, No. 1274 (November 25, 1963), 830–31.

by foreign aid appropriations came from American steel mills; for the first 9 months of 1963, 87 percent was purchased from U.S. producers. In 1960, 11 percent of the nonferrous metals financed under foreign aid came from the United States; for the first 9 months of 1963, 92 percent were purchased in the United States. For fertilizer the percentage rose from 17 percent to 97 percent. And similar figures could be given for many other products.

Furthermore, the restriction of foreign aid spending to U.S. goods and services means that a substantial share of U.S. exports in some lines is now financed by our foreign aid program. For example, in calendar year 1962, one-third of U.S. exports of locomotives, one-third of U.S. exports of fertilizer, and 21 percent of U.S. exports of iron and steel products were among the commodities purchased under the foreign aid program to assist the economic development of countries in Asia, Africa, and Latin America.

Under these new policies the foreign aid program today accounts for a relatively small and declining element in the U.S. balance-of-payments deficit. The outflow of dollars under foreign aid next year is estimated at about a half billion dollars—far smaller than the $2.5 billion spent abroad each year by U.S. tourists, or the nearly $3 billion invested abroad each year by U.S. business.

I do not believe these facts are as well understood in the Congress as they need to be. Some Members of the House of Representatives who voted several weeks ago for a substantial cut in this year's foreign aid bill apparently did so in the mistaken belief that the cut would reduce the U.S. balance-of-payments deficit by an equivalent amount. In fact, the major appropriation items that were cut by the House—Alliance for Progress lending, development lending elsewhere in the world, and military assistance—are tied virtually 100 percent to U.S. procurement. The main direct effect of the House cut therefore would be to reduce U.S. exports, not to reduce the balance-of-payments deficit.

The facts I have cited thus far demonstrate that the U.S. foreign assistance program today has a major effect in financing U.S. exports of goods and services, and a relatively small and declining effect on the U.S. balance-of-payments deficit.

Foreign aid today in overwhelming degree takes the form of U.S. goods and services—not U.S. dollars—going out to help the underdeveloped countries. And in the process, according to a private planning group's estimate, American assistance to the developing countries is responsible for at least several hundred thousand American jobs.

Impressive as these statistics are, they tell only part of the story of the impact on the American economy.

Our foreign aid programs include a series of measures designed to encourage and assist U.S. private investment in the underdeveloped countries. We strongly believe that U.S. private capital and know-how can make a major contribution to economic development, not only in Latin America but in Africa and Asia as well.

Over and above the immediate impact on U.S. exports and foreign investment, the aid program, in the process of helping in the economic development of peoples in Asia, Africa, and Latin America, is acquainting them with U.S. goods, opening up markets for U.S. businesses, and establishing favorable conditions for U.S. private investment abroad.

Our biggest present export customers are the developed countries of Western Europe and Japan, whom we assisted in the 1940's and early 1950's, and where aid financing is no longer necessary. In the period from 1950 to 1962, our exports to Europe doubled. Our exports to Japan have tripled in the past decade.

In the developing countries, AID-administered economic assistance programs are now playing a major role in introducing U.S. products and paving the way for an economic growth that will surely lead to expanded markets for U.S. exports. There are already signs that in some developing countries trade is beginning to fol- there were increases in U.S. commercial exports (not aid-financed) of 14 percent to Taiwan, 28 percent to Colombia, and 76 percent low aid, as it did in Europe. As examples, over the past 5 years to Israel.

I cite these figures not as a justification for foreign aid. Its justification rests on broader grounds. But I bring them to your attention to show that the cost of foreign aid is not the drain on American gold supply, economy, or taxpayers that it is sometimes pictured to be. The President requested for fiscal year 1964 a program costing $4.5 billion. This is a large sum of money, but it should be kept in perspective. It represents 0.7 percent of our gross national product and 4 percent of the Federal budget. Our economy has been operating in recent years with $35–$40 billion of unused capacity; total mutual defense and assistance expenditures are only about 10 percent of that unused capacity. It surely cannot be argued that this amount constitutes a serious strain on our national resources, nor can it be argued that it is an excessive burden for the wealthiest nation in the world. . . .

33. *Aid and the Balance of Payments*[3]

[EDITOR'S NOTE: *This is an excerpt from a statement David E. Bell originally made before the Senate Committee on Banking and Currency. Later, during the 1965 hearings on foreign aid, the statement was submitted to the House Committee on Foreign Affairs.*]

MR. BELL: Mr. Chairman, thank you for the privilege of appearing before this Committee. As Administrator of the Agency for International Development, I am particularly pleased that these hearings are being held, for they present an excellent opportunity to give the facts to the Congress, and to attempt to clear up some of the misconceptions surrounding the relation of aid to our balance of payments.

Foreign aid is by its very nature closely involved with the flow of payments. Thus each action and step taken by AID is and must be evaluated from the point of view of our balance-of-payments situation.

The foreign aid program provides goods and services to other countries which they cannot obtain through normal means—through their export earnings and through obtaining capital on commercial terms and by private investment. A successful aid program is one which enables the recipient country to strengthen its economy to the point where it can obtain goods and services it needs for steady expansion and growth by normal trade and normal capital movements, and without further need for aid grants and soft loans. This is what was achieved in Western Europe under the Marshall Plan, and has since been achieved in Japan, Spain, Greece, Taiwan, and other countries.

It is plainly important to seek to carry out this important national program, like any other, at minimum cost to the United States.

In the first years of the U.S. foreign aid program after World War II, during the Marshall Plan and most of the 1950's, our aid appropriations were, in general, spent wherever in the world prices were lowest. During the Marshall Plan period, of course, the

[3] SOURCE: *Foreign Assistance Act of 1965*, Hearings before the House Committee on Foreign Affairs, 89th Cong., 1st sess. (Washington, D.C.: Government Printing Office, 1965), pp. 1277–81.

United States was the only major source in the world for most of the goods those countries needed. Therefore most of the aid dollars, although not tied to U.S. procurement, were spent in this country. Later in the 1950's the revived European economies became increasingly effective competitors for U.S. aid purchases.

Beginning in 1959, in response to the changed situation of the U.S. balance of payments, our policy respecting aid purchasers was changed. Today, with small exceptions, aid appropriations can only be spent in the United States, for goods and services produced in this country. This has undoubtedly raised the cost to the Federal budget of providing a given amount of goods and services under the aid program, since some items are being purchased with aid appropriations in the United States which could be bought more cheaply in other countries. But our present policies are intended to minimize the adverse effect of the aid program on the balance of payments, even if that results in some increased cost to the budget.

There are two approaches to measuring the impact of AID's expenditures on the balance of payments. The first, which might be called the accounting approach, measures the direct result of the AID spending: are the dollars appropriated by the Congress spent directly in this country or spent abroad or transferred to another country or to an international organization.

Under this method of measurement, which is similar to the Department of Commerce figures on the balance of payments, during fiscal year 1964—the latest data available—the gross adverse effect on the U.S. balance of payments of AID's economic assistance programs was about $513 million.

We have now received preliminary estimates for the calendar year 1964 which show substantial further improvement. The payments abroad dropped to about $400 million. This is offset by repayments of past assistance extended by AID and predecessor agencies of over $150 million, making a net effect of about $250 million.

The current expenditure rate under our economic assistance program is almost exactly $2 billion per year. Thus in 1964, for every dollar of economic aid extended, 20 cents showed as a current adverse impact in our balance of payments—not considering current or future receipts.

Put the other way round, 80 percent of AID's expenditures last year represented not dollars going abroad, but steel, machinery, fertilizer, and other goods and services purchased in the United States.

Under these circumstances, of course, a cut in AID appropriations would primarily reduce U.S. exports, and would have only a very small effect on the balance of payments.

Moreover, the proportion of appropriations spent in the United States is rising. Eighty-five percent of new obligations are being committed for direct expenditure in the United States. . . .

This then is the accounting measure of the direct flow of dollars abroad resulting from our economic aid program.

The true net economic effect of foreign assistance on our balance of payments cannot be measured so simply. This is because there are indirect effects not revealed by the direct accounts. A substantial portion of the dollars that go out under our aid program, to the United Nations, for example, comes back through regular commercial channels for purchases of U.S. goods.

Dollars which go out and enter the economy of a less developed country may be used later by that country to buy needed goods in the U.S. market or may go through trade channels to a third country, which will use the dollars for purchase of goods in the U.S. market.

These are examples of the so-called feedback effect; which means that the effect of aid outflows on the U.S. balance of payments is overstated, because dollar outflows to a considerable extent are immediately reflected in increased U.S. export sales for dollars.

But there is another indirect effect in the opposite direction. When an aid recipient is able to buy U.S. imports under a tied loan; that is, has a letter of credit opened in a U.S. bank which can only be spent in the United States, then that country may use the tied dollars to buy goods that it would have otherwise bought with dollars it already owns. These other dollars—free exchange—are thus available for other purchases either in the United States or elsewhere. This is the so-called substitution effect; meaning that to some extent aid-financed imports are substituted for imports that would have been bought with free dollars and, to this extent, the effect of tied aid on the U.S. balance of payments is understated.

There are no good estimates of the size of the feedback and substitution effects. Only indirect evidence is available. With respect to the question of how much substitution occurs, for example, it is clear that most of the less developed countries have severe shortages of dollars, and need more goods from the United States than they can afford, even with the addition of aid. Furthermore, statistics do not indicate that a dropoff in commercial trade occurs when there is an increase in aid. Quite the opposite. The most frequently cited example is Latin America. While expenditures under the Alliance for Progress have been increasing over the past 3 years, so have Latin American purchases from the United States through regular commercial channels. In fact, according to preliminary estimates, commercial U.S. exports to Latin America increased by $500 million in 1964 alone. Thus it is the best guess of the economists who have studied these matters that the amount of substitution is relatively small.

Over-all, it is our conclusion that the indirect economic effects of aid on our balance of payments roughly balance each other and, even allowing for some variation from time to time, the true effect of aid on our balance of payments would not differ very much in either direction from the figures shown by the accounting estimates referred to earlier.

To sum up, our balance-of-payments figures show, by the accounting measure, the share of our expenditures made directly for U.S. goods and services is 80 percent and rising, and the share paid to foreigners and international organizations is 20 percent and falling. These figures do not take into account indirect effects, but it is our best guess that they would be little different if they did. AID dollars spent abroad which return quickly in payment for commercial exports roughly offset the amount of AID financing for goods that would have been exported anyway. As nearly as we can tell these two imperfections roughly cancel each other out and 15 to 20 percent is a valid indication of the real adverse impact of aid on the U.S. balance of payments. . . .

Looking beyond the immediate present, the foreign aid program has a number of effects which are positively beneficial to our balance of payments.

First, our aid today is overwhelmingly in the form of dollar repayable loans, unlike the situation under the Marshall Plan, when 90 percent of our aid was in the form of grants. Future repayments of interest and principal on today's loans will be a positive factor in our balance of payments.

Secondly, the evidence is plain that countries which with our aid achieve steady economic growth become increasingly better markets for U.S. exports and more attractive places for U.S. investment abroad. Over the last 15 years our exports to Europe have doubled and our exports to Japan have tripled. As other countries

—Spain, Greece, Taiwan, and so on—gain economic momentum and our aid comes to an end the same kind of result is evident.

Moreover, the aid program in case after case has directly led to the introduction of American products and services in other countries, and to follow-on markets unrelated to the aid program. Aid has in fact been one of our best export promotion mechanisms. . . .

34. *Congressional Interest in the Domestic Impact of Aid*[4]

[EDITOR'S NOTE: *Legislators like to be able to justify expensive programs in terms of the immediate economic interests of their constituents. However, this is difficult to do with the aid program. In the following excerpt from a Congressional hearing, Senator George Aiken* (R., *Vermont*) *questions Eric Johnston, then Chairman of the International Development Advisory Board.*]

SENATOR AIKEN: Mr. Johnston, a short time ago I had a letter from a supposedly well-informed constituent insisting, as many others do these days, that the budget be cut very materially.

He does not seem to take kindly to my suggestions as to where the budget could best be cut, so this morning I got a letter from him presenting the solution to this problem, and that is to cut out the foreign aid program because that does not affect us at home except that it comes out of our pockets. If we could cut that out, we would have that much more money for ourselves.

I have had the mistaken idea that the foreign aid program did contribute somewhat to the gross national production of this country: I was wondering if your organization has made any study as to what extent the $3.8 billion appropriation for foreign programs last year did contribute to the $412 billion gross national product of this country.

MR. JOHNSTON: Senator, we have made no specific study of this problem as being outside of our field, but I do want to say this to you and to the constituent who has written you, foreign relations have a more profound effect upon America than any other single factor.

The huge budget that we now have is the result of our foreign relations, past as well as present. What happens in other countries

[4] SOURCE: *The Foreign Aid Program*, Hearings before the Senate Special Committee to Study the Foreign Aid Program, 85th Cong., 1st sess. (Washington, D.C.: Government Printing Office, 1957), pp. 301–3.

has a profound effect upon the tax load that we bear, upon the Defense Establishment we have to support, upon the public debt and the interest that we have to pay on it, upon the disposition of our surpluses abroad, upon a whole group of subjects.

If we are going to have stability in the world, we do not feel that you can have that stability just in America.

We cannot live alone and like it. We have got to live as a part of the world. Therefore the world must have some stability. If we can contribute to that stability of the world by what we consider to be a very small portion of our total income, if that contributes to the stability of the world so that we can have peace and can avoid slaughter of human beings and can avoid expenditures for war, then certainly it contributes to the development of America and to the well-being of your constituent.

SENATOR AIKEN: Yes. Some of our correspondents, however, resolve their problems to the common denominator of the dollar. They want to know how many dollars it takes out of our pockets. I think we have to show them how many dollars remain in our pockets and how much these programs contribute to the gross national product of this country, because that is the language that they understand.

It is pretty difficult to talk with them on social and moral grounds sometimes. But I believe you point out, out of the $3.8 billion appropriated last year, some $2 billion of it went for military hardware and equipment.

MR. JOHNSTON: Right.

SENATOR AIKEN: That certainly all comes back to this country; doesn't it?

MR. JOHNSTON: Most of it is spent in this country, some for outmoded military equipment of only marginal value to us.

SENATOR AIKEN: It was produced by our own economy.

MR. JOHNSTON: That is right.

SENATOR AIKEN: The metal came from our mines and furnished work for the miners and income for the owners.

The railroads don't carry those things free, I am sure. They never did for me.

MR. JOHNSTON: I am sure they don't. They have not started that.

SENATOR AIKEN: And isn't it safe to say that $3 billion in a business could be multiplied several times over in estimating its contribution to the gross national product?

MR. JOHNSTON: I think that might be true, but only if we were faced with unemployment in this country.

The best answer to your constituent, it seems to me, was given by the President of the United States in his speech yesterday before the Advertising Council. He said that the great aspirations of mankind for peace must take precedence over our desire to reduce taxes, over our desire for immediate material comfort.

SENATOR AIKEN: Very well.

Now how are we going to sell this situation to the people who are very critical of foreign aid programs? How are you going to show them that perhaps instead of taking money out of their pockets, it puts money in their pockets?

MR. JOHNSTON: That is a very good question you have asked and in my opinion one of the most important questions that you have asked.

The most important thing we can do, Senator, is to make clear to the American people how much money is being spent and what it is doing for them.

They should know that most of the foreign aid money is for military hardware and the support of the military establishments of our allies. This is as much a part of our national defense as is the purchase of tanks for our own army. Furthermore, 90 percent of all military aid funds are spent right here in the United States.

They should know that only a small part of total foreign aid is for economic development abroad. Certainly, it is less than $1 billion out of the $3.8 billion appropriated under the Mutual Security Act for this fiscal year. And incidentally, 75 percent of all economic aid funds are spent in the United States.

They should be told that we hope that this small amount of money will help to produce healthy conditions abroad so that the causes of war can be reduced. If this happens, our economic aid expenditures will have saved untold amounts of money and lives. . . .

35. Congress and Aid: 1962[5]

[EDITOR'S NOTE: *In the 1962 hearings on foreign aid, Senator Alexander Wiley (R., Wisconsin) spoke on the impact of aid on the domestic economy. His interest is similar to that expressed earlier by Senator Aiken (see Document 34)*].

SENATOR WILEY: Just before I came here, I received a telephone call from a prominent businessman who is quite a bit agitated about the money we were voting. I am interested in getting your

[5] SOURCE: *Foreign Assistance Act of 1962*, Hearings before the Senate Committee on Foreign Relations, 87th Cong., 1st sess. (Washington, D.C.: Government Printing Office, 1962), pp. 20–21.

answer why this $4.8 billion is justified at this time. In other words: (1) how many jobs does it create in this country, (2) how much of this money stays here, and (3) is there a deterrent element to war in the program?

I think, sir, that you have to do an awful good job for the country so it will see the real basic reasons for our continuing the expenditures of these vast sums.

I say this telephone call was from a very levelheaded fellow, a businessman. All of which I feel means that there is a tremendous responsibility upon this administration.

You have different groups. General Walker testified yesterday. You have the Birch group and others that are causing a great segment of the American people apparently to wonder—as this fellow said this morning—"Are we going nuts?" I did the best I could to explain to him a few things.

Now, I am giving you the opportunity. You are representing this country in a department that means a great deal. You have the confidence of a great many people.

I think we should know and get a breakdown. People get an idea you are just taking this money and shoving it out.

I think probably I have said enough. Now it is your turn.

SECRETARY RUSK: Thank you very much, Senator Wiley. I do believe that we in the administration must accept responsibility for explaining and defending this program to the American people.

I am sure that Members of Congress who vote upon it feel the same obligation to their own constituents. And I am happy to comment on certain questions that you raised.

On the matter of jobs, our best estimate is—and this can only be an estimate—is that some 700,000 jobs do turn on the activities of the foreign aid program, in its purchases, its services, and all the rest of it.

SENATOR WILEY: That is, it will take 700,000 Americans to produce the American goods that the program needs.

SECRETARY RUSK: At least that many are involved in the production of the goods and services which are utilized in the program; yes, sir.

SENATOR WILEY: Does that include the delivery?

SECRETARY RUSK: Yes—in most part.

Now, on the percentage spent in this country, we anticipate that about 78 percent of it would be spent here this year, and that figure continues to go up. If you count military assistance and Public Law 480, it would be in the order of 85 percent.

But we are very much aware of the impact of the management of the AID program on the gold problem, and are trying to manage it with prudence in the light of our general position in gold.

Now, on the matter of the importance of the program, Senator, it is true that the cost of this program rests upon every taxpaying home in the country, and that means practically all Americans. One of the things that we are constantly having to impress upon our friends abroad is that these funds do not come out of some mountain somewhere, where we go in and shovel out this money from some mysterious source. This comes out of taxes, and every taxpayer has his share in it. So we do not minimize the burden of this program on the American people.

But let me also emphasize, Senator, that the stakes in this program reach into every home.

We have, for example, at the present time, American troops in every continent, doing their duty with respect to the preservation of peace and freedom in this world. The kind of world in which we are going to be living in these next several years ahead of us will have a great deal to do with what kind of homes we are going to be able to have here in this country, whether we shall be able to live out our lives in reasonable sanity, plan our families' futures, get on with the great unfinished business of our own country.

This will be basically affected by what is happening in other continents—because if they are disturbed, if they are in revolution and turmoil, if they are the victims of aggression, then there is no serenity here for us in this country.

And so we believe that just as the costs move into every home, so do the returns, so do the stakes, so do the goals, so do the targets. And we feel that it is of fundamental importance for us to do what we can—and here we are talking about less than 1 percent of our gross national product—to do what we can to get on with this business of building a peaceful world that we have committed ourselves to on a bipartisan basis for the last 20 years in our country. And this too is important to all of our citizens.

We don't minimize the burden. We don't minimize the stakes. And I am one of those who thinks that we must not abandon the field to the enemy. We must continue this effort in many ways. AID is one of them. And the burdens to us are burdens which we not only can afford, but burdens which we cannot dare not to bear. . . .

XII

Agriculture and Foreign Aid

Most foreign-policy decisions are influenced to some extent by domestic political considerations. Nowhere is this better illustrated than in the use of agricultural commodities as a form of foreign aid. P.L. 480 activities, which constitute one of America's largest aid programs, are not considered primarily in terms of foreign policy by many Legislative and Executive officials. Instead, they are perceived merely as a convenient means for Congress and the Department of Agriculture to get rid of huge amounts of surplus commodities that cause too many embarrassing questions about the cost of subsidizing farmers.

The interplay between domestic and international politics is amply illustrated by the role agriculture plays in the American aid program. The main points of controversy have been: (1) Should the "cost" of P.L. 480 activities be charged against the Department of Agriculture or against the Department of State, i.e., against foreign or domestic policy? (2) To what extent can surplus agricultural commodities, such as wheat, cotton, tobacco, soy beans, and rice, be substituted for dollars in the aid program? (3) To what extent can the "local currencies" acquired through P.L. 480 "sales" be used as a substitute for dollars in the aid program? (4) What is the effect of surplus-commodity disposal on the recipient nation? (5) What is the effect of such disposal on agricultural exports of nonrecipient nations?

36. *The Problem Foreseen*[1]

[EDITOR'S NOTE: *In 1950, Gordon Gray (see Document 6, Chapter IV) accurately forecast the problems of the coming decade with regard to the relation between agriculture and foreign policy.*]

A basic objective of U.S. agricultural policy is to improve the economic position of the American farmer by increasing his real in-

[1] SOURCE: Gordon Gray, *Report to the President on Foreign Economic Policies* (Washington, D.C.: Government Printing Office, 1950), pp. 84–87.

come. Given this objective, agricultural policies tend ordinarily to be formulated predominantly within the framework of domestic economic problems, circumstances, and considerations. Despite its preeminently domestic orientation, however, our agricultural policy has broad ramifications which make it in fact, if not by design, a fundamental part of our foreign economic policy. By and large, those aspects of our peacetime farm policy which bear most directly on our foreign relations were not formulated with particular foreign policy objectives in mind, but have, in the main, developed out of the basic elements of our farm programs. It should not be surprising, therefore, that there are important points of conflict between our farm programs and our foreign economic policies.

The foreign policy implications of our agricultural programs are of great importance because of the central position of the United States in the international agricultural economy. In 1949 or 1949/ 50, for example, the United States supplied about 39 percent of the world's wheat exports, about 49 percent of the cotton exports, and 41 percent of the tobacco exports. Likewise, the United States took 28 percent of the world's sugar exports and 21 percent of the wool exports. Thus U.S. agricultural policy is a matter of vital concern to the rest of the world. We should continue more vigorously to seek to reach both our domestic agricultural and foreign objectives, in ways which will achieve a closer compatibility between them.

A present keystone of our agricultural policy is the price-support program, under which the Federal Government maintains a floor under the prices of many farm products, either through direct public purchases or through nonrecourse loans. In wartime or other emergency circumstances when the demand for agricultural products is very great relative to production capacity, price supports have served the very useful purpose of minimizing farmers' risks and thus encouraging maximum production. The use of price supports during and immediately after World War II was a major factor in making possible the enormous increases in our output of farm products, and in providing supplies of food and fiber which saved many foreign countries from extreme hardship.

At the other times, however, in the absence of inflationary pressures, price supports have tended to maintain a level of farm prices which tend to encourage a volume of production of many commodities in excess of the amount saleable at the support price. Unless output is restricted, a surplus is produced which cannot be sold in the market at the support price, and which must necessarily be acquired and held by the government. In this situation, government stocks tend to grow unless the market price rises above the support price, in which case the government is permitted by law to sell its holdings in the market, or unless the government is able to dispose of its stocks at cut prices, plus certain other charges, for special uses which will not compete with sales in the regular market.

When total stocks in relation to prospective production and requirements for a price-supported commodity reach the point at which, under present legislation, it is no longer considered feasible to allow stocks to increase further, controls become necessary. These controls take the form of acreage allotments, marketing quotas, and marketing agreements or orders, restricting the amount which each producer is allowed to sell. The purpose of these measures is to reduce the supply of the commodity to the amount which can be sold in the market at the support price, so that government holdings need not increase further.

Given these basic components of our long-range farm policy, certain consequences follow, which have a direct bearing on our foreign economic relations. *First*, the increase in prices of some important agricultural exports, which often results from the provision of price supports, raises the cost of vital imports to foreign countries and thus tends to reduce their real incomes. This is one factor which has often led foreign countries in self-defense to expand their own frequently inefficient production of agricultural products, thus reducing their reliance on imports, and to encourage the use of substitutes for imports, such as synthetic fibers instead of cotton. Both of these reactions tend ultimately to reduce the foreign market for U.S. agricultural exports and to involve a wasteful use of productive resources.

Second, when price supports raise domestic prices above the world prices, imports of internationally-traded commodities would begin to flow into the United States in abnormally large volume unless special measures were applied to control imports. In the absence of such measures, the United States Government would be supporting, not only the domestic price, but the world price as well. Consequently, the price-support program has led to the imposition of import quotas and import licensing of a number of agricultural products. Moreover, in order to facilitate the liquidation of stocks of some commodities acquired through support operations, absolute embargoes have been applied to the importation of these products. Some, at least, of these restrictions reduce imports below the levels which would prevail in the absence of both domestic price supports and special import controls, which may impair the real income of the United States and of foreign countries or increase their need for outside aid.

Third, in these cases in which the support program raises domestic prices substantially above world prices, U.S. exports will diminish or disappear at the same time as governmental stocks are increasing. When this happens, a variety of pressures are brought to bear to induce the government to get rid of its surpluses abroad. Sporadic subsidization of exports, through special payments to exporters or through the sale of government stocks at cut prices, or special provisions in our foreign aid programs, are methods which are occasionally used for this purpose. . . .

37. *Politics and Public Law 480*[2]

[EDITOR'S NOTE: *Although "sales" of surplus commodities abroad are administered by the Department of Agriculture, it is the State Department that must handle complaints from governments of third countries who find that their exports have been hurt. Therefore, the State Department has traditionally been less enthusiastic about the P.L. 480 program than some other agencies. In the 1957 hearings on P.L. 480, Senator Hubert Humphrey (D., Minnesota), then a member of the Senate Committee on Agriculture and Forestry, was trying to dispel the idea that the program was primarily a way of "exporting" the American agricultural "problem." It is worth noting that those who were really interested in foreign policy would have little incentive to make the cost of foreign aid appear larger; whereas those who were really interested in domestic problems would be tempted to make the cost of agricultural subsidies look smaller. Thus, the fact that Humphrey called so much attention to the foreign-policy aspects of P.L. 480 probably indicates that he himself was more interested in the domestic impact. The second portion of this excerpt contains the testimony of Assistant Secretary of Agriculture Earl Butz on an official tour he had recently completed.*]

SENATOR HUMPHREY: I hope these discussions can clear up one thing. Government attitudes seem to have unfairly invoked a double standard in regard to American agriculture's vital contribution

[2] SOURCE: *Policies and Operations Under Public Law 480*, Hearings before the Senate Committee on Agriculture and Forestry, 85th Cong., 1st sess. (Washington, D.C.: Government Printing Office, 1957), pp. 52–55, 131–33.

to United States foreign aid programs.

When we spend billions for guns, tanks, and planes to give to our allies overseas, everybody accepts it as necessary to our national defense and security—and nobody complains about subsidizing General Motors, Boeing Aircraft, Remington Arms, or any of our big industries producing such weapons.

But whatever we spend trying to send food to the men who will have to handle those guns, tanks, and planes seems to be written off in everybody's mind as just subsidizing American farmers.

The truth is both are investments in national security—and both are entitled to public support in the same light.

At our opening yesterday we heard testimony from officials of the Department of Agriculture and the Department of State. They were exploratory discussions which I hope we can continue further at a later date. There still does not seem to be a full appreciation even in these agencies of the tremendous force for freedom in our possession or enough energetic imagination toward putting our abundant food supplies to use for that purpose.

Agriculture has done a good job trying to look out for agriculture's interest in this program, but I am convinced it should be raising its sights. They are so busy pointing to what has been done, they are overlooking the tremendous opportunities to do more, and they have undersold their own contribution by having given the public the idea that our surplus was a terrible liability instead of going out and proving what an asset it can be.

The State Department seems to regard its responsibility primarily as a watchdog to prevent surplus disposal from interfering with trade by any of our allies, instead of grasping the full significance of having at its disposal something the whole world needs and something we possess in a greater degree—so far—than the Communist world.

I hope before these hearings are over, all of these agencies sharing to some degree responsibility for this vital program can lift their sights from their own little orbits long enough to embark on bold, imaginative use of our food resources as an instrument of peace and freedom—and be willing to give farmers credit for creating a great national asset instead of berating them for wrapping some kind of millstone around our necks. . . .

SENATOR AIKEN: Mr. Chairman[3] . . . I would like to say that I share your concern that so much is charged up against agricultural

[3] Senator Allen J. Ellender (D., Louisiana).—ED.

programs which very properly should be charged against other programs. However, it was my impression that it was Congress rather than the executive agencies that wrote the laws providing for this chargeoff against agriculture for benefit derived by other agencies of Government.

SENATOR HUMPHREY: I think the Senator is absolutely right. I don't want my remarks to be interpreted as indicating that the chargeoff was due to anything that the agencies were doing. I merely say that in what limited inquiry I have made thus far as an individual, most of the discussion around Public Law 480 has indicated that, well, this so-called surplus is a problem with which we are stuck; let's see what we can do with it. All I am saying is that I haven't heard the Treasury Department speak of the gold in Fort Knox, Kentucky, as a problem, to use an analogy, and it seems to be about the largest surplus of any one metal we have, because it is all stored.

SENATOR AIKEN: I think that the Department has done a pretty good job in disposing of surpluses, a large percentage of them going to needy people overseas. . . .

SENATOR HUMPHREY: I thoroughly agree. As I say, the Department of Agriculture has done a very good job trying to look out for agriculture in this program. But I still believe one of the purposes of these hearings is to coordinate the efforts of the different agencies of Government, because so many of them are involved in the operation of Public Law 480. We cannot ignore the fact that we have made the involvement in Congress.

SENATOR AIKEN: Any conflict between Agriculture and any other agency or any difference of opinion is not new. I have been here going on 17 years, and that same difference of opinion has existed ever since I came here. I expect that it existed before I came to Washington. It is just a natural rivalry to see which agency can do the most good in this world.

SENATOR HUMPHREY: I don't mind that kind of rivalry, Senator, if the agencies will just work on that basis.

. . . .

[Mr. Butz is introduced.]

SENATOR HUMPHREY: . . . I know that you recently made a rather extensive tour, in your capacity as Assistant Secretary of Agriculture. I wonder if you would be willing to tell us from your observations on your tour whether you witnessed or heard of a need for food in various countries which you visited.

Did the additional need of food come to your attention?

MR. BUTZ: Well, yes, it certainly did, Senator. I may say that in some of those countries, particularly in the Near East, I got there just a few days after you had been there and I think I observed the same things that you observed.

There is, of course, need for food in many parts of the world. This is not new—

SENATOR HUMPHREY: Not at all.

MR. BUTZ: This has been true ever since recorded history, as you well know. The need for food is relative.

I observed, as you did, Senator, that in some of these countries Public Law 480 shipments of food has helped a great deal in alleviating food shortages and alleviating human suffering and bolstering the economies of the country, and strengthening our own security, I think, by strengthening our friendly nations.

On the other hand, I was a bit distressed in some of these countries, Senator, and I think I might as well lay it right on the table now, by what I conceive to be a growing attitude on the part of the officials of some of these countries—that is not true of all of them—that they could use what dollar exchange they had available and what pound exchange they had available, or whatever hard currency exchange they might have, to buy nonfood items because it was now possible to use their local currency, of which they always have plenty, to buy the food items under Public Law 480.

I was not pleased with this—what I conceived to be a growing tendency on the part of certain foreign officials to think this way. Because I think we ought always to be in there fighting to have our agricultural exports get as large a share of the dollars spent by foreign countries as possible.

This is a continuing market and a permanent market and the kind of market we want to encourage.

I think I would go so far as to say that we have used Public Law 480, I think, as a positive factor in foreign policy—I am sure we have. It is on the plus side. It is only natural, therefore, I think, that some of our own officials abroad begin to look on this thing as something that they can use as a factor in promoting good relations between the United States and the country where they are stationed. You and I would feel identically the same way if we were in that situation.

Therefore, I think there is a tendency even for them to regard this as something that could be continued perpetually. What I am saying is that I think there is a tendency on the part of our foreign government officials, as well as some of our own people, to a lesser extent, to feel that the primary purpose of Public Law 480 might become the promotion of a foreign policy rather than the disposal of surpluses, which we hope are a temporary phenomenon in this country.

SENATOR HUMPHREY: I think that is a very basic observation. There may be honest differences of opinion. This is one of the things that we will want to go into, as to whether or not this is to be considered a disposal operation from here on out, or whether it is to be considered a part of the foreign policy.

I have mixed emotions about this, to be very candid with you. On the question of your observation relating to certain officials looking upon Public Law 480 as a means of obtaining necessary food items, and thereby reserving their dollars or their sterling—

MR. BUTZ: Or hard currency, whatever it might be.

SENATOR HUMPHREY: Or hard currency, for capital items, this is something upon which there are two schools of thought. The schools of thought are as follows: That these countries with which we are dealing are friendly countries. Most of them are recipients under the mutual security program. The dollars that many of them have are very limited, and they all need capital goods. I talked to officials who said:

Isn't it better that they should buy pipe, pumps, build hydro-electric dams, buy diesel engines, railroad track with dollars because this is something that has a way of replacing income? I mean it isn't something that disappears like food; it is something that is productive, generates more productivity and possibly a greater, more solid base for the economy? Therefore, isn't it better to use the dollars, since they are spent in the United States, most of them, to use the dollars for capital goods, industrial goods, which are needed to broaden the base of their economy, and during that period that they are getting this base of the economy firmed up a bit, to rely as much as they can upon the use of their local currencies for purchases of food, particularly if we have any need for that local currency?

MR. BUTZ: Senator, I quite agree with that. From the standpoint of the recipient country, I think this is sound policy.

What I am saying is that from the standpoint of the Department of Agriculture, and I should think from the standpoint of sound United States national policy, we in Agriculture ought always to be trying to build up our dollar exports just as much as we can. We ought to protect ourselves so that no country gets the idea that it can get its food supply indefinitely without spending dollars for it.

SENATOR HUMPHREY: Well, let me just stay with you on this for just a moment because I think there are two issues that you have raised here which are at the crux of the whole discussion of the developments under Public Law 480. Number one, is this strictly a disposal program or is this to be an arm of American foreign policy? That is number one. Number two, about the fulfillment of food needs under Public Law 480, in some areas, even at the expense of some dollar sales for food commodities. Now I thoroughly agree with the northern European country thesis, such as you have mentioned here, under barter, that a number of countries that have entered barter operations are countries that have dollars. Their economies are strong and there is just very little reason, at least on the surface, for assuming that they would need Public Law 480 goods. But when you get down into a country where they have such a limited number of dollars that the choice is between whether they are going to buy wheat, which will be consumed in 30 days, or whether they are going to buy electrical wiring for a rural electrification development, which may last 25 or 30 years, and thereby improve their general productivity, then the question comes: What are you going to do, providing that in both instances the United States is going to supply the capital? Because that is what happens in many of these countries. What we have been doing, in fact, is buttressing up, firming up, their dollars to buy food with dollars which we supplied, thereby giving them both our food and our dollars. Then we firm them up with dollars to buy the diesels or the generators, or the wire or the cement, whatever may be necessary in the capital improvement program.

MR. BUTZ: Senator, I cannot see that it makes any real difference there so far as U.S. policy is concerned, as long as you say we are giving them the dollars both for the food and for the cement and electric wiring—as the illustrations you used.

If we are giving them the dollars for both, from purely a partisan point of view, from Agriculture, if I may speak that way—

SENATOR HUMPHREY: Yes.

MR. BUTZ: I would like to protect the dollar market for foodstuffs so that someday I do not have to win it back starting from zero.

SENATOR HUMPHREY: I see your point of view and as Assistant Secretary of Agriculture you have your immediate professional obligation to your Department and the manner in which it is operated.

Mr. Butz: And to the agriculture industry of America.

Senator Humphrey: To the agriculture industry. That is what the Department represents.

But it is also bothering me about the public relations involved here. When we sell 50 tanks to a country and Chrysler Motors builds those tanks, or whoever builds them—they are a fine company—no one ever says that we are subsidizing the automobile industry by building the tanks. But if you go out and sell 50,000 or 50,000,000 bushels of wheat to the same country that got the tanks, the farmers are criticized for subsidy. And the only reason you are sending the wheat is because the people are so weak they could not even drive the tanks unless you fed them—that is not an exaggeration, you know. We have had to have nutritional programs in a country to first feed the soldiers before we could put them in the tanks. We got tanks there before we got healthy enough people to even put in the tanks.

Now, when you buy the wheat from the farmer or the Commodity Credit, somebody raises the flag and says, "This is a subsidy." My question is—I am rather naïve about this—who gets subsidized, the motor company that sells the tanks or the farmer, or the Commodity Credit, who sells the wheat? Why do you call one a subsidy and not the other? They are both needed.

Mr. Butz: They are both a subsidy.

Senator Humphrey: No, they are both an expenditure.

I think this [is] the part that bothers the Department of Agriculture, and the farm community, that whenever they sell under Public Law 480 it is charged up all the time as a loss. Well, the military equipment we send over is a total loss once it gets there. Something like buying an automobile, the minute you drive it out of the garage, you have already lost $500 without even getting across the street.

Mr. Butz: I may say that is charged as a mutual security appropriation, too.

Senator Humphrey: Right. That is the point, it is charged up as a part of our foreign policy and that is one of the questions I was asking earlier, in that list of possible points of interest in this hearing, that maybe we should be charging up more of these Public Law 480 developments, not to the Department of Agriculture, but as a part of the total security program of the country. . . .

38. The State Department View of Public Law 480[4]

[EDITOR'S NOTE: *Thomas C. Mann, then Assistant Secretary of State for Economic Affairs and now Under Secretary of State for Economic Affairs, presented the State Department view in the 1959 hearings on extension of P.L. 480.*]

MR. MANN: Mr. Chairman and members of the committee, thank you for this opportunity to present the views of the Department of State on general aspects of the administration of Public Law 480. The Department of Agriculture has already testified at some length and I assume that the Committee wishes me to direct my remarks primarily to the foreign policy aspects of the program.

I wish to say in the beginning that the existence of agricultural surpluses in our country provides us with an opportunity to improve standards of health and nutrition, to promote a more rapid rate of economic growth through development loans and grants from sales proceeds, to increase commercial marketings by expansion of food consumption, and to help nations cope with the difficult task of providing food for rapidly expanding populations.

The Department of State is therefore interested in finding ways to utilize our agricultural surpluses in the most effective way possible in the service of humanity and freedom. . . .

There are, however, a number of considerations which we believe deserve the particular attention of this committee and of the Congress.

First, there is a limit on the quantity of our surplus agricultural commodities which can be disposed of under Public Law 480 without injury to our economy, the economies of our friends and allies who export the same commodities, and the economies of the recipient countries themselves.

Countries with convertibility and balance-of-payments problems find it advantageous to purchase food with local currency, especially since a substantial part of the currency is returned to the country in long-term, low-interest loans for economic development. It is, therefore, not surprising that they sometimes seek Title I commodities not only to obtain agricultural products which they

---

[4] SOURCE: *Extension of Public Law 480*, Hearings before the House Committee on Agriculture, 86th Cong., 1st sess. (Washington, D.C.: Government Printing Office, 1959), pp. 199–208.

would find it difficult to pay for in convertible currencies but as a substitute for commercial transactions for which they can allocate foreign exchange. If we were to permit this, our own commercial sales would inevitably decline, as would those of our friends and allies. This is why we strive to avoid displacing normal marketings.

It is sometimes thought that excessive disposals of agricultural surpluses are harmful only to those economies whose commercial exports are displaced.[5] But the disposal of excessive quantities can be harmful to the recipient country itself.

For one thing, it can discourage domestic agricultural development by reducing producer incentives. The Argentine nation is today paying the price of austerity largely because its agricultural production, on which its economy rested, sharply declined because of previous price policies which removed the producers' incentive to raise livestock and grains. The reduction in agricultural production, in turn, contributed directly to balance-of-payments difficulties which we have been helping to alleviate and to inflation and rising costs of living which it is not so easy to remedy quickly and painlessly.

Countries which are striving for rapid economic growth need all of the exchange they can get for the purchase of capital imports. Our disposal program contributes to their ability to buy these needed imports. But this advantage can be offset if their agriculture declines and a situation of dependence on foreign food is created which they cannot hope to pay for in the foreseeable future. This could in time result in a serious problem for them as well as for us and for the free world.

When a Department of State officer was discussing this general problem the other day before another committee, he correctly pointed out the recipient countries themselves may find that other parts of our program displace their exports and reduce their export earnings. He said:

A good example of this type of problem was brought out by a statement made by a delegate from Pakistan to the GATT meeting in November 1958. He said that his country had greatly benefited from the U.S. surpluses and he thanked the U.S. Government. But he pointed out that the disposal by the United States of cotton surpluses had resulted in lower foreign exchange earnings from Pakistan's cotton exports, and he went on to express his fear that the situation was getting worse, observing that in the first quarter of 1958 as com-

[5] Canada is especially vociferous in complaining about the effect of P.L. 480 on its wheat exports.—Ed.

pared with the first quarter of 1957, Pakistan's foreign exchange earnings from cotton had dropped nearly 50 percent.

. . . It certainly would not make sense to the American taxpayer for us to tear down with one hand what we are trying to build with the other. This point was made recently by a representative of a country which has received substantial dollar aid from the United States. He said that his government greatly appreciated this assistance but could not understand why the United States was, at the same time, displacing his country's normal marketings by sales of Public Law 480 tobacco.

It is of course difficult to mark the precise line where our agricultural disposal program would do more harm than good. Consumption varies from year to year especially in a commodity like cotton where so much depends on whether the textile industry is in a recession or a boom period. Disasters due to natural causes may temporarily reduce crops and conversely a good crop year can create a burdensome surplus disruptive of market stability. The ability of importing countries to pay for their food imports is another variable.

Psychological attitudes also vary and determine, for example, whether buyers accumulate stocks or cease buying in the hope that lower prices will prevail later. At times, market stability and the attitudes of other exporting nations are governed not so much by what we actually do in administering our disposal program but what they fear we might do. Because we are such a large producer of agricultural products and because our stocks are so large, we have, in the eyes of the entire free world, an obligation to act in a responsible way.

We have developed a procedure for dealing with this problem which works remarkably well considering all the variable and sometimes complex factors involved in each and every transaction. This procedure was recently explained in these words.

After a request for Public Law 480 commodities is received—let us take a hypothetical example of Country A, which has asked for 900,-000 tons of wheat—we analyze the historical trade patterns for a past representative period. We evaluate the information concerning such factors as existing stocks, domestic production, estimated consumption, foreign exchange resources, and total import requirements. On the basis of the results we can determine approximately how much wheat we can put into Country A without impairing normal commercial imports from the United States and other suppliers. Let us assume for instance, that 600,000 tons turns out to be a reasonable amount to offer under Title I. We then consult the other suppliers and explain what we have in mind. We point out that available data show that Country A should be required to import 300,000 tons of wheat on a regular commercial competitive basis, that we believe this leaves room for them as well as ourselves to maintain our respective normal commercial exports to Country A and that we would like to have their views. If we have done our job well and our estimates are reasonable and realistic, the other suppliers will agree with us and express their sincere appreciation for taking their interests into account. . . .

THE CHAIRMAN:[6] Now another thing that I don't think Congress intended you should do; there was some statement which indicated that before you put through a transaction or approved a proposal you conferred with the officials of friendly governments.

MR. MANN: Yes, sir.

THE CHAIRMAN: And if you sell them on the idea and they pat you on the head and say they appreciate the time you are taking and the time you have taken, you go on with it, but if they don't appreciate and approve it the whole thing is out.

MR. MANN: No, Mr. Chairman. I think there is a great misunderstanding about foreign governments.

THE CHAIRMAN: . . . We are primarily interested in getting rid of these surpluses and we don't care how you do it and under what authority. We have told you we want the commodities sold for dollars first and then for foreign currencies or then donate them.

MR. MANN: I think there is no disagreement, Mr. Chairman, because we have done that a pretty good clip.

THE CHAIRMAN: We haven't been able to give it away. We can't even give food away to starving people.

MR. MANN: We have disposed of about $1.4 billion in the process in the last year.

THE CHAIRMAN: And you have acquired an additional amount. So just look at what has happened to our surplus. In 6½ years the surplus has gone up from less than $2.5 billion to $9 billion.

MR. MANN: Yes.

THE CHAIRMAN: In the meantime you have sustained gigantic losses. We disposed of the dairy stocks and we did not sell it but gave it away to the tune of $1.5 billion.

If we go on in the years of 1960, 1961, and 1962 as we have been going on in the last 6½ years look where we will be 5 years from now. We have got to do something in the future that we haven't

[6] Representative Harold D. Cooley (D., North Carolina).—ED.

done in the past. I am groping around trying to find some way that we can improve this program.

MR. MANN: Of course the basic cause of this surplus is something we are not talking about today. We agree with you completely that to the extent that we can with Public Law 480 or commercial sales or any other way maximize our agricultural exports, whether you have barter or dollars or rupees, we want to do that. All I am saying is that you cannot without disrupting world trade dump the whole total of our excess onto the world market. There is a level beyond which it is not in our interest to pass. It is a matter of judgment. Our judgment is that we are putting our surplus on the market now at just about as great a clip as we can without injuring the economies of our country and other countries.

THE CHAIRMAN: If that is true then our situation is hopeless.

MR. MANN: If we can maximize that without doing damage to commercial trade we are in favor of doing it.

THE CHAIRMAN: If we are doing all we can at the present time and if you don't think we can do any better than we have been doing then our situation is hopeless; isn't that true?

MR. MANN: I believe myself that the magnitude of the program last year is not insignificant.

THE CHAIRMAN: Yes, I know, but it has not accomplished what we wanted to accomplish.

MR. MANN: Which is to take care of all our agricultural surplus?

THE CHAIRMAN: We want to dispose of our surplus agricultural commodities. That is the program contemplated by Public Law 480, and we want to do what we can to improve our foreign relationship with the people of the free world.

What are we going to do with all the wheat stored in the Liberty ships at Hampton Roads and all over the country?

MR. MANN: Dispose of as much as we can without breaking world markets.

THE CHAIRMAN: It has been there 5 or 6 years. Will you leave it there another 5 or 6 years?

MR. MANN: I think we are getting into another area of how much the world can purchase and consume, and part of the problem is a matter of production.

THE CHAIRMAN: Mr. Teague.

MR. TEAGUE:[7] Lest the Secretary get the impression that everyone on this committee does not see any merit in his statement

[7] Representative Charles M. Teague (R., California).—ED.

which, as I interpret it, emphasizes the importance of our over-all trade relations and maintaining relations with important allies to us around the world, I feel as one member that what he has done is worthy of very considerable and careful consideration by this committee.

THE CHAIRMAN: I certainly have anticipated in the preparation and passage of the provisions to which Mr. Mann referred that we will give due consideration to the interest of friendly nations, but not permit them to veto everything he proposes to do.

MR. TEAGUE: I do not interpret anything the Secretary said as giving a right to veto. He said he consults with the nations that have problems and it is important to our commercial relations and trade that we maintain a spirit of cooperation with these friendly countries. It seems to me that is what the Secretary is saying.

THE CHAIRMAN: His concluding statement is, "If we have done our job well and our estimates are reasonable and realistic, the other suppliers will agree with us and express their sincere appreciation for taking their interests into account."

That means to me that if you don't get their appreciation and thanks you don't go any further.

MR. MANN: Let me clarify that. Number one, no country has a veto on what the U.S. Government does.

Number two, I don't recall in the last year a single transaction that was canceled out because of objections of a foreign government. We discussed such things as the quantity we would ship without breaking the price, whether there would be a normal marketing provision or whether it should not be a global marketing provision and things of that sort. I would say that the area of disagreement has been very, very small and never have we withdrawn from a transaction because a foreign government objected to it when we were convinced we were right. I want to make that very clear.

THE CHAIRMAN: Can you give us an instance of a single transaction which you have consummated over the protest of a foreign friendly power?

MR. MANN: Oh yes, I can do that. This is a public hearing and I don't know whether we should get into that but I can tell you that we have disagreed and gone ahead. . . .

XIII

Population and Foreign Aid

It has become commonplace to designate the population explosion as the second most serious social problem facing twentieth-century man—the first, of course, being war. What, however, has the population problem to do with foreign aid? It is not simply a matter of whether the United States should give aid for use in population-control programs, nor is it merely a matter of whether population-control efforts should be a prerequisite to receiving American aid —although both of these questions are important. Insofar as foreign aid aims at increasing per capita incomes in underdeveloped

TABLE 7

LESS-DEVELOPED COUNTRIES: AVERAGE ANNUAL GROWTH RATE OF
GNP, POPULATION, AND PER CAPITA GNP, 1957/58 TO 1963/64[a]
(*In Per Cents*)

	Annual GNP Growth Rate[b]	Annual Population Growth Rate[c]	Annual Per Capita GNP Growth Rate
Latin America			
Argentina	0.6	1.7	−1.1
Bolivia	3.5	2.3	1.2
Brazil	5.3	3.1	2.2
Chile	3.3	2.3	1.0
Colombia	4.6	2.8	1.8
Costa Rica	4.1	4.0	0.1
Ecuador	4.3	3.2	1.1
El Salvador	5.7	2.9	2.8
Guatemala	4.5	3.0	1.5
Honduras	3.6	3.1	0.5
Jamaica	3.9	2.0	1.9
Mexico	5.3	3.1	2.2
Nicaragua	5.3	2.9	2.4
Panama	4.9	3.0	1.9
Paraguay	2.2	2.2	0.0
Peru	6.4	2.3	4.1
Trinidad and Tobago	6.0	3.0	3.0
Venezuela	4.5	3.8	0.7
Far East			
China (Taiwan)	7.1	3.1	4.0
Korea	4.7	2.9	1.8

TABLE 7 (*continued*)

	Annual GNP Growth Rate[b]	Annual Population Growth Rate[c]	Annual Per Capita GNP Growth Rate
Far East (*continued*)			
Malaya, States of	5.9	3.1	2.8
Philippines	4.9	3.2	1.7
Thailand	7.4	3.0	4.4
Vietnam	3.5	2.8	0.7
Near East			
Cyprus	3.6	1.2	2.4
Greece	6.2	0.7	5.7
Iran	4.7	2.4	2.3
Israel	10.5	3.6	6.9
Jordan	9.5	2.9	6.6
Turkey	4.0	2.9	1.1
South Asia			
Ceylon	3.5	2.5	1.0
India	4.4	2.3	2.1
Pakistan	4.5	2.5	2.0
Africa			
Ethiopia	4.5	1.4	3.1
Ghana	5.1	2.5	2.6
Kenya	3.5	2.9	0.6
Malawi	2.1	3.0	−0.9
Morocco	2.0	3.1	−1.1
Nigeria	3.3	2.0	1.3
Rhodesia	3.6	3.3	0.3
Sudan	4.5	2.9	1.6
Tunisia	4.7	2.6	2.1
Uganda	3.4	2.5	0.9
Zambia	4.7	2.9	1.8

[a] SOURCE: *Foreign Assistance, 1965*, Hearings before the Senate Committee on Foreign Relations, 89th Cong., 1st sess. (Washington, D.C.: Government Printing Office, 1965), p. 113.

[b] GNP growth rates are AID estimates based largely on official national statistics.

[c] Population growth rates are based on data from AID countries, the United Nations, and other sources.

areas, population growth is a major determinant in the effectiveness of aid. As Table 7 shows, an increase in GNP may be gobbled up by a growth in population, even to the extent that individuals are in a worse position than they were before.

Only in recent years, however, has American policy begun to take account of the interdependence of the effectiveness of aid programs and the rate of population growth. A Roman Catholic

President, immune to charges of anti-Catholicism, initiated the first hesitant steps toward a realistic assessment of the relevance of population data to aid policy.

39. *Eisenhower Reconsiders*[1]

[EDITOR'S NOTE: *During the summer of 1965, Senator Ernest Gruening (D., Alaska), Chairman of the Senate Government Operations Subcommittee on Foreign Aid Expenditures, conducted hearings on population problems as they related to the aid program. The following is an excerpt from a letter submitted by former President Eisenhower. The letter is dated June 18, 1965.*]

DEAR SENATOR GRUENING:

I am complimented by your invitation for me to comment on the many problems arising out of the extraordinary and rapid increase in the world's population. I am taking advantage of your suggestion that should it be more convenient to me to submit a written statement than to appear before you in person, this would be satisfactory to your committee.

As a first comment I must say that I am delighted that your committee is concerning itself with this subject, one that I consider constitutes one of the most, if not the most, of the critical problems facing mankind today.

While it is true that there remain great areas of the world in which there are still unexploited resources for food production and of irreplaceable subsurface minerals, it is still quite clear that in spite of great technical progress in production of the necessaries of life, we are scarcely keeping up, in over-all production and distribution, with the requirements of burgeoning and underfed populations. Moreover, since the earth is finite in area and physical resources, it is clear that unless something is done to bring an essential equilibrium between human requirements and available supply, there is going to be in some regions not only a series of riotous explosions but a lowering of standards of all peoples, including our own.

Ten years ago, although aware of some of these growing dangers abroad, I did not then believe it to be the function of the Federal

[1] SOURCE: *Population Crisis*, Hearings before the Subcommittee on Foreign Aid Expenditures, Senate Committee on Government Operations, 89th Cong., 1st sess. (Washington, D.C.: Government Printing Office, 1965), pp. 6–7.

Government to interfere in the social structures of other nations by using, except through private institutions, American resources to assist them in a partial stabilization of their numbers. I expressed this view publicly but soon abandoned it.

After watching and studying results of some of the aid programs of the early 1950's, I became convinced that without parallel programs looking to population stabilization all that we could do, at the very best, would be to maintain rather than improve standards in those who need our help.

We now know that the problem is not only one for foreign nations to study and to act accordingly, but it has also serious portents for us.

I realize that in important segments of our people and of other nations this question is regarded as a moral one and therefore scarcely a fit subject for Federal legislation. With their feelings I can and do sympathize. But I cannot help believe that the prevention of human degradation and starvation is likewise a moral—as well as a material—obligation resting upon every enlightened government.

If we now ignore the plight of those unborn generations which, because of our unreadiness to take corrective action in controlling population growth, will be denied any expectations beyond abject poverty and suffering, then history will rightly condemn us. . . .

40. *The Draper Report on Population and Aid*[2]

[EDITOR'S NOTE: *The Draper Report contained far-reaching implications for the aid program (see Document 25, Chapter VIII). Among them was the emphasis it placed on the relation between aid and the population growth rate. The recommendations based on an understanding of this relation, however, did not receive much attention in Washington until recently.*]

No realistic discussion of economic development can fail to note that development efforts in many areas of the world are being offset by increasingly rapid population growth.

In 1950 the world population was estimated to be about 2.5 billion. This represented an increase of approximately 1 billion in the

[2] SOURCE: President's Committee to Study the United States Military Assistance Program, *Composite Report* (Washington, D.C., August 17, 1959), I, 94–97.

previous 50 years. If present growth rates continue, there would be a further increase of nearly 4 billion in the second half of the 20th century. This would more than double the 1959 population of the world within the next 40 years—a period much shorter than the life expectancy of those just now reaching voting age. Problems connected with world population growth will be among the most serious to be faced by the younger generation of today.

A large part of the world population is at present underfed. The United Nations estimates that from 1950 to 1955 the world's population increased at an annual rate of 1.5 percent, with the population in many underdeveloped countries increasing at double this rate. World food production is barely keeping pace with the increase in population in the world. However, the increase in food production in most of the underdeveloped countries has been falling behind the increase in population.

The seriousness of this problem is increased by the fact that the major population growth is taking place in the economically underdeveloped areas, where annual rates of 3 percent are not uncommon. Unless the relationship between the present trends of population growth and food production is reversed, the already difficult task of economic development will become a practical impossibility.

The present rapid rates of population growth result primarily from a decrease in mortality rates rather than from a marked increase in fertility rates. Public health campaigns, especially in the less developed areas, have been phenomenally successful in many countries. In some instances, death rates have been cut by as much as 30 percent in a single year and 50 percent in the short span of 10 years. This is a great humanitarian achievement. Nevertheless, continuation of the traditionally high fertility rates meanwhile results in rapid population growth.

Although experience in the more developed countries suggests that present high fertility rates may eventually fall more into line with the decreased mortality rates, these high fertility rates are normally a part of deeply rooted cultural patterns, and natural changes occur only slowly. In many countries, national production is failing even to keep pace with population growth, and per capita gross national product and food supplies are therefore decreasing rather than increasing.

Government leaders in many of the less developed nations recognize that the only hope for their people lies in accelerating the normal adjustment to the rapidly declining mortality rate. Few countries have set up the necessary programs, although broad acceptance has been found in those areas where programs have been established. Most of the countries lack the large numbers of trained social and public health workers needed to implement an effective program.

Basically, the problems of rapid population growth and of adequate economic progress must be faced and solved by the individual countries. The United States and the other more advanced countries can and should be prepared to respond to requests for information and technical assistance in connection with population growth. Such information will help to point up the seriousness of the problem, and to encourage action in countries where population pressures exist. Such information is also useful in defining the areas in which initial efforts will be most effective. Recognizing an immediate problem created by the rapid growth, the United States should also increase its assistance to local programs relating to maternal and child welfare.

We Recommend: That, in order to meet more effectively the problems of economic development, the United States (1) assist those countries with which it is cooperating in economic aid programs, on request, in the formulation of their plans designed to deal with the problem of rapid population growth, (2) increase its assistance to local programs relating to maternal and child welfare in recognition of the immediate problem created by rapid population growth, and (3) strongly support studies and appropriate research as a part of its own Mutual Security Program, within the United Nations and elsewhere, leading to the availability of relevant information in a form most useful to individual countries in the formulation of practical programs to meet the serious challenge posed by rapidly expanding populations. . . .

41. *The State Department View: 1962*[3]

[EDITOR'S NOTE: On November 30, 1961, William T. Nunley, a State Department official, delivered a speech in which he outlined the department's view of the population explosion as a problem for U.S. foreign policy. The interesting aspects of this speech consist not only in what is said but in what is left unsaid.]

[3] SOURCE: William T. Nunley, "Address to the National Conference on International Economic and Social Development," *Department of State Bulletin*, XLVI, No. 1175 (January 1, 1962), 22–25.

In speaking about world population problems and their relationship to economic and social development, I want to begin by identifying myself. I do not pretend to be speaking in a purely personal capacity, although some of my observations are necessarily personal. I am an officer of the Department of State and have served for 15 years under three administrations. I am currently assigned as a Special Assistant to the Under Secretary of State. It is therefore my intention to explain as best I can the current attitudes of the Department of State with respect to international population problems.

The essential task of the Department of State is to advise and assist the President in the conduct of international relations. As you know, President Kennedy's Administration has become popularly known as "the New Frontier." I believe this label is altogether appropriate. Henry David Thoreau once defined a frontier as something that is "neither east nor west, but wherever a man faces a fact." During the last year many Americans have been deeply impressed by the determination of President Kennedy and his top officials to face the hard, undiluted, and undecorated facts of our national and international life. This willingness to face facts—to come to grips with the facts that are known and to ferret out the facts that are still unknown—provides the principal explanation of the State Department's attention to international population problems.

We have all heard a great deal about the "world population explosion." However, I sometimes suspect that this metaphor has produced more confusion than enlightenment. For example, I recently heard a story about a little girl who asked her mother to let her watch some people explode. At the same time, there are a handful of relatively mature citizens who write sincere letters to the State Department which sometimes seem to suggest that we should devote less attention to such problems as the Berlin crisis, Southeast Asia, disarmament, international trade, collective security, and so forth, and instead concentrate a much larger portion of our diplomatic energies upon attempting to regulate the private lives of men and women 10,000 miles away.

Please understand that I am not questioning the reality of the "population explosion." The world's population is growing at an alarming rate. It is probable that the three-billionth human being was born some time this year. According to the best available demographic estimates, 3,000 babies will be born before I finish speaking tonight. So maybe I'd better hurry along.

In the eyes of the State Department, population problems are significant primarily because of their economic implications. This applies to families, communities, and nations alike. I realize that if I had 12 children instead of 4, my house would be a lot noisier than it is now, although this possibility sometimes seems pretty incredible. But my big problem would still be food, clothing, shelter, and popsicles.

I also realize that some people are worried about the prediction that, at some future date—say 2100 A.D.—the entire planet may require a "standing room only" sign. While such a dismal situation may indeed lie within the realm of theoretical possibility, the prospect is not giving me and my colleagues any sleepless nights. During the months and years immediately ahead we shall probably spend a great deal more of our time worrying about an equally theoretical and even drearier prospect—the possibility that human life may be wholly extinct by 2100 A.D.

In any event, from the viewpoint of the State Department the fact that India, for example, has about 400 million people is intrinsically neither good nor bad. This would hold true even if India's population should increase to 600 million or 800 million. The important question is whether these people can be fed, clothed, and sheltered, given the necessities of life and some of the comforts, given the means to educate themselves, to preserve their freedom, and to attain greater material and spiritual growth.

While demographic statistics are highly unreliable, a few broad generalizations are possible. Any child born into the non-Communist world today has a two-to-one chance of being born into a nation where the average per capita income is less than $5 per month.

This is the really important fact. It is important not only to the child himself, his family, his community, and his nation, but it is also immensely important to the United States of America. It is important in terms of our ethical and religious values, in terms of our domestic prosperity, in terms of our political freedom, and in terms of our ultimate survival. When an American understands this fact, it doesn't matter very much whether his heart is dripping with the milk of human kindness or whether he is as selfish as Scrooge. It is no longer possible for any man or nation to be safe in a world where two-thirds of the people are on the verge of starvation.

Some Truths and Uncertainties

What I have said leads to some fairly obvious conclusions. The State Department has given little attention to the population problems of the economically advanced nations, which are able to provide a fairly decent standard of living to most of their citizens. We are concerned primarily with the population problems of the lesser developed nations. Even here, we are not concerned with population problems per se but only with population problems as they may relate to economic and social development.

When we begin to consider this relationship, we find ourselves upon a small island of miscellaneous truths surrounded by a vast ocean of ignorance and uncertainty. Let me give some examples.

First, we know there is a substantial and intricate relationship between economic growth and population growth. More specifically, we know that our economic assistance programs have a continuing impact upon population growth, although this impact has never yet been deliberate and is usually unconscious. However, the nature and extent of the interaction between economic development and population growth is often hazy. For example, public health programs tend to reduce the death rate and thus accelerate population growth, but also increase the productive capacity of the labor force. Similarly, rural development may reinforce a village way of life favorable to high fertility but may simultaneously produce new opportunities for women which compete with the traditional role of childbearing.

Second, we know that worldwide economic growth is well ahead of worldwide population growth. But this doesn't mean much to people who are hungry. Moreover, as we look into the future we cannot be sure whether the problems produced by population growth will ultimately be resolved by reducing the rate of population growth, by technological breakthroughs in the production of goods and services, by commercial arrangements which permit a better distribution of goods and services, by mass emigration, or by various combinations of these alternatives.

Third, we know there are tremendous variations in the population problems of different countries. In some lesser developed countries the present ratio between economic development and population growth is favorable. In other instances the rate of population growth is so high that a particular country is not yet achieving, even with considerable American economic assistance, a per capita rate of economic growth that is sufficient to satisfy the aspirations of its people and to assure political and social stability. In two or three countries the current rate of population growth is actually higher than the rate of economic growth. In many countries, however, we are unable to draw any very useful conclusions, because there is no reliable information about the actual rate of population growth, the actual rate of economic growth, the relationship between the two, the probable social and political consequences, and probable future trends.

Fourth, we know that certain citizens in foreign countries believe that their governments need a deliberate policy and effective program of population control. However, these citizens suffer many uncertainties. They are often unclear as to existing facts and future probabilities concerning both population growth and economic growth. They sometimes fail to appreciate the difference between population control and birth control and also do not know what techniques are available in each case. Population growth, of course, is affected by a great many factors other than birth control. These may include the mobility of workers, the minimum marriage age, kinship obligations, the system of land tenures, urbanization, and so forth. But no one knows very much about the methods by which governments may deliberately bring these factors into play so as to produce predictable results.

The citizens mentioned often do not know how to persuade their governments to adopt a definite program, and the government itself may not yet know how to obtain the cooperation of its population or how to achieve the results desired without conscious cooperation. Even where all other conditions are favorable, a government may lack the resources or technology to carry out an effective population control program.

As a consequence, very few governments have as yet adopted anything resembling an active program of population control, although several have adopted measures which make it easier or harder for individual families to regulate births. Moreover, I can say quite categorically that no government has ever yet requested any specific assistance from the United States in controlling population growth. . . .

If what I have said sounds confusing, let me assure you that the basic facts are confusing. However, I want to urge the members of this audience—and every other person in the United States who may be interested in population problems—to undertake or stimulate further research into all aspects of these problems, especially with reference to their relationship to economic and social advancement in the lesser developed countries.

Meanwhile I can tell you fairly simply what the Department of State is doing and what it is not doing. First, we are thinking about population problems and talking about them. Second, we are attempting to get other people to think and talk about these problems—to stimulate individuals, organizations, and governments to add to the total store of knowledge on this subject. Finally, we are prepared to consider, on their merits, certain types of requests for assistance to other governments. In fact, we have already begun to advise and assist a few governments in their efforts to acquire additional knowledge about their own population problems, specifically in the conduct of censuses.

I haven't the slightest idea what we will be doing 1 year or 10 years from now, because we are standing at the edge of a jungle that is largely unexplored. However, there are certain things which I feel certain that the United States Government will *not* do. We will not attempt to impose population controls upon other governments or peoples. We will not make population control a condition of our economic assistance to other countries. We will not advocate any particular technique of population control in preference to other techniques.

Our refusal to do these things is not based upon political timidity. It is based in part upon the lack of information by our Government and other governments. It is also based upon certain inescapable facts of international political life—the nature of the relationships among free governments and the relationship of governments to peoples.

In any event, our ultimate objective is clear. Our Government intends to continue providing economic assistance to the lesser developed nations. I do not know whether or not the United States Government will ever consciously provide specific assistance in controlling population growth, and I am even less certain whether we will ever offer assistance in support of birth-control programs. At the present moment, incredible as it may seem to some Americans, birth control is not a major issue in most parts of the world. It certainly is not a policy objective of the United States Government. Our real objective was stated by Under Secretary [George W.] Ball in Vienna only a few weeks ago, when he said that what we want to do is to make sure that every birth everywhere in the world will some day be accompanied by a birthright.

42. *AID Policies on Population: 1965*[4]

1. *What is the U.S. policy on population?*
On January 4, 1965, President Lyndon B. Johnson said in his

[4] SOURCE: Agency for International Development, *AID Policies on Population* (Washington, D.C.: Department of State, March 2, 1965); here reprinted from *Population Crisis*, Hearings before the Subcommittee on Foreign Aid Expenditures, Senate Committee on Government Operations, 89th Cong., 1st sess. (Washington, D.C.: Government Printing Office, 1965), pp. 86–87.

State of the Union message: "I will seek new ways to use our knowledge to help deal with the explosion of world population and the growing scarcity of world resources."

2. *Does AID advocate family planning policies for developing nations?*

No. AID's role is not that of an advocate. The United States opposes any effort to dictate population policies to another country.

On their own initiative over the past several years, growing numbers of less developed countries have either instituted operating programs in the field of family planning or are considering such programs. There are major programs underway in India, Pakistan, Korea, Taiwan, Ceylon, Hong Kong, and Jamaica. Pilot programs or significant action-research programs are being carried out in Thailand, the United Arab Republic, and Tunisia.

3. *Does AID advocate any particular method of family planning?*

AID does not. It is the U.S. position that in publicly supported health services, every family should have complete freedom of choice in accordance with its conscience with respect to what methods, if any, it uses.

4. *Does AID regard the adoption of official family planning policies as a self-help condition for receiving U.S. aid?*

No.

5. *Does AID volunteer assistance to other nations on family planning?*

No. AID assistance is provided on specific request only. The growing concern with population problems has resulted in an increasing volume of informal requests for information and assistance in relation to this problem.

Requests for assistance in this field, as in others, will be considered only if made or approved by appropriate host government authorities. Such assistance would, in any case, merely be additive to the host country's own efforts and assistance from other sources.

6. *What assistance will AID provide?*

AID has long given assistance in the development of health services and the training of health personnel. Assistance has also been given in developing official statistics, including population censuses and vital statistics. In February, 1965, AID provided a $400,000 grant to a Latin American research center in Santiago, Chile, Centro para el Desarrollo Economico y Social de America Latina, for studies in family size and population growth.

Since 1962 AID has encouraged the collection and analysis of population growth data and study of attitudes about family planning, but until recently requests for information and assistance in family planning have been referred to appropriate private agencies.

AID now considers requests for technical assistance including the training of family planning workers. Where appropriate, the requests will continue to be referred to private agencies.

AID will also consider requests for commodity assistance. AID will not consider requests for contraceptive devices or equipment for manufacture of contraceptives.

Items that could be provided by AID include vehicles and educational equipment for use in maternal and child health and family planning programs. We are also prepared to receive requests to assist in local currency financing of such programs.

7. *What countries have already requested assistance from AID?*

In addition to requests for demographic help and assistance to public health programs, AID has received indications that requests may be forthcoming from Pakistan, India, South Korea, Taiwan, and possibly other countries. These involve such items as vehicles, educational equipment, local currencies, and technical assistance.

8. *How is AID organized to provide assistance?*

Requests for assistance will be handled, as in any other field, on a case-by-case basis.

Agency headquarters has furnished AID missions with general reference materials and technical publications dealing with a wide range of subjects from demography to family planning.

The Population Reference and Research Branch, organized in the Health Service of AID's Office of Technical Cooperation and Research (TCR), serves as the AID focal point for information and coordination in the population field. Consultants have been appointed in the demographic, economic, medical, and public health aspects of the population field.

The Latin America Bureau created a population unit and requested each Latin American AID mission to appoint an officer to be responsible for population matters.

Every AID mission is being instructed to assign one of its officers, as Latin America missions have done, to become familiar with the problems of population dynamics and program developments in the country and to keep the mission director, country team personnel and Washington headquarters appropriately advised.

9. *Is AID the only source available to the less developed countries for assistance with population problems?*

By no means. Substantial assistance has been made available by private institutions. Leadership has come from the Rockefeller Foundation, the Ford Foundation, and the Population Council for action research projects in Puerto Rico, India, Jamaica, Pakistan, Taiwan, Korea, Tunisia, Chile, and Thailand.

In addition several foreign governments offer assistance in family planning programs upon request from developing countries.

43. *Foreign Aid and Population Control*[5]

[EDITOR'S NOTE: *On June 14, 1965, Senator Joseph S. Clark (D., Pennsylvania) delivered the following speech in the Senate. It was subsequently submitted to the 1965 hearings on population crisis.*]

Mr. President, I wish to devote my remarks today principally to a single aspect of the foreign assistance program. It is an aspect which has, I believe, been neglected in the past, and which, if it is not faced and considered now with the utmost seriousness, will make the remainder of our assistance program at best irrelevant and at worst self-defeating. I refer to the problem of overpopulation and the measures which must be taken to deal with it.

In his State of the Union address, the President made a courageous commitment. "I will seek new ways," he said, "to use our knowledge to help deal with the explosion in world population and the growing scarcity in world resources." The urgency of the President's language was not misplaced. The United Nations Population Commission has estimated that in 1964 world population increased by 2.1 percent, the largest increase in history. In the less developed countries the increase was approximately 2.5 percent, a rate which if it remains constant, will produce a doubling of population every 28 years. Present world population, at the latest reckoning, stood at something over 3 billion. The Population Commission has published its estimated projections for the rest of the century, based upon as comprehensive a consideration of relevant social and economic factors as is possible in the present state of statistics and the science of demography. The projection which the Commission considered the most plausible was predicated on the assumption that fertility would begin to decline in many developing countries within a decade or two, as a consequence of expected

[5] SOURCE: *Population Crisis*, Hearings before the Subcommittee on Foreign Aid Expenditures, Senate Committee on Government Operations, 89th Cong., 1st sess. (Washington, D.C.: Government Printing Office, 1965), pp. 78–80.

economic, social, and cultural advances, and the increasing efforts of some governments to encourage family planning. According to this projection, world population will rise to 4.3 billion by 1980, and to over 6 billion by the year 2000. This expected doubling of world population in 40 years is frightening enough in itself. But within these figures there lies another set which should command even more apprehensive attention. It seems certain that of the total increase the share of the underdeveloped countries will rise substantially. During the 1950's their share was already about 75 percent of the increase. Between 1960 and 1980 it is expected to be 83 percent, and between 1980 and 2000, 86 percent.

Stated differently, of the 1.3 billion increase in world population expected in the next 15 years, 1,079 million will occur in the poor and underdeveloped countries of the world, only 221 million in the rich and developed countries. With respect to the expected 1,700 million increase between 1980 and 2000, 1,463 million will occur in the poor countries, only 283 million in the rich countries. As a consequence of the differential growth rates, the less developed regions would increase their share of total population from 67 percent in 1960, to 72 percent in 1980, and 76 percent by the end of the century.

By the end of the century slightly more than three out of every four human beings will be living in countries which are today incapable of providing a standard of living adequate to feed, clothe, and shelter their people in minimum decency.

These are the bare facts of the situation. They carry a message which has particular significance for the foreign aid program, and therefore for our deliberations today. For the quantity and value of the economic aid which we provide for the countries of Asia, Africa, Latin America, and other parts of the world cannot be measured without reference to the number of people it has to serve. Our economic aid program is designed, among other purposes, to assist in the creation of viable political economies in parts of the world where they do not now exist, and where they are not likely to exist for many years to come. This will be a long and arduous process in the best of circumstances. If it is to stand a chance of success, the essential ingredients of any political economy—the population factor as well as the investment and productivity factors—must be viewed as a whole. It is not particularly encouraging, for example, to discover that in Venezuela, although the annual growth rate of GNP in the last 6 years has been 4.5 percent, the population growth rate has been 3.8 percent—leaving a real, per capita GNP growth rate of only 0.7 percent; and this is particularly disturbing when one considers that in this relatively rich South American country per capita GNP today is only $765. A similar situation may be observed in many of the developing countries, with the growth of GNP barely keeping pace with the growth of population, let alone achieving a real growth rate which offers the prospect of a developing economy in the foreseeable future. . . .

It is clear from these figures that any discussion of foreign aid, and any application of a foreign aid program, which omits, or understates, or ignores, or tries to forget about the problem posed by overpopulation is quite unrealistic. And yet this speech comes near the end of the debate on the foreign aid bill and the subject of population control has still to be mentioned.

There are those who argue that overpopulation can be coped with by a better distribution of the world's resources, by the settling of vacant and fertile land, and by the rapid development of potential sources of food and production which have not yet been exploited. There are others who make their case against programs of population control by asserting that because manpower is a vital prerequisite of productivity, such control will have in the long term a detrimental effect on a country's economy. But when they are matched with the terrible fact that already nearly two-thirds of the world's inhabitants go to bed hungry each night, these contentions are sophistry of a peculiarly tragic nature. The fact is that the untapped sources of production cannot possibly be exploited fast enough—even supposing that their full exploitation would be sufficient to satisfy the needs of 6,000 million people by the year 2000, which is itself a dubious assumption. Immediate action is needed to curtail fertility in many areas of the world, but especially in those areas to which the bulk of the foreign aid in this bill is directed.

In an amendment to the Foreign Assistance Act of 1963, proposed by Senator Fulbright, Congress gave its first express authorization for the expenditure of some AID money on research into problems of population growth—although this was not the first time AID had spent some money for this purpose. The Secretary of State and the Administrator of the Agency for International Development reported to the Foreign Relations Committee, during the hearings on the present bill, the extent of AID's activity in the field of population control. The Agency has, of course, long given assistance in the development of health services and the training of health personnel in many countries. Thus, death control has speeded population growth. A few years ago the Agency began to help with the compilation of statistics and other data depicting population trends. It is now giving technical assistance in the training of family planning workers, and financial assistance for the purchase of vehicles and educational materials to be used in family planning programs where such assistance is requested. Each AID mission has been directed to assign one of its officers to become familiar with the problems of population dynamics and control programs in the host country. All these are welcome developments, and show some appeciation of the importance of the problem.

However, this is not nearly enough. These few, gingerly taken steps are hardly a proper reflection in practice of the giant strides which have been made in the intellectual recognition of the problem or the need to move immediately to solve it before the deluge of unwanted babies overwhelms us. Certainly the progress which has been made to date on the question of birth control is only the small beginning of a fulfillment of the President's enlightened promise in the State of the Union address.

At present the Agency will not consider requests for contraceptive devices or equipment for the manufacture of contraceptives. The policy is based on the argument that this is one facility which a developing country can and should provide for itself. Perhaps we should leave manufacture and distribution of devices to free enterprise in the developing countries. Moreover the actual manufacture and distribution of contraceptives by AID would doubtless be strongly opposed by large sections of the American people. However, it is further stated by AID that the Agency "does not advocate family planning or any method of family planning." This was said in a recent speech by Dr. Philip R. Lee, the Director of the Agency's Health Service, and it clarifies a point which remained somewhat obscure in administration testimony before the committee. The Secretary of State acknowledged that overpopulation was a serious problem, but the thrust of his testimony was that it would be improper for the U.S. Government even to go to the governments of aided countries and explain to them that, in the opinion of AID, their birth rates were too high to make effective the economic aid they were receiving. In my judgment, this is a dangerously timid approach. I believe that AID should be advocating the institution of voluntary family planning programs as a necessary condition to meeting the rising tide of unfed mouths and unfulfilled aspirations in these countries—and thus preventing American aid from being poured down a rat hole.

The health programs of AID as already noted have played a major part in the eradication of disease and the reduction of the death rate experienced in many parts of the world. This interference with the natural ecology of underdeveloped regions is, of course, a humanitarian act of unquestioned good. But it does create its own problems. In particular it compounds the dangers of a high fertility rate. Thus, the United States has itself contributed substantially to the world's poverty, through keeping alive children who can only be reared in hunger and squalor. This is an especially compelling reason for AID to take the lead in an immediate attack on the problem by advocacy of voluntary family planning.

I appreciate that no universally valid laws exist which govern the interaction of population growth and economic development. It is indispensable to study the demographic, economic, and cultural circumstances of each country and each society, because each country differs as to the degree of the problem and the receptivity to family planning programs. I certainly do not advocate the compulsory imposition of family planning by the United States on any of the countries which we aid. It has been suggested that aided countries should be required to show evidence of serious attempts to check the population explosion as a precondition for receiving U.S. economic aid. But this would be unwise for two reasons. First, the principle which governs all our aid programs must continue to be sustained: the government of the host country must retain the final right of decision over the programs it wishes to accept. This should not be abrogated by what would be, in effect, an ultimatum. In an area which is as sensitive as family planning, it is especially important that the absolute rights of the host country be recognized. The second reason for rejecting the creation of a precondition is that it would not be the most efficient way, at this stage, of meeting the population problem itself. A blanket rule of that sort would inevitably disregard the real differences existing in the various countries, both as to the intensity of the problem and as to the nature of the best solution.

What is needed is a change of attitude on the part of Government agencies involved in aid to the developing countries. AID should now move on from its attitude of limited response to initiatives made by aided governments, to an attitude of active proselytising of the cause of voluntary family planning, in the many countries where that would be appropriate. From my own discussions with AID officials in the field I know that many of them are very seriously concerned with the population problem, and are anxious to do as much about it as they can. But I question whether their urgency is matched by the directives they receive from their superiors in the State Department. Several ambassadors in the Latin American countries, for example, have not fully grasped the importance of the problem. Some of them seemed to take the view that this was hardly something for them to meddle in. There may have been a time when such a negative attitude was appropriate, but that time has long passed.

If the attitude is not changed, I repeat, the purposes of our aid program—and, indeed, our aspirations for a world of peace, stability, and universal comfort—will be placed in jeopardy. Our aid will become an even smaller drop in an even vaster ocean. The national economies which we seek to support will slip further and further behind in their struggle to achieve a solid base. As we well know, communism thrives on the unfulfilled expectations for a better life of the people of the underdeveloped nations. If we fail to do all we can to help them recognize and combat their population problems, their disappointments will be our responsibility—and we shall have to pay the penalty in increasing tensions between "haves" and "have nots," and perhaps, ultimately, war.

Visions of the world in 50 years' time as a place of famine, congestion, and deprivation of every sort are speculative but not fictitious. They are so terrible that many people do their best to forget them, or to pretend that they do not exist. It is clear that this is an attitude of folly. We must look the specter in the eye and apply ourselves as best we can to the task of exorcising it. As the most powerful nation in the world, and the nation with the most pervasive influence, we have the greatest responsibility to encourage younger nations, with these pressing problems, to take the prudent path toward economic stability. One aspect of our encouragement lies in the programs of health, shelter, food, investment, education, and modernization. These will remain at the heart of our philosophy of economic aid. But a second aspect—one which is fundamentally unseverable from the first—is the need to encourage a drastic reduction in the level of fertility. I urge my colleagues and the Agency for International Development to give this greater emphasis than they have done hitherto.

XIV

Conclusion

Aid activities have changed radically since 1945. Loans have supplanted grants; Latin America and Asia have replaced Europe on the receiving end; international aid agencies have multiplied; surplus food has become important; and so on. Some issues, however, have recurred in the great debate over foreign aid. These have been presented through the preceding readings; they concern: (1) loans vs. grants, (2) multilateral vs. bilateral aid channels, (3) Legislative control, (4) the balance between military and economic aid, (5) the role of the private sector, (6) the relation of aid to trade, (7) the domestic impact of the aid program, (8) the place of agriculture in foreign aid, and (9) the population explosion. Most of these issues are touched upon in the final reading—a report commissioned by President Kennedy. The Committee to Strengthen the Security of the Free World was created to prepare the report, and General Lucius D. Clay was named Chairman.

The Clay Report, as it came to be known, had a long line of predecessors—reports issued in 1950, 1951, 1954, 1957, and 1959. Each of these studies had been solicited by a President in an effort to strengthen support for the aid program in Congress and among the informed public. Traditionally, such reports had concentrated on lecturing Congress and the American people regarding their international obligations and on scolding them for not supporting a more substantial aid program. The Clay Committee, however, argued that the United States was attempting to do "too much for too many" and recommended a smaller, better administered program. Instead of addressing their criticisms to Congress and the public, the committee reproved the Executive Branch. Note the following passage, for example:

> The Committee recognizes that its recommendations to decrease or abolish aid in a number of countries and otherwise to tighten standards will be difficult to implement and provoke charges that they are "politically impossible" in terms of good U.S. relations with countries concerned.

If this passage had been written by previous study committees, it would probably have said the following:

> The Committee recognizes that its recommendations to increase aid in a number of countries will be difficult to implement and provoke charges that they are "politically impossible" in terms of *good Congressional relations with constituents.*

The effect of the Clay Report on the 1963 aid program was disastrous. Hostile legislators argued that the program was so rotten that even the President's hand-picked advisers wanted it cut. In fact, the aid appropriations bill went unpassed until December—halfway through the fiscal year for which it was intended.

In a reading of the Clay Report, one should be especially alert to the following questions: Is there evidence of a military bias? Does the report focus on long-term or short-term goals? Does it give enough attention to the popuation problem? What concept of the world situation underlies the report? Is the report internally consistent?

The Clay Report provides a fitting conclusion to a book devoted both to foreign-aid analysis and to presenting the raw material for such analysis.

44. *The Clay Report*[1]

March 20, 1963

The President of the United States

DEAR MR. PRESIDENT:

Three months ago, you asked this Committee to examine the scope and distribution of U.S. foreign military and economic assistance and to recommend any changes we believed desirable for its optimum contribution to strengthening the security of the United States and the free world. This report embodies our general views on how the foreign assistance programs should be conducted. Our views concerning specific countries have been discussed

---

[1] SOURCE: The Committee to Strengthen the Security of the Free World, *The Scope and Distribution of United States Military and Economic Assistance Programs* (Washington, D.C.: March 20, 1963).

at length with the Administrator of the Agency for International Development. We have not included the Export-Import Bank or its lending activity within the scope of this study.

I. U.S. Foreign Aid Since World War II

At the end of the war, only the United States had the strength and resources to fill the power vacuum into which international Communism sought to move. To strengthen the free world, the United States then embarked upon an extensive foreign assistance effort which has lasted well over a decade. First, the special programs for Greece and Turkey, the Marshall Plan, and U.S. contributions through new international organizations were undertaken. This was followed by the establishment of Point Four's technical assistance operations, to help less developed countries build a basis for further development, and a military-economic program designed to increase the ability of nations bordering the Communist bloc to resist Russian or Chinese imperialism. More recently, the United States added capital loan assistance on generous terms and surplus agricultural commodities to its longstanding Export-Import Bank and technical assistance operations and embarked on a sustained program, including its participation in the Alliance for Progress, of economic aid to less developed countries.

Questions and Criticisms

Each of our Presidents since foreign aid began has repeatedly expressed his judgment that this assistance is essential to the national interests of the United States and to the curtailment of Communist efforts in all parts of the world. Criticisms of aid activity, its burden on the already heavily pressed taxpayer, and the prospect of its prolonged continuation, however, have raised questions concerning the nature and conduct of these programs. There has been a feeling that we are trying to do too much for too many too soon, that we are overextended in resources and undercompensated in results, and that no end of foreign aid is either in sight or in mind.

There are aspects of these programs which justifiably concern or perplex our citizens. It is clear, for example, that economic and social growth can be achieved only if it is based on an internal expression of will and discipline, without which external aid is of little value. Yet, many of the countries which have received our aid have not fully performed their part of the assistance bargain with their own resources. Moreover, we have not adequately conditioned our aid in many cases on the achievement of such performance. Indeed, we may find ourselves, in effect, granting a number of continuing subsidies because it is argued that their denial would create instability and lose us good will.

It is obvious, also, that the process of economic development is a long one and will be limited at the outset by the absence of trained manpower and adequate local institutions. Moreover, their absence in turn limits the capacity of these countries to absorb aid effectively. The miracle of postwar recovery in Western Europe was made possible by the application of temporary aid to countries whose well-established economic, political, and social systems, and trained manpower could use it wisely. In the less developed nations, most of these conditions do not exist. Moreover, the rapidity of population growth in many areas increases the magnitude of the development problem and accentuates social unrest.

There is evidence the American public feels strongly, too, that other prospering industrialized nations, having recovered their economic strength since the war with our assistance, should assume much more of the foreign aid burden than they are now carrying.

There has been increasing concern as well over the contribution of foreign aid to the persistent deficits in our international balance of payments—12 in the last 13 years. These deficits have produced a sustained decline in our gold stock and a marked increase in foreign-owned dollar balances, with a resulting loss in our international liquidity. Upon international dollar convertibility at the existing gold parity rest the international payments mechanism which has evolved since the war, the economic health and prosperity of the United States and its friends, and our role of political, economic, and financial leadership in the free world. Our commitment to the convertibility of the dollar is essential to the accomplishment of the objectives we properly seek abroad, including those of our foreign assistance programs.

There are other factors which trouble our citizens as well. While there is some awareness of the competence, dedication, and even gallantry on the part of many in the assistance programs, they believe that the quality of many others has not been adequate. They know also that the volume of aid and number of aid-giving sources in the free world have increased substantially and that the number of sources has created difficult problems of effective coordination. They are concerned, too, that we have aided countries which are unaligned with us or even in opposition to us.

Recent Progress

Certainly the Agency for International Development (AID) is now aware of the criticisms directed against our foreign aid programs. The Act for International Development of 1961 is a good one. The consolidation of aid agencies, improvement in personnel, reduction in marginal activities, better analysis of development requirements, and increased insistence on self-help pursuant to the Act have been steps forward, as has the shifting of aid from a subsidy to loan basis in several countries and the establishment of target dates for terminating aid in others. Amendments to the Act in 1962 also have been helpful, especially the Hickenlooper Amendment, requiring suspension of aid to countries expropriating privately owned U.S. property without adequate compensation, and the provision banning aid to Communist countries except in extraordinary circumstances.

The harmful effect on our international accounts also has been mitigated by tying U.S. economic aid to procurement in this country, a step which was necessary despite its undesirability as a general and continuing practice. This tying of aid has become increasingly effective to the point where, from a figure of 50 percent of expenditures in 1962, less than 20 percent of U.S. aid commitments in fiscal year 1964 is expected to add to a negative balance. It is estimated that this balance will have been cut in half, from about $1.2 billion in 1960 to $500–$600 million for 1964, while the direct financing of U.S. exports of goods and services in the same period will have tripled, going from $600 million to about $2 billion a year. Moreover, further efforts are being made to reduce this drain.

Also, more countries are becoming independent of U.S. aid through the successful combination of our assistance and their own internal efforts. Greece, Israel, and the Republic of China [Taiwan] are expected soon to reach the point where their external financial requirements can be met by conventional loans from the Export-Import Bank, the International Bank for Reconstruction and Development, and other sources. The Philippines, also, under its present vigorous leadership, is moving to a similar position.

II. Present Status and Future Guidelines

Even with due consideration for improvements, however, much remains to be accomplished. While we are concerned with the total cost of aid, we are concerned even more with whether its volume is justified and whether we and the countries receiving it are getting our money's worth. We believe that we are indeed attempting too much for too many and that a higher quality and reduced quantity of our diffuse aid effort in certain countries could accomplish more. We cannot believe that our national interest is served by indefinitely continuing commitments at the present rate to the 95 countries and territories which are now receiving our economic and/or military assistance. Substantial tightening up and sharpened objectives in terms of our national interests are necessary, based on a realistic look at past experience, present needs, and future probabilities.

There should be no doubt, however, of the great value of properly conceived and administered foreign aid programs to the national interest of the United States and of the contribution of the foreign assistance dollar in such programs to the service of our nation's security. We live in a world in which poverty, sickness, instability, and turmoil are rife and where a relentless Communist imperialism manipulates this misery to subvert men and nations from freedom's cause. A foreign aid program is one instrument among many which we and other developed countries adequately can afford and vigorously must use in the defense and advancement of free world interests. It is our purpose in this report to point out how this essential program can be strengthened for this purpose, and our criticisms and proposals here should be viewed in the light of this objective.

There is ample evidence of the need for aid and that it can be successful under proper circumstances. While it may be argued that the cost of Marshall Plan assistance to the U.S. taxpayer was larger than necessary, it is clear that its provision made possible the rebuilding of a free world nucleus with the strength to withstand and forestall Communist pressure. Presently, there are many countries in the less developed areas which wish to be free of Communist domination but lack the political or economic strength to maintain their independence without help from more fortunate nations. If countries with a will to be free are to become or remain so and if their governments are to prove to their peoples that the democratic, non-Communist route to political and economic well-being is the better one, some form of external assistance to their internal efforts is necessary.

To examine the utility of our assistance programs objectively, one must bear in mind their basic purposes. In this year's programs, over $1 billion was allotted for direct military assistance to countries on the bloc's periphery which are allied with us or each other in defense against Communist attack. These countries also received about $700 million in economic aid to support their military effort and otherwise add to their stability and growth. These funds represent 44 percent of the total foreign assistance appropriation. If we add to this the military and economic support of Vietnam and Laos and of other border countries which wish to retain their independence, though not allied with us or with other countries in common defense, total expenditures for military support and accompanying economic aid in the border areas aggregate $2.8 billion or 72 percent of total appropriations. Dollar for dollar, these programs contribute more to the security of the free world than corresponding expenditures in our defense appropriations. If one adds to this sum our assistance under the Alliance for Progress, about 15 percent of the total program, and our contributions to international organizations of which we are members, amounting to $150 million, the total reaches 91 percent of current foreign assistance appropriations. This does not mean, of course, that these programs are exempt from constant re-examination in the light of their necessity and effectiveness, but it indicates the major purposes which foreign assistance presently serves.

In asking whether we receive optimum value from our assistance programs, we must know what we seek and what it is we expect. We must not be disappointed if nations which receive our aid do not always agree with us. If our assistance strengthens the will and capacity of a country to remain independent and helps it move toward political and economic stability, our money will have been wisely spent.[2] If our aid simply postpones the inevitable day of financial and national reckoning then we have wasted our substance and helped the country not at all. It is for this reason that aid to countries which are avowedly neutral and sometimes critical of us may be in order, so long as their independence is genuine, their over-all behavior responsible, and their use of their own resources prudent and purposeful.

We must be clear as well as to the kind of economic systems we attempt to foster and assist. Our aid should help create economic units which utilize not only limited government resources wisely but mobilize the great potential and range of private, individual efforts required for economic vitality and rapid growth. The broad

[2] Is this statement consistent with the following paragraph?—ED.

encouragement of these efforts requires incentives, as Mr. Khrushchev recently has emphasized in seeking to improve his own economic system. However, there have been too many instances in which foreign economic aid has been given without regard to this fact and to the historic form, character, and interest of our own economic system. We believe the United States should not aid a foreign government in projects establishing government-owned industrial and commercial enterprises which compete with existing private endeavors. While we realize that in aiding foreign countries we cannot insist upon the establishment of our own economic system, despite its remarkable success and progress, we should not extend aid which is inconsistent with our beliefs, democratic tradition, and knowledge of economic organization and consequences. Moreover, the observation of countless instances of politically operated, heavily subsidized and carefully protected inefficient state enterprises in less developed countries makes us gravely doubt the value of such undertakings in the economic lives of these nations. Countries which would take this route should realize that while the United States will not intervene in their affairs to impose its own economic system, they too lack the right to intervene in our national pocketbook for aid to enterprises which only increase their costs of government and the foreign assistance burden they are asking us to carry.

The argument that aid should be given for "political" as well as "economic" reasons also must be carefully examined. The problem in extending aid lies in distinguishing between those judgments which are wise, encompassing as they do the full range of economic, political, and other factors in long-term perspective, and those which are unwise. Whether a country ought to receive aid from the U.S. is a question of our enlightened self-interest; however, the kind and basis of aid provided thereafter—except when paramount military security or other extraordinary circumstances are involved—are questions to be determined on economic grounds. Here, as in other instances, the United States must establish sound benchmarks for its own performance and stick to them, whatever the vagaries of ephemeral world opinion.

Some aid projects have come into being as gifts to prove our esteem for foreign heads of state, hastily devised projects to prevent Soviet aid, gambles to maintain existing governments in power, leverage for political support, and similar reasons. While a certain amount of this is unavoidable, there have been too many exceptions to the rule. Insofar as others believe we accept promises in lieu of performance, respond to careful campaigns against our embassies, pay higher prices for base and other settlements if negotiations are long and unpleasant enough, and give unjustified aid in the hopes of precluding Soviet assistance in marginal cases, to that extent the firmness of U.S. negotiating positions loses credibility, our efforts to make aid more effective by getting local self-help are weakened, and U.S. Congressional and domestic backing for aid is undermined.

We seek not to create difficulties for our official representatives around the world, beset with responsibilities to maintain good relations and concurrently urge foreign governments to take difficult steps in the interest of a better but uncertain future. We wish only a better understanding of this problem by our official representatives and those who would judge and assist them.

We are convinced that the United States must take more risks for the purpose of obtaining performance from foreign governments, be more willing to live with charges that it is insensitive to other countries' needs, and accept the consequences that in some countries there will be less friendly political climates.

III. Findings

The conclusions of our examination embrace the nature of U.S. interests and programs in various areas of the world, general matters concerning the free world development assistance effort, and aspects of U.S. programs deserving special comment. We will consider them in that order.

The Border Areas

In examining our national interest in foreign military and economic assistance, the direct relationship to free world security is most evident in the defensive strengths of those nations which, in their contiguity to the Communist bloc, occupy the frontier of freedom. Many of these countries are our allies, and some belong to alliances with which we are associated. Several of these nations are carrying defense burdens far beyond their internal economic capacities. These countries are now receiving the major portion of U.S. foreign assistance but are also providing more than 2 million armed men ready, for the most part, for any emergency. While their armies are to some extent static unless general war develops, they add materially to free world strength so long as conventional military forces are required. Indeed, it might be better to reduce the resources of our own defense budget rather than to discontinue the support which makes their contribution possible.

This does not mean that the military assistance program in this area does not need present and continuing review. We are convinced that in several of these countries, indigenous forces are larger than required for their immediate mission of defense and not large enough to assume other missions. There, phased reductions of a very substantial order appear practical, after further careful examination, without unduly sacrificing immediate effectiveness. This would not only lessen the cost of military assistance but reduce related supporting economic assistance as well. Moreover, the amount of economic support for these military programs could be further reduced in at least one instance if long-delayed internal financial reforms were undertaken.

There are a few other border countries whose military forces presently are of value largely for internal security purposes. Even though they belong to alliances with which we are associated, we believe the present level of support to these forces, particularly with sophisticated weapons, cannot be considered as essential to the security of the free world. In these countries, which have substantial resources of their own, significant reductions of military and economic assistance are in order.

In addition there are other countries in this border area, particularly in Southeastern and Western Asia, to which we provide economic assistance and, in some cases, military equipment, though they are neither allies nor members of alliances with which we are associated. We believe most of this military assistance is not essential to our own or free world security, and we cannot recommend continued supply of this equipment. Also, economic assistance provided to some of these countries on the basis of past agreements is beyond that necessary for our interests. While firm commitments to these countries should be honored, economic aid should be phased down in some cases and phased out in others.

In our consideration of border countries, we have not attempted to analyze the substantial cost of our efforts in Laos and Vietnam, since the nature of present U.S. commitments there precludes useful examination by this Committee. While we recognize that the foreign aid program must be flexible in view of rapid changes in today's world, it was not designed for combat zones; we suggest consideration be given to making provision for such areas other than in our foreign aid program.

In any review of front line countries, special attention must be given to India, even though it is not an ally. We have provided economic assistance to India for some time, most of it as part of a multilateral undertaking which obtains aid from other sources. Recently, we have agreed to extend military assistance on a parity with similar aid from the United Kingdom and other Commonwealth countries. The importance of this program frequently has been misunderstood in view of past expressions of Indian foreign policy and certain aspects of its internal philosophy. India has recently proved, however, that it is determined to maintain its independence from Communist domination. Together with our ally, Pakistan, it is the only area of South Asia able to offset the Red Chinese colossus. Unless their freedom and economic growth continue, there can never be a balance of power in Asia and our own involvement in this area could be indefinite and infinitely more costly. Thus, we believe that in the interest of our own and free world security, economic and military assistance to India, as well as to Pakistan, must continue under present circumstances. However, it would be difficult to justify continued economic assistance at present rates unless other free world countries continue and extend their support on terms comparable to our own.

We cannot leave this area of the world without special reference also to Indonesia. Because of its population, resources and geographic position, it is of special concern to the free world. However, we do not see how external assistance can be granted to this nation by free world countries unless it puts its internal house in order, provides fair treatment to foreign creditors and enterprises, and refrains from international adventures. If it follows this path, as we hope it will, it deserves the support of free world aid sources.

On the western end of the bloc periphery, Greece and Turkey are moving toward increased security and well-being. Both of these important nations, however, are still in need of military assistance and economic support, and Turkey will require both forms of assistance for some time to come. We believe that other NATO members should increase their contributions to these countries to the point where they bear a proportionate share of the burden and that the proportion of our own assistance should be reduced accordingly. Elsewhere in Europe, there is no apparent need for further military or economic assistance other than for the fulfillment of existing commitments.

Africa

As we consider the African nations, immediate security interests are less evident than in countries adjacent to the Communist bloc. The United States does have a stake in helping to create a climate of stability and growth in freedom, however, and the Communists have already displayed their interest and subversive potential in this area. Also, the new countries of Africa in most cases have maintained close ties with the former metropoles without impairment of their full independence, and the latter in turn have displayed considerable willingness to help meet the assistance needs of these young nations. The Committee regards Africa as an area where the Western European countries should logically bear most of the necessary aid burden. In fact, this is proving to be the case. Almost all nations formerly under French aegis are now receiving heavy French assistance, largely in grants. We welcome this present arrangement, based on past relationship, and trust it will continue. Similarly, the new nations formerly under British rule should look largely to the United Kingdom for economic assistance, and we hope that this experienced nation will continue to provide it. The new Overseas Development Fund of the European Economic Community also should prove a major source of help.

It can always be said that in fragile, new, developing countries, the United States must provide aid lest they accept it from Communist nations with resulting political penetration and eventual subversion. We cannot accept this view. We believe these new countries value their independence and do not wish to acquire a new master in place of the old one; there already have been instances on the continent to corroborate this belief. While our aid programs in this area are generally new, experience has shown they tend to increase. In the light of its other responsibilities, the United States cannot undertake to support all of the African countries, especially when their ties with other free world nations are largely elsewhere.

In the northern and northeastern area of the African continent, with the exception of surplus agricultural commodities, most of our assistance has gone to countries in which we have military bases. In general, future economic aid to countries in this area should either be curtailed as existing commitments are fulfilled or substantially reduced, except for technical assistance—the primary present need—and Public Law 480 shipments of agricultural commodities. Beyond this, further direct aid should be limited to loans for particular projects with economic justification and on terms appropriate to the financial abilities of the countries concerned.

Elsewhere in Africa, our economic assistance programs should be similarly limited. We should fulfill specific programs in Nigeria and Tanganyika to which we are committed, as with Tunisia in

North Africa. As these commitments are completed, further U.S. aid should be confined to participation in multilaterally supported programs.

With regard generally to U.S. military assistance to African countries, we must bear in mind that the chief burden of helping these nations to enhance their internal security capabilities again falls logically on the former metropoles, with which most of these countries have retained police and military relationships. In some cases, small-scale and supplementary U.S. training programs and internal security assistance may be justified, and limited activity in a few countries where we maintain bases is in order. Small programs and missions should be terminated elsewhere. We believe the problems created by military assistance programs in the African countries generally would be greater than those they would forestall or resolve.

The Congo merits particular mention. While recognizing that the United States has encouraged the United Nations to assume great responsibilities there, we believe the United States also has contributed proportionately more than its share to the task assumed. We believe the United States should attempt to maximize the economic assistance of other nations to the Congo and that its own contribution should be not more than half the total economic aid provided for the next few years, after which external assistance beyond conventional means could be discontinued to this potentially rich country. We believe also that military aid and expenditures should be reduced as rapidly as possible, consistent with and designed to improve the internal security problem which now exists.

Latin America and the Alliance for Progress

Because of the unusual importance of and difficulties in this area, the Committee has given it special attention.[3]

The Alliance for Progress—predicated on a joint endeavor to achieve for the Latin American peoples economic progress and social justice with free institutions and political liberty—was born in the face of a formidable inheritance. Political and economic instability, habits of government, and social rigidity in Latin America, ambivalent emotions toward U.S. power and influence in the hemisphere, deteriorating Latin American terms of trade, vacuums of political leadership and technical skill, the absence of U.S. and

[3] Does Latin America occupy an unusually important place in United States foreign policy?—ED.

Latin American institutional structures adequate to deal with these problems, and increasing Communist efforts to exploit them—these and other conditions combined to argue for both the urgent necessity and short-term impossibility of the Alliance.

Our offer of a multilateral Alliance and our performance subsequent to that offer should have proved the strength of our commitment to this program. Latin American understanding of and willingness to fulfill the undertakings of leadership, self-help, and self-discipline agreed to in the Punta del Este charter, however, with notable exceptions have yet to be proved.

Now that the first and organizational phase of this complex enterprise is completed, we believe the United States should increase its efforts to achieve greater Latin American performances beyond promises under the charter. This insistence on national economic and social performance, notwithstanding the internal and international political problems involved, is necessary, both because of and despite the primary importance of this area to the United States. The United States and Latin America cannot allow another Castroite-Communist Cuba to come into existence. And while adequate and timely U.S. aid is necessary to reduce the political, economic, and social instability which could lead to such an end, as always it can be no more than a catalytic agent to supplement the attitudes and actions of indigenous governments and societies. No matter what the amount of outside assistance, nothing will avail to promote rapid progress if Latin American leaders do not stimulate the will for development, mobilize internal savings, encourage the massive flow of private investment, and promote other economic, social, and administrative changes.

With this in mind, the Committee believes the following in order:

1. The United States should continue to make unmistakably clear that the Alliance for Progress is a long-term venture of extraordinary complexity and scope, demanding a decade or more of sustained effort by all involved to attain truly significant results. Accordingly, the United States will not accept empty praise or unjustified criticism of the Alliance as substitutes for Latin American performance. Also, the American public should cease to judge the Alliance on whether it has accomplished in two years what must take much longer. Indeed, care must be taken even now to assure that U.S. assistance does not exceed amounts that can be usefully absorbed without encouraging even less effort and discipline on the part of government to the south. It should be recognized that de-

mand for rapid results could lead to expenditures which would ultimately defeat their purpose.

2. While the Alliance has spurred some progress in Latin American willingness and ability to make necessary changes, the United States and hemispheric organs of the Alliance should make even more clear to the governments and publics of the hemisphere that they are serious about self-help, fiscal reform, and other changes. The United States should indicate it expects the achievement of certain attainable goals over the next few years, with continued assistance meanwhile conditioned on reasonable progress toward that end. In doing so, we must recognize there are various reasons for nonperformance by Latin governments apart from their unwillingness, including legislative resistance, opposition from powerful private interests, shortages of able civil servants and technicians, and the absence of certain institutions. While we should not seek quickly what we have no right to expect, there are certain vital fields where improvements can and must take place; without them, Latin America has no hope for real progress and no claim to external assistance.

3. The United States should be increasingly more specific on the self-help and reforms it seeks and do so on a country by country basis. At the top of such a list are the goals of monetary stability, sound financial and social budgeting, reductions and eventual elimination of subsidies to government enterprises, tax systems and administration which contemplate raising local revenue levels, stimulating private local and foreign investment and distributing the tax burden more fairly, and measures for the better utilization of land designed to increase agricultural productivity and credit, expand and diversify agricultural exports, encourage rural development, and increase income on the lower levels of society.

4. Assistance should be concentrated heavily on those countries which undertake to meet the principles established in the Charter of Punta del Este.

5. We must continue to assume leadership with Latin Americans in stimulating the offering of incentives to the private sector which are required if Latin development goals are to be attained. Impediments to the growth of private enterprise must be identified and treated, the shallowness and harm of doctrinaire biases against responsible private enterprise exposed, new sources of credit opened to medium and small Latin American businessmen, and foreign investment encouraged in the confidence that all governments now have means to protect themselves against potential abuses. Agita-

tion for the expropriation of foreign enterprises and for nationalization of private productive ventures is hardly conducive to the mobilization of private local and foreign capital investment and is destructive to rapid economic progress. Latin America must be encouraged to see its essential choice between totalitarian, inefficient, state-controlled economies and societies on the one hand and an economically and politically freer system on the other, realizing that a society must begin to accumulate wealth before it can provide an improved standard of living for its members. We believe the increasing acknowledgement that proper incentives to the private sector are required for dynamic growth must be accompanied by sustained U.S. and Latin American efforts and decisions at all levels of government policy and action. With such a basis, a more progressive Latin private enterprise spirit, substantial foreign investment which receives no more and no less than fair treatment, and other Alliance aid, the development of Latin America would be assured.

6. While the United States must employ the judicious withholding of funds as well as their timely award to encourage necessary internal reform, neither granting nor withholding funds is of value if incapacity and not unwillingness is the source of the problem. What is needed in such instances is an internal effort to build new institutions and external provision of the technical advice and backing needed in connection with these changes. It will take an extraordinary mobilization of United States and other talent to make such external advice sufficiently broad and incisive to be effective in the near future.

7. Normally, the financing of most local costs of economic and social development is borne by the recipient country, as external assistance is provided in the form of foreign exchange. Thus far, this has not been the case with the Alliance for Progress. We do not believe the United States should continue to finance such costs directly or through the Inter-American Development Bank except in countries which are moving to mobilize their own resources for this purpose and to build the local institutions and procedures necessary to channel them into productive investment. Even there, this interim assistance while the mobilization of funds takes place should not be provided in amounts which deter Latin American governments from raising their own potentially ample funds and should be terminated in countries where it has this effect.

8. The United States should continue and expand its efforts to assist the freer trade and economic integration of this region, with

special note of the importance of wide and nondiscriminatory Latin American access to the Common Market and to the economic development and increased human well-being which would be stimulated by a free Latin American economic community.

9. Finally, we would stress the importance of Latin American governments consulting with and enlisting in the pursuit of their development programs the support of industrial, financial, labor, cooperatives, and other leaders who believe in the goals of the Alliance.

With regard to U.S. military assistance programs in Latin America, training, civic action programs, internal security assistance where necessary, and military equipment of a small arms or communications nature should be continued and the remaining activity eliminated. Latin American military forces are not required for hemispheric defense in the event of external attack, and U.S. supply of modern, sophisticated equipment in response to the pressures of local military prestige contributes to dangers which outweigh whatever temporary value they may be designed to serve.

Sharing the Assistance Effort

One must begin by giving due credit to the revived nations of Western Europe and Japan, as well as Canada, for taking up an increasing share of the burden of economic assistance to the less developed countries. Bilateral economic assistance from the governments of these nations rose from about $1 billion in 1956 to $2 billion in 1961. It is estimated that the comparable figure for 1962 is $2.1 billion and for 1963 will be $2.5 billion. While increasingly substantial sums have become available from these countries, only France is spending on as generally favorable terms as we are. With the exception of France, assistance from other free nations has to a substantial extent been in the form of hard loans to finance exports from the lending countries. Moreover, their aid includes obligations under reparations agreements and assistance to dependent overseas territories for which they are responsible.

We are convinced that the burden of sustaining foreign assistance to the less developed countries is falling unfairly upon the United States and that the industrialized countries can and should do more than they are now doing. The present inequity is even more apparent when one adds defense expenditures to economic assistance to determine the national shares in the total expense of protecting and advancing the free world's well-being. This matter is of even greater concern when one considers the negative U.S. balance of payments.

The United States has been working on this problem for several years. The Development Assistance Committee of the Organization for Economic Cooperation and Development also has been striving for improved performance by the governments concerned and should be encouraged in its efforts. In addition, however, this matter should be the subject of systematic U.S. representation at the highest levels of government. Among our specific aims should be for Italy, despite her special problems, to allocate budgetary funds for aid, expand volume and liberalize terms, Canada to raise the volume of aid, the United Kingdom to lower interest rates and increase the volume of its aid to independent, developing countries, Germany to raise its volume and soften terms, France to soften its aid terms outside of Africa, and Japan to soften its terms.

The importance of improving loan terms—including maturities, interest rates, and grace periods—is particularly apparent in the case of those nations undertaking comprehensive development programs. Unless the lending terms of other countries improve greatly and approach U.S. terms, international consortia and coordinating groups for such countries as India, Pakistan, Turkey, and Nigeria will saddle these countries with impossible debt-service requirements and U.S. funds would pay for these short-term and short-sighted debts. In this connection, we would note our belief that the International Bank for Reconstruction and Development and the Organization for Economic Coordination [Cooperation?] and Development should establish minimum terms for loans eligible to be considered as part of their consortia and other collective arrangements.

Other developed countries cannot, in a realistic world, be expected to assume their proper proportions of the assistance effort so long as we are apparently willing to bear more than our fair share.[4] The United States should make clear its views to aid-giving and aid-receiving countries, since both have a role to play in its improvement. The United States, other aid-providing countries, and the respective aid-receiving countries concerned should seek some understanding on the latter's borrowing patterns as developing nations. This is especially important for those countries which would utilize soft-term U.S. loans for repaying continuing hard-term loans from other sources. Also, developing countries must re-

---

[4] Is this an invitation to Congress to cut the aid budget?—Ed.

frain from accepting inappropriate terms of aid and actively seek better terms from their various lenders.

Multilateral Aid

The importance of increasing the amount and improving the nature of aid provided for developing countries leads directly to the subject of multilateral assistance from the free countries.

We believe that both multilateral and bilateral assistance programs will have important roles in the foreseeable future. We also believe that the interests both of the United States and of the developing nations will be best served by the gradual shifting to effective international administration, free of the complications arising from membership of the Soviet Bloc, of as large a share of the responsibility for developmental investment as the cooperation of other free world aid-giving nations makes possible.

A multilateral organization, having no political or commercial interests of its own to serve, is able to concentrate on obtaining the greatest possible return, in terms of economic and social development, for each dollar of aid funds invested. It is also better able to limit its assistance to projects which are soundly conceived and executed and to condition the financing of such projects upon appropriate economic performance by the recipient country. Moreover, conditions imposed by an international, cooperative organization are not so susceptible to the charge that they infringe on the sovereignty of the recipient country; even if they offend national sensitivities, they do less damage to the fragile fabric of comity among nations than when such resentment is directed against a single country. Also, to the extent that international administration integrates funds contributed by a number of countries, it avoids the difficult problems of coordination which arise when aid is provided by many independent sources.

International administration of development assistance, of course, will realize the advantages cited only if it is effectively organized. In this connection, we would point out that the International Development Association (IDA), an affiliate of the International Bank for Reconstruction and Development, is a ready-made instrument to accomplish these purposes. To the extent that the United States and its partners can agree to increase the use of IDA as a common channel for aid funds, we will have achieved many of our common objectives—a fairer sharing of the burden and the effective and coordinated use of the assistance provided on terms both appropriate to the needs of the recipient countries and impartial as among the commercial interests of the contributing nations. . . .

IV. FUTURE U.S. ASSISTANCE PROGRAMS

We are convinced that barring extraordinary developments, U.S. security interests will require maintaining our military assistance program for some years to come, though it should be reduced progressively as the economic capacities of recipient nations improve. We believe that in a few years, the basic need for such assistance can be served by an annual appropriation of $1 billion. It should be noted that the Department of Defense also contemplates the phased reduction of military assistance to this figure, though it believes it cannot be attained until fiscal year 1968. We believe further that the supporting assistance which supplements major military aid in several countries will continue to be necessary, though it should be possible to reduce this type of assistance in such cases sharply over a three year period.

For the present, however, we are convinced that reductions are in order in present military and economic assistance programs. Mindful of the risks inherent in using an axe to achieve quickly the changes recommended, the Committee recommends these reductions be phased over the next 3 years. This should permit the fulfillment of most past aid commitments and others which might be revised somewhat in the light of actions by the countries concerned. While dollar savings from these changes will be substantial, though not immediately great in relation to the total program, the changes wrought should permit aid to be more effective now and in the future.

The Committee recognizes that its recommendations to decrease or abolish aid in a number of countries and otherwise tighten standards will be difficult to implement and provoke charges that they are "politically impossible" in terms of good U.S. relations with countries concerned. The Committee recognizes as well that the political problems of pulling back from ongoing aid programs are much greater than those created by U.S. refusals to extend aid where none previously has been given. Nonetheless, we believe these actions must be undertaken and can be effected by diligent diplomatic effort over a 1- to 3-year period.

We hesitate to translate our recommendations into precise dollar terms. This would require in addition to our current examination, detailed review of programs now under consideration and judgments on the firmness of understandings arising from past negotiations with foreign governments. We have stated program criteria which affect the number of countries receiving aid and the nature of that assistance. AID informs us that if our criteria were now in effect, present programs would be reduced by approximately $500 million, and there would be additional reductions in the following years as some of these programs were phased further down or out. We recognize the necessity of fulfilling present commitments which in some cases will delay the point when these criteria can be in full application and the existence of other commitments which could require increased funds in the future.

Beyond the period at hand, the future of economic assistance is not predictable. It depends on many factors, including the capacity of countries to absorb aid usefully, their pursuit of internal policies which justify our external assistance, the pace at which sound multilateral institutions can increase their volume of activity, and the continued confidence of the free world in the stability of our economy. Once the objectives of the economic assistance program have been sharpened and operations improved, it will be easier to judge how much in the way of new resources should be provided yearly to facilitate the kind of economic growth in the developing countries which is in our national interest to support. In the long run, as more and more of the developing countries establish viable economies, there will be less need for extraordinary external assistance. As we approach this point, we can look for repayments of interest and principal on AID loans to provide an increasing share of the funds necessary for the economic assistance program. While repayments on AID loans in fiscal year 1964 will amount to only $5 million, they will increase gradually thereafter. Moreover, there is approximately $2 billion in outstanding dollar repayments of economic assistance loans from other sources, not including Export-Import Bank loans. The reappropriation of these repayments as well as those on AID loans could provide a revolving fund which could make possible a reduced appropriation of new resources needed yearly for the program.

In making our recommendations for present reductions, we recognize that future emergencies and unknown challenges are likely to arise. The President of the United States must have the flexibility to meet such contingencies, and nothing in this report should be construed to limit him from doing so as future circumstances require. It is for this reason that we strongly favor the provision of an ample Contingency Fund in the annual aid appropriation.

V. Conclusion

These, Mr. President, are our views and recommendations. We express to you our appreciation for the candor and cooperation of the officials of the agencies concerned who have helped in our examination, especially the new and vigorous Administrator of AID, whose attitude and ability has impressed us greatly.

In submitting this report, we hope to have been responsive to the concerns which moved you to create this Committee and to repose your confidence in us as members.[5] The reductions recommended in current activities should not be construed as minimizing the importance in principle of foreign assistance. On the contrary, we believe these programs, properly conceived and implemented, to be essential to the security of our nation and necessary to the exercise of its world-wide responsibilities. If our recommendations are accepted, they should assist the programs in meeting these objectives.

Our examination of U.S. foreign assistance programs and consideration of them in this report has been based upon the sharp criterion of their value to the security of our country and of the free world. We would not express ourselves adequately, however, if we failed to note the further interests of our country and of our people in the purpose and effect of these programs. For this reason, we would point out that the need for development assistance and a U.S. interest in providing it would continue even if the cold war and all our outstanding political differences with the Communists were to be resolved tomorrow. This is so not merely because it is part of the American tradition to be concerned with the plight of those less fortunate than ourselves. This is so not merely because it is in our national self-interest to assure expanding markets for our production and reliable sources of supply of necessary raw materials. It is because the people of the United States hope to see a world which is prosperous and at peace that we believe those nations which are seriously striving to promote their own development should be helped by us and by our partners to create and maintain the conditions conducive to steady economic progress

[5] As a matter of fact, the Committee probably was not responsive to the concerns which motivated the President to appoint it.—Ed.

and improved social well-being within the framework of political freedom.[6]

Respectfully submitted,[7]
LUCIUS D. CLAY, *Chairman*
ROBERT B. ANDERSON
EUGENE R. BLACK
CLIFFORD HARDIN
ROBERT A. LOVETT
EDWARD S. MASON
L. F. McCOLLUM
HERMAN PHLEGER
HOWARD A. RUSK, M.D.

[6] Whereas previous reports usually began with a paragraph like this one, the Clay Committee seems to have added it more or less as an afterthought.—ED.

[7] George Meany, also a member of the Committee, submitted a dissenting statement.—ED.

List of Abbreviations

AID	Agency for International Development
CCC	Commodity Credit Corporation
CIAP	Inter-American Committee for the Alliance for Progress
DAC	Development Assistance Committee
DLF	Development Loan Fund
ECA	European Cooperation Administration
ECOSOC	United Nations Economic and Social Council
ERP	European Recovery Program
FAO	United Nations Food and Agriculture Organization
FOA	Foreign Operations Administration
GATT	General Agreement on Tariffs and Trade
IBRD	International Bank for Reconstruction and Development
ICA	International Cooperation Administration
IDA	International Development Association
IDB	Inter-American Development Bank
IFC	International Finance Corporation
IMF	International Monetary Fund
ITO	International Trade Organization*
MAP	Military Assistance Program
MSA	Mutual Security Agency
MSP	Mutual Security Program
NAC	National Advisory Council on International Monetary and Financial Problems
NATO	North Atlantic Treaty Organization
OAS	Organization of American States
OECD	Organization for Economic Cooperation and Development
OEEC	Organization for European Economic Cooperation
P.L. 480	Public Law 480, Agricultural Trade Development and Assistance Act
SUNFED	Special United Nations Fund for Economic Development*

* Proposed but never brought into being.

259

UNEDA	United Nations Economic Development Administration*
UNEPTA	United Nations Expanded Program of Technical Assistance
UNESCO	United Nations Educational, Scientific and Cultural Organization
UNRRA	United Nations Relief and Rehabilitation Administration
UNSF	United Nations Special Fund
USAID	United States AID Mission (replacing USOM)
USOM	United States Operations Mission
WHO	World Health Organization

* Proposed but never brought into being.

Recommended Further Reading
on Foreign-Aid Analysis

ASHER, ROBERT E. *Grants, Loans, and Local Currencies: Their Role in Foreign Aid*. Washington, D.C.: Brookings Institution, 1961.

BALDWIN, DAVID A. *Economic Development and American Foreign Policy: 1943–62*. Chicago: University of Chicago Press, 1966.

BLACK, EUGENE R. *The Diplomacy of Economic Development*. Cambridge, Mass.: Harvard University Press, 1960.

BROWN, WILLIAM ADAMS, JR., and REDVERS OPIE. *American Foreign Assistance*. Washington, D.C.: Brookings Institution, 1953.

COFFIN, FRANK M. *Witness for Aid*. Boston: Houghton Mifflin, 1964.

FEIS, HERBERT. *Foreign Aid and Foreign Policy*. New York: St. Martin's Press, 1964.

GOLDWIN, ROBERT A. (ed.). *Why Foreign Aid?* Chicago: Rand McNally, 1962.

LISKA, GEORGE. *The New Statecraft*. Chicago: University of Chicago Press, 1960.

MASON, EDWARD S. *Foreign Aid and Foreign Policy*. New York: Harper & Row, 1964.

MILLIKAN, MAX F., and DONALD L. M. BLACKMER (eds.). *The Emerging Nations: Their Growth and United States Policy*. Boston: Little, Brown, 1961.

MILLIKAN, MAX F., and W. W. ROSTOW. *A Proposal: Key to an Effective Foreign Policy*. New York: Harper & Bros., 1957.

MONTGOMERY, JOHN D. *The Politics of Foreign Aid*. New York: Frederick A. Praeger, 1962.

O'LEARY, MICHAEL K. *American Politics and Foreign Aid*. New York: Atherton Press, 1966.

SCHELLING, THOMAS C. *International Economics*. Boston: Allyn & Bacon, 1958.

WESTWOOD, ANDREW F. *Foreign Aid in a Foreign Policy Framework*. Washington, D.C.: Brookings Institution, 1966.

WOLF, CHARLES, JR. *Foreign Aid: Theory and Practice in Southern Asia*. Princeton, N.J.: Princeton University Press, 1960.